A COMMON HUNGER

Joan G. Fairweather

A COMMON
HUNGER

Land Rights in Canada and South Africa

UNIVERSITY OF
CALGARY
PRESS

Published by the
University of Calgary Press
2500 University Drive NW
Calgary, Alberta, Canada T2N 1N4
www.uofcpress.com

We acknowledge the financial
support of the Government
of Canada through the Book
Publishing Industry Development
Program (BPIDP) and the Alberta
Foundation for the Arts for
our publishing activities. We
acknowledge the support of the
Canada Council for the Arts for our
publishing program.

Canada

Canada Council   Conseil des Arts
for the Arts   du Canada

LIBRARY AND ARCHIVES OF
CANADA CATALOGUING IN
PUBLICATION:

Fairweather, Joan G., 1939–
A common hunger : land rights in
Canada and South Africa /
Joan G. Fairweather.

(Africa, missing voices series
1703–1826 ; no. 3)

Includes bibliographical references
and index.

ISBN 10: 1-55238-192-7
ISBN 13: 978-1-55238-192-2

1 Native peoples – Land tenure –
   Canada.
2 Indigenous peoples – Land
   tenure – South Africa.
3 Native peoples – Canada –
   Claims.
4 Native peoples – South Africa
   – Claims.
5 Native peoples – Canada –
   Government relations.
6 Indigenous peoples – South
   Africa – Government relations.
I Title.
II Series.

K738.F83 2006   333.2
C2006-904197-0

Cover design, Mieka West.
Internal design & typesetting,
Jason Dewinetz.

To my parents.

Contents

Part Two ⊙ *Reclaiming the Land*

Part Three ◉ *Dealing with Legacies*

Preface

This comparative history of two former British colonies – Canada and the Republic of South Africa – focuses on the response of indigenous peoples to their experience of European colonization and domination.[1] While the methods and political objectives of dispossession differed in many important ways, the alienation of land had devastating consequences for the aboriginal peoples of both countries. Today, by reclaiming rights to the land and an equitable share in the wealth-producing resources they contain, the first peoples of Canada and South Africa are taking important steps to confront the legacies of poverty that characterize many of their communities.

On a visit to South Africa in October 2001, I took a journey that led me to the heart of the land rights issue. A community in the Richtersveld, 600 kilometres north of Cape Town, was reclaiming traditional land belonging to the state-owned diamond company, Alexkor Ltd. The case, which was similar to many aboriginal land claims in Canada, was unusual in South Africa. The Richtersveld land claim was based on both racial discrimination and aboriginal rights – the first such case in South Africa's history. Henk Smith, the community's lawyer, encouraged me to visit the area and meet some of the people.

As we drove north from Port Nolloth along the tarred coastal road to Alexander Bay (where the Alexkor headquarters are located), the diamond company's presence was everywhere. Two rows of tall, barbed wire fences had been erected along the road, sealing off the mining operation from intruders. Beyond the tailings dumps we could see hydraulic excavators, bulldozers and dump trucks at work extracting the diamond-bearing ore from the beach terraces. On the road inland from Alexander Bay, where the Gariep (formerly Orange) River flows into the sea, the ubiquitous Alexkor fences lined the road on both sides. Along the river valley, irrigation plants produced lush fields of crops and green pasture-land; across the road, in stark contrast, penned ostriches grazed on the

Alexkor Ltd diamond mine.

sparse vegetation. When the tarred road became an unpaved track, I knew we had left Alexkor property behind. At the remote, dirt-poor settlement of Sanddrif (one of the five villages involved in the land claim) a meeting of community leaders was already in progress. The Richtersveld community's struggle to regain control over their traditional lands had been long and costly. Earlier that year, their case had been rejected by the Land Claims Court in Cape Town and now their hopes rested with the Appeal Court. If this also failed, their final resort would be to appeal to the Constitutional Court. Alexkor seemed to hold all the cards, but the community was not about to give up. They had no other choice.

My visit to the village of Sanddrif helped to crystallize the themes of this book and provided fresh insights into the motivation and strategies of indigenous peoples to regain control over their land and their lives. The plight of the Richtersveld community – and their determination to restore hope and dignity to their villages – epitomizes the experience of local inhabitants worldwide whose lands and resources have been taken over by European settlers (and now by large corporations) for their own use and profits. While hunger for land and human dignity is one of the most destructive and enduring consequences of European colonization, it has also become the catalyst for cultural renewal and political change.

The research for this project has progressed through several phases of my life. In the 1960s, as an undergraduate student at the University

Ostrich farm near Alexander Bay, Northern Cape.

of South Africa (UNISA) I learned about South Africa's history from the perspective of its white population. In the 1980s, having emigrated to Canada, I became involved in the work of International Defence and Aid Fund for Southern Africa (Canada). Part of my role in this organization was to research and help to disseminate information about the violation of human rights under the apartheid regime.[2] In the 1990s, my interest in aboriginal justice expanded to Canada's treatment of its indigenous peoples. The parallels and differences between South Africa and Canada with respect to aboriginal rights became the topic of my M.A. thesis at the University of Ottawa in 1993: *Is This Apartheid? Aboriginal Reserves and Self-Government in Canada, 1960–1982.* The final phase of my research for this book came in the late 1990s when I returned to South Africa to work as an archivist at the Mayibuye Centre for History and Culture in South Africa at the University of the Western Cape near Cape Town.

Most of the primary sources on early European settlement were found in the National Archives of Canada (now Library and Archives Canada), the Cape Archives and State Library in Cape Town, the South African National Archives in Pretoria and the State Library of Victoria in Melbourne. The chapters on land claims and the legacies of injustice in Canada are based on documentation in the Law and Medical Libraries at the University of Ottawa and in the reading room of the Inuit Tapirisat of Canada in Ottawa. Publications produced by the Department of Land Affairs and the Land Claims Commission, the Surplus People Project, the

Legal Resource Centre and the Program for Land and Agrarian Studies (PLAAS) at the University of the Western Cape provided essential background on land claims in South Africa.

A variety of secondary sources relating to Canada and South Africa as well as Australia and New Zealand were consulted, some recently published, others dating from the nineteenth century. Books, conference papers and journal articles on aboriginal rights, and the complex legal and constitutional constraints on aboriginal justice, were of vital assistance in the preparation of this manuscript. Of particular relevance to this study were publications that have come out of South Africa in recent years, including critiques of South Africa's Truth and Reconciliation Commission by African theologians and academics.

This analysis of land rights in Canada and South Africa is divided into three parts: Dispossession, Reclaiming the Land and Dealing with Legacies. A brief discussion of land rights in Australia and New Zealand is provided in the Appendix.

Part One covers a broad sweep of history from the arrival of Europeans on the shores of North America and southern Africa in the sixteenth century to the present. This four-hundred-year overview is provided on three levels: human, legal and political. Chapter One traces the human interaction between aboriginal and non-aboriginal peoples from first contact to early European settlement. These are the defining stories of wars, epidemics, enslavement, exploitation and, above all, territorial dispossession whose legacies are being challenged by present generations of first Canadians and South Africans. Chapters Two and Three present an analysis of the legal and political foundations of aboriginal-state relations in Canada and South Africa and the struggle of the indigenous peoples for sovereignty and constitutional rights. Central to the discussion are contrasting histories of treaties, reserves, civil rights and policies of segregation and assimilation.

Part Two examines the ways in which indigenous communities are reclaiming control over their ancestral lands and the wealth-producing resources they contain. In Chapters Four and Five, a selection of case histories illustrates the extent to which litigation and negotiated settlements have restored dignity and a measure of prosperity to indigenous communities. Chapter Six focuses on issues of self-government and land tenure as they relate to Canada's First Nations and to South Africa's former bantustans.

The broader issues relating to land justice and the legacies of colonialism and apartheid in Canada and South Africa are discussed in Part Three. Chapter Seven is about the poverty and loss of human dignity associated with land loss and why land rights are critical in restoring hope and healing to landless communities. The final chapter draws comparisons between South Africa's Truth and Reconciliation Commission (TRC) process and Canada's Royal Commission on Aboriginal Peoples (RCAP), both of which took place during the 1990s. As instruments of restitution, neither commission can claim any notable success: meaningful reconciliation requires changes in state policies that address the ongoing hunger for land and dignity in aboriginal communities.

The choice of terms for the peoples of Canada and South Africa requires some explanation. The indigenous peoples of both countries are referred to generically as "first peoples" or "aboriginal peoples." Although "Indian" – the name erroneously given to the local people of the Americas – is controversial (and easily confused with South Africans of Indian origin), it is used here to refer to members of registered bands who are governed under Canada's Indian Act. These groups are also referred to as First Nations, a term that has come into use since the 1970s. The adjective "native," favoured by North American Indians, is used sparingly in this comparative study because of its highly negative connotations in South Africa. "African" is used as both a noun and an adjective, and refers to South Africa's indigenous Bantu-speaking inhabitants. The term "black" is also used in reference to Africans but appears most often as a collective term for Africans, Euro-Africans (classified as "Coloureds" by white governments) and South Africans of Indian descent, who shared a common experience of oppression under white supremacist governments.

Canadians and South Africans of European descent are generally referred to as "white" or "non-aboriginal." The term "Afrikaner" refers to white South Africans whose home language is Afrikaans. In the eighteenth and nineteenth centuries, these descendants of Dutch, German and French immigrants were referred to as "Boers" (Dutch for farmer) or as "Trekboers" (frontier farmers) or "Voortrekkers" (meaning pioneers or those who travel ahead).

MAP 1

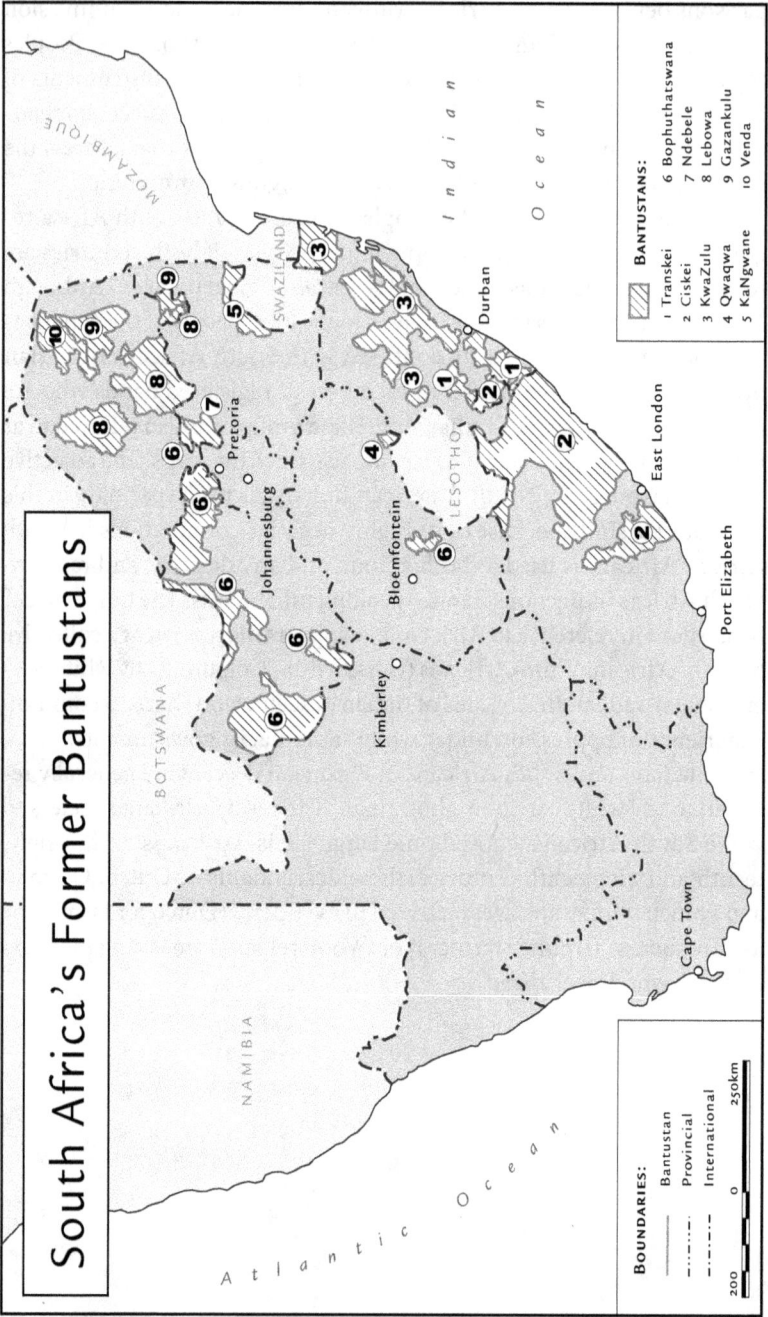

South Africa's Former Bantustans

BANTUSTANS:

1 Transkei   6 Bophuthatswana
2 Ciskei   7 Ndebele
3 KwaZulu   8 Lebowa
4 Qwaqwa   9 Gazankulu
5 KaNgwane   10 Venda

BOUNDARIES:

—————— Bantustan
·—·—·— Provincial
–··—··— International

200   0   250km

Map by Dariusz Ciach.

MAP 2

South Africa's Provinces, 1994

MOZAMBIQUE

Kosi Bay

I n d i a n   O c e a n

Pietersburg

LIMPOPO

KWAZULU-NATAL

MPUMALANGA

KWAZULU

SWAZILAND

Durban

GAUTENG

Pretoria

Ladysmith

LESOTHO

NORTH WEST

Mogopa

Vaal

ORANGE FREE STATE

Orange

Kimberley

Fish

CAPE

Kei

EASTERN CAPE

Port Elizabeth

BOTSWANA

Orange

NORTHERN CAPE

NAMIBIA

Sanddrif

Alexander Bay

WESTERN CAPE

Cape Town

A t l a n t i c   O c e a n

BOUNDARIES:

-·-··- Provincial
-·-··- International

Rivers

○ SelectedCities

250   0   250   500

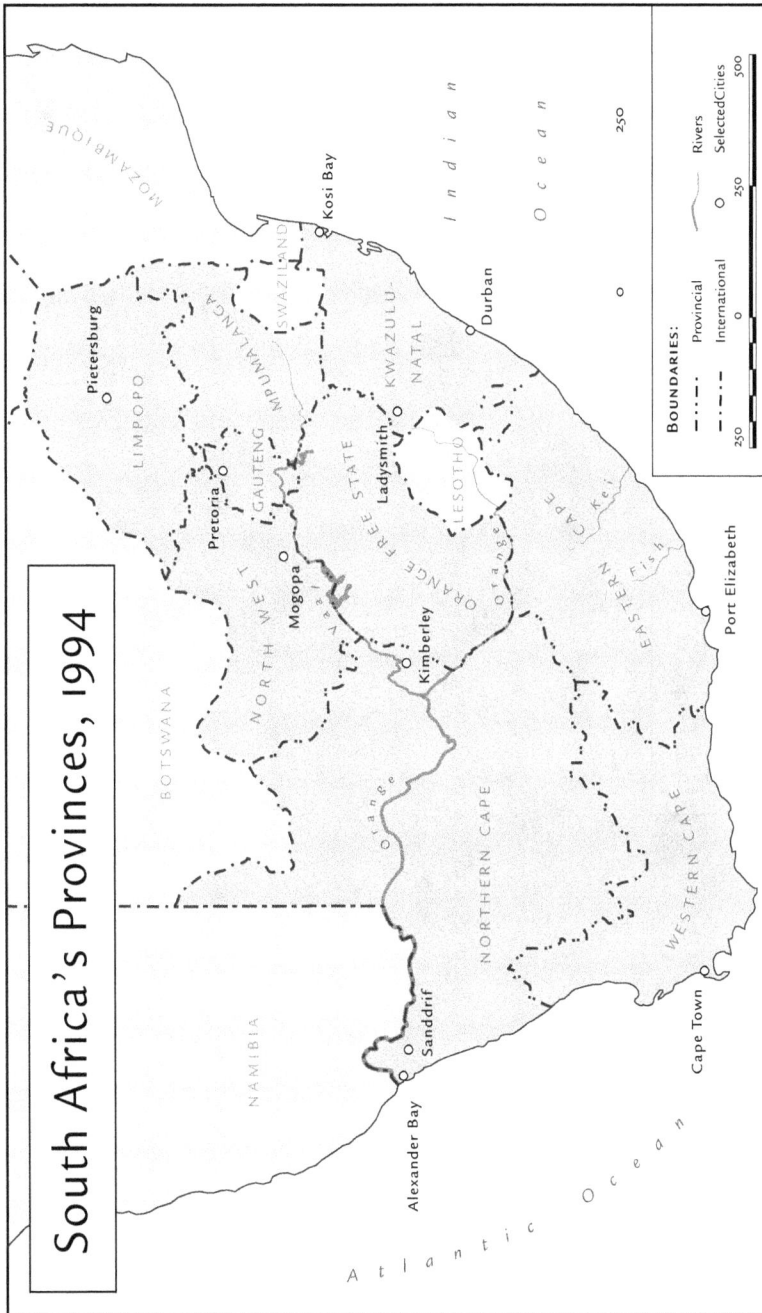

Map by Dariusz Ciach.

MAP 3

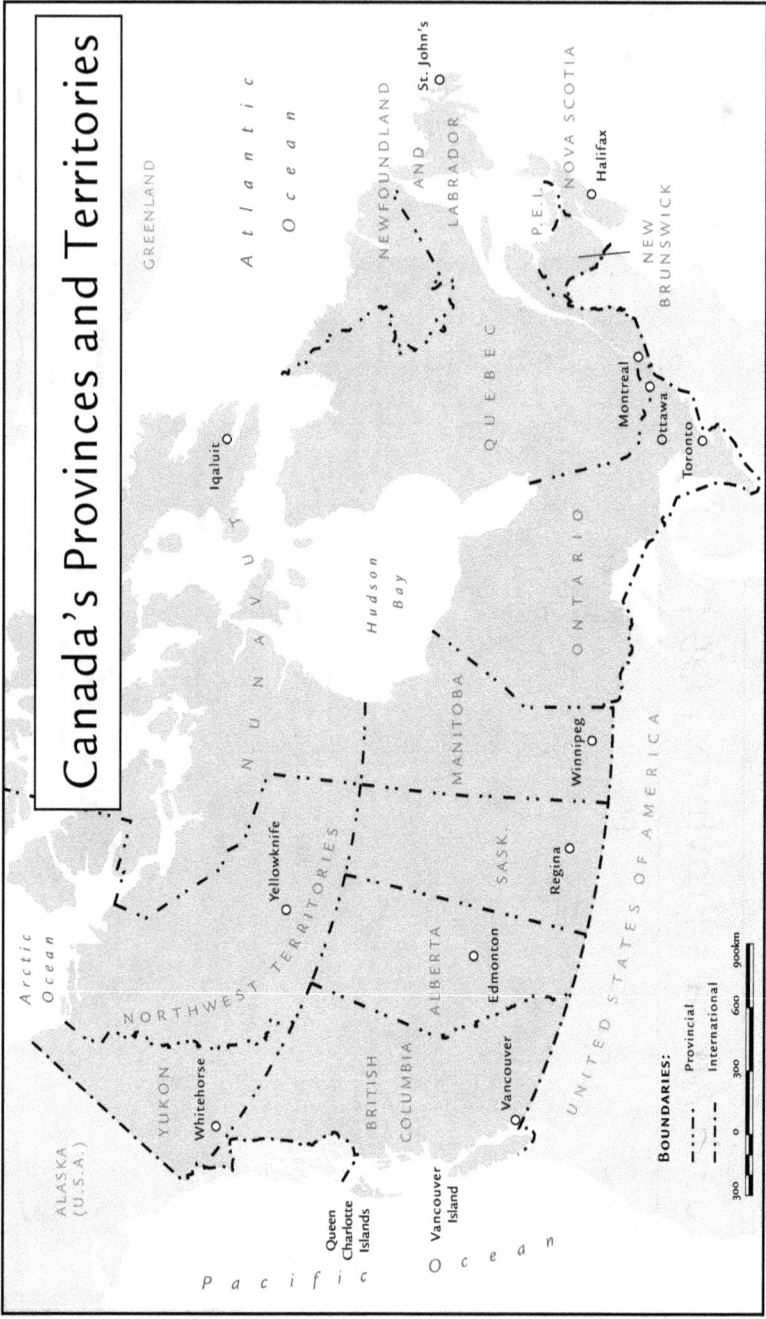

Canada's Provinces and Territories

GREENLAND

Atlantic Ocean

NEWFOUNDLAND AND LABRADOR

St. John's

NOVA SCOTIA

Halifax

P.E.I.

NEW BRUNSWICK

QUEBEC

Montreal

Ottawa

Toronto

Iqaluit

Hudson Bay

ONTARIO

N U N A V U T

MANITOBA

Winnipeg

SASK.

Regina

Arctic Ocean

NORTHWEST TERRITORIES

Yellowknife

ALBERTA

Edmonton

YUKON

Whitehorse

BRITISH COLUMBIA

Vancouver

UNITED STATES OF AMERICA

ALASKA (U.S.A.)

Queen Charlotte Islands

Vancouver Island

Pacific Ocean

BOUNDARIES:

–·–·– Provincial

–··–··– International

300 0 300 600 900km

Map by Dariusz Ciach.

MAP 4

Major Land Claim Areas

GREENLAND

Atlantic Ocean

St. John's

Halifax

Montreal
Ottawa
Toronto

②

Iqaluit

Hudson Bay

①

Winnipeg

U N I T E D   S T A T E S   O F   A M E R I C A

Yellowknife

Regina

③

Arctic Ocean

⑤

⑦

Edmonton

④

Whitehorse

⑥

Vancouver

ALASKA
(U.S.A.)

Pacific Ocean

300   0   300   600   900 km

LAND CLAIM AREAS:

1. Tungavik Federation of Nunavut
2. James Bay Territory
3. Inuvialuit Settlement Region

4. Council for Yukon Indians
5. Dene Nation and Métis Association of NWT
6. Gitxsan and Wet'suwet'en Territories
7. Lubicon Nation Land Claim

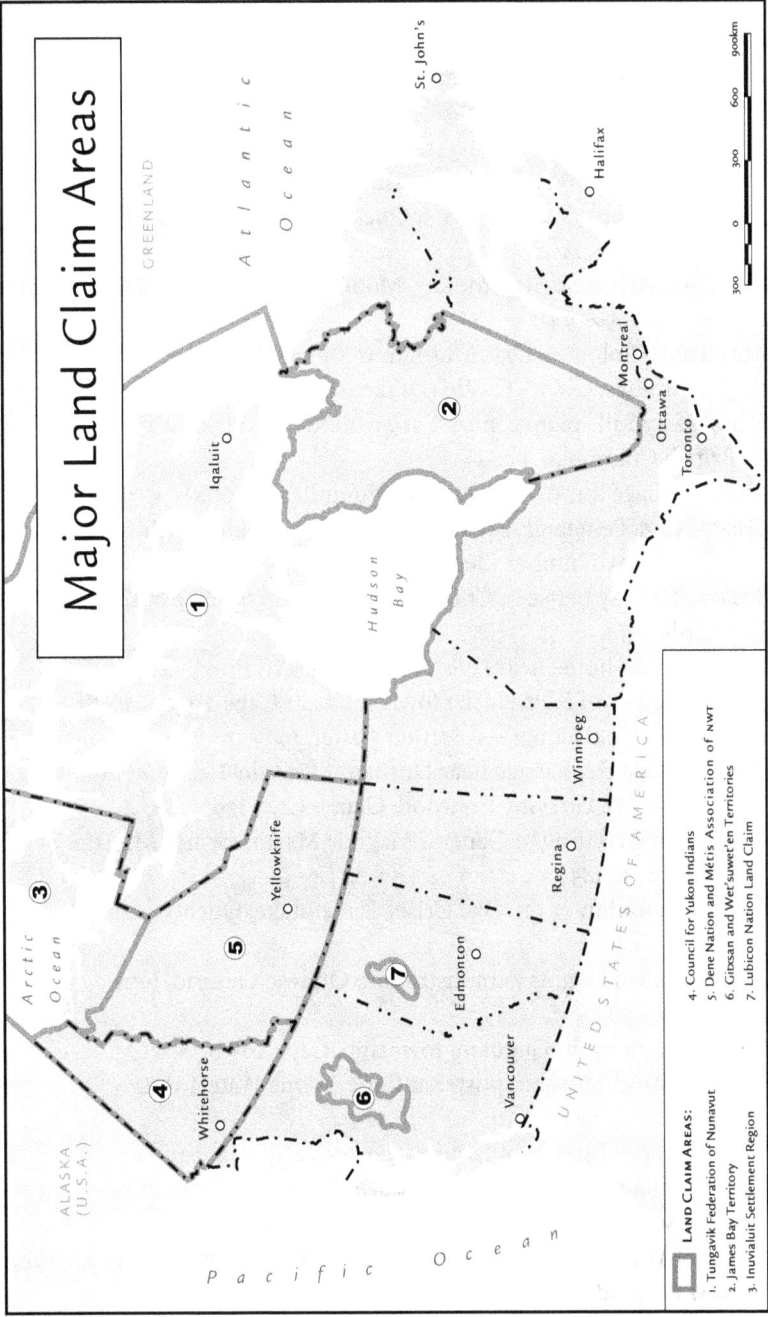

Map by Dariusz Ciach.

LIST OF MAPS

ACKNOWLEDGEMENTS

I am grateful for this opportunity to recognize and thank all those who contributed in special ways to this book. My mentors were the friends and colleagues who shared their knowledge and passion with me: Cornelius Jaenen, Olive Dickason, Poppie Rabalao, Al Cook, Peter Carstens, Peter Colenbrander and Rodney Davenport. Others who inspired and assisted me in various ways along the journey were: Margaret Back, Bob Acton, Douglas and Mary Anglin, Patricia Kennedy, Dariusz Ciach and Wilma MacDonald in Ottawa; Mary Miliano and Peter and Christine Fensham in Australia; Jenny Bean and Kirstin Brown in New Zealand; and François and Molly Bill, Jacob Tshabangu, Kamseela Govender, Henk Smith and Willem Louw in South Africa. Thanks as well to Nancy Mucklow in Kingston for her skillful editing and belief in the importance of this book.

My family and friends, who have shown their support in many different ways, made this project possible. I want to thank my husband, Ian Fairweather especially for his constant support and valuable assistance. My final word of appreciation goes to Jean Wilson, who took an interest in this book from its inception and is truly its "godmother."

Introduction

The indigenous peoples of Canada and South Africa share a common hunger for land and human dignity due to their experiences of colonization and dispossession. However, comparing the history of land rights in these countries presented a number of challenges.

Geographically and demographically Canada and South Africa could not be further apart. Canada is a northern country – the second largest in the world – blessed with many waterways, forests, mountains and vast open spaces. The majority of Canada's population of just over thirty-one million is primarily of European descent (mainly British or French) with the aboriginal peoples (Indian, Inuit and Métis) forming about 4 per cent of its total population. By contrast, South Africa, the most southerly country on the African continent, is not much bigger than the province of Ontario.[1] Although it is rich in minerals (notably gold and diamonds), South Africa is limited in critical resources like arable farmland and water, vital to support its population of forty-four million people. Unlike Canada where the aboriginal population is a tiny minority, the vast majority of South Africa's population is African. In 1996, the size of the various population groups was recorded as follows: 33.7 million Africans, 5.3 million white South Africans, 3.7 million Euro-Africans and one million people of Asian descent.[2]

The political histories of Canada and South Africa are also very different. Colonized in the seventeenth and eighteenth centuries by France and Britain, the Confederation of Canada was established in 1867 comprising four provinces: Ontario, Quebec, New Brunswick and Nova Scotia.[3] Over the following decades, the country expanded from east to west across the continent and today consists of ten provinces and three territories. (Map 4, *xix*.) The province of Quebec, which is predominantly French-speaking, has had an active separatist movement since the 1970s. Although the Canadian Constitution was repatriated in 1982, Canada remains a member of the British Commonwealth. The Governor General

1

is the official head of state, representing the British monarch.[4] Canada has
two official languages: English and French. South Africa has developed
along different lines. It was colonized by the Dutch and then the British
in the seventeenth and eighteenth centuries. The Union of South Africa
(established in 1910 from two British and two Boer colonies) had four
provinces and two official languages: English and Afrikaans.[5] In 1961,
South Africa became a republic, having already withdrawn its membership from the British Commonwealth. In 1994, after its first democratic
elections, South Africa was invited to rejoin the Commonwealth. The
country is now divided into nine provinces and has eleven official languages: English, Afrikaans and nine African languages.[6] (Map 2, *xvii*.)

The issue of indigenous land rights is complex and controversial in
both countries. Even the term aboriginal (or indigenous) is problem-
atic. Who, in fact, *were* the original occupants? Over the centuries, the
continents of North America and southern Africa have been inhabited
by successive waves of peoples. Wars and displacement of one group by
another took place long before Europeans arrived. In this study, the term
"indigenous peoples" refers to descendants of the original or pre-colonial
inhabitants of a territory or geographic area who, despite the legal status
imposed on them by the dominant society, retain some or all of their
social, economic, cultural and political institutions.

For all their differences, South Africa and Canada have a number of
things in common that relate to the issue of land rights. The indigenous
peoples of Canada and South Africa comprise not one but many nations, each with their own languages, cultures, histories and ancestral
territories. Among the fifty-two bands and nations claiming land rights
in Canada are the Innu, Mi'kmaq and Maliseet in the Atlantic provinces,
the Algonquin, Iroquois and Ojibway in eastern Canada, the Lubicon
Cree, Blackfoot and Peigan nations in the Prairie provinces, the Inuit,
James Bay Cree and Dene in the northern territories and the Nisga'a,
Haida, Gitxsan and Wet'suwet'en on the west coast. (Map 3, *xviii*.) South
Africans are similarly diverse in cultural origin. The major African or
Bantu-speaking peoples of South Africa are the Zulu, Xhosa, Tswana,
Pedi, Ndebele, Tsonga, Venda and Sotho nations. Other groups of in-
digenous South Africans include the Griqua, Nama (Khoikhoi) and San,
most of whom have adopted Afrikaans as their mother tongue.

For all their diversity, the indigenous peoples of Canada and South
Africa have similar reasons for reclaiming rights in their ancestral lands.
Since the arrival of Europeans on their shores, the wealth of both countries (from mining, industry, farming and technology) has been exploited
and monopolized by the non-indigenous, settler community. Although

the traditional economies of Canada's first nations and indigenous South Africans differ considerably, their means of production have historically been embedded in the land and the products of the land. Reclaiming control over the land and resources is therefore a question of economic and cultural survival for many indigenous communities. The poorer the community, the more vital their need for access to land and natural resources. Subsistence farming in South Africa and hunting and trapping in Canada are traditional ways to ward off hunger in times of need, but they require sufficient land and a protected environment to make them viable and fruitful.

In post-apartheid South Africa, the recognition of land rights is both a constitutional issue and a question of national security. The Constitution of 1996 assures every South African the right to own land. However, most of the land and its wealth-producing resources remain in the hands of the white minority, while the vast majority of people remain landless and poor. At the same time, the threat of civil war still hovers over this fragile democracy. In neighbouring Zimbabwe, conflict over land rights has escalated into anarchy. The African National Congress government has established mechanisms designed to avert such a catastrophe in South Africa. But for these mechanisms to succeed, the Land Claims Commission and Constitutional Court must ensure that land restitution takes place in a timely fashion.

In Canada, the recognition of aboriginal land rights has received little political attention thus far although the human rights of its indigenous peoples are at stake. While aboriginal Canadians represent a tiny minority of Canada's population, their numbers are increasing, and social problems (poverty, health care, housing, education and unemployment) are also escalating. The social conditions of many aboriginal communities in Canada are a source of national shame and reveal a hypocrisy that is all too apparent to native Canadians who bear the brunt of anachronistic government policies. Political activism within aboriginal communities has intensified since the early 1970s. Canada's First Nations, Inuit and Métis are now confronting governments and the courts with demands for compensation for the loss of land and culture and for recognition of inherent aboriginal rights.

ABORIGINAL RIGHTS AND INTERNATIONAL LAW

The history of indigenous land rights in southern Africa and North America began five hundred years ago. In the years following the first European forays into the New World in the fifteenth century, the legal authorities realized that special laws were needed to deal with the indigenous inhabitants of the colonies and the lands they occupied. More important still was the need to ensure that once European sovereignty had been proclaimed over an occupied territory, rival European states could not establish similar proprietary rights over the same territory. In other words, they required an internationally recognized law to ensure the undisturbed occupation of the lands and jurisdiction over the peoples of their colonies.

Yet a long period of lawlessness preceded the era of treaties and proclamations. The Spanish conquistadores of the fifteenth century followed no law except rapacious greed. Their campaigns of extermination against the Indians of Hispaniola left behind a legacy of dispossession and exploitation that plagues the region to this day. By 1496 (four years after Christopher Columbus landed on the Caribbean island of Taino, thinking he had arrived in India), the Spaniards were in complete control of the West Indies. Mexico, Peru and Cuba were soon to follow.

Following the practice of the day, the conquistadores claimed title to the New World in the name of the King of Spain and Christianity merely by planting a flag in the soil. Priests accompanying the soldiers would read the *Requerimiento* to the defeated tribes, demanding that they acknowledge their allegiance to the Spanish Crown and adopt the Christian faith. Failure to comply resulted in either death or forced labour. In 1510, the conquistadores introduced a forced labour system known as *ecomienda*. The Crown not only gave land to individual Spaniards (usually soldiers) but allotted them Indians to work the land for them. While the Indians were not officially enslaved, they received no wages, and their life was one of involuntary servitude. Thus, for many years the *ecomienda* model under the King of Spain was the only legal code governing the southern colonies.

In the sixteenth century, two Spanish advocates of aboriginal rights challenged the legitimacy of Spanish claims in the Americas. One was Bartolomé de Las Casas, a Dominican priest, and the other was Francisco de Vitoria, a theologian. Both men based their views on the classic concept of *jus gentium* (the equality of humankind) and its founding principle of natural law. Their publications and lectures, which became known as the Spanish School, laid the foundations for a more enlightened approach to colonization. However, both de Vitoria and Las Casas were men of their time and their arguments were laced with ambiguities. De Vitoria declared on the one hand that "Indians are rational beings and true owners of their lands and estates." However he also proclaimed that the Spanish were entitled to retaliate if the Indians refused to trade with them – by declaring war, occupying their cities and enslaving them.

Las Casas also preached conflicting messages. He defended the right of Indians to resist Spanish aggression but also insisted on the Spanish right to Christianize Indians; indeed that this was their sacred mission to the New World. Thus, the dispossession continued and the system of forcing indigenous peoples to work for their colonizers became a model for European imperial powers throughout the next two centuries.

In most parts of the world, the mere act of "discovery" remained a justification for colonization for at least another century. In 1670, Canada's northern region, known as Rupert's Land, was declared the private property of a band of English adventurers, thereby beginning the imperial invasion of Canada. Inuit writer Zebedee Nungaq observes with some irony that, "by some sleight of hand, by some fluke [my ancestors] became tenants in our own ancestral homeland."[7] A century later, Australia and New Zealand were colonized under similar circumstances. In 1788, under the justification of first possession, the British government declared sovereignty over the land and people of Australia. New Zealand followed a few decades later. (See Appendix).

In the eighteenth and nineteenth centuries, as competition for new colonies intensified, international lawyers looked for new arguments to justify European settlement. The question of the moral and legal entitlement of colonizers to discovered territories was raised by eighteenth century Dutch jurist Hugo Grotius:

> Discovery confers no rights unless the area was uninhabited.
> Indeed, the Indians, when first discovered by the Spanish ...
> were idol worshipers and wrapped in serious error. Nonetheless,
> they had full sovereignty, both over public and private property
> which was their natural right which could not be taken away.
> Thus it is heretical to believe that those outside the faith do not
> have full sovereignty over their possessions, for this reason:
> plunder is not excused by the fact that the plunderer is a
> Christian.[8]

New theories of law emerged in the latter part of the eighteenth century to replace the high-minded but largely unaccepted concepts of natural law. These new positivist theories provided a legal loophole for imperialism. Unlike natural law, which considered indigenous rights to be based on notions of human equality and Christian morality, positive law abandoned traditional codes of ethics altogether. Proponents of positive law argued that since indigenous populations pursued migratory lifestyles and did not occupy territory in any formal sense, they had no proprietary rights to their land. By portraying indigenous peoples as primitive and uncivilized, European states asserted that lands they occupied were *res nullius*, a term derived from Roman property law meaning without an owner.

The positivist argument was supported by United States Chief Justice John Marshall, one of the most influential legal minds of the time. In the case of *Johnson v. McIntosh* in 1823, Marshall declared:

> Although we do not mean to engage in the defense of those principles which Europeans have applied to Indian title, they may, we think, find some excuse, if not justification, in the character and habits of the people whose rights have been wrested from them ... the tribes of Indians inhabiting this country were fierce savages, whose occupation was war, and whose subsistence was drawn chiefly from the forest. To leave them in possession of their country was to leave the country a wilderness.[9]

Sixty years later, positivist reasoning was used to justify the Partition of Africa. The Berlin Conference (1884–85), which defined the entire continent of Africa as no-man's-land, allowed European nations (Britain, France, Belgium, Italy, Germany and Portugal) to stake out their claims to the entire continent, thereby denying Africans the right to their ancestral homes. In his *Principles of International Law* of 1895, T.J. Lawrence asserted that all territory " not in the possession of states who are members of the family of nations, must be considered as *terra nullius* and therefore open to occupation."[10]

In North American law, a distinction came to be made between the proprietary rights of so-called civilized inhabitants (settlers) and the aboriginal rights of the indigenous inhabitants. The historical rationale for the distinction can be explained as a combination of expediency and paternalism. In the first place, the distinction was designed to prevent conflict with rival European nations competing for possession of the American continent. But there was also a marked degree of paternalism about the requirement that Indian lands could only be alienated by order of the Crown. As Marshall explained in his 1823 judgment, although the rights of the original inhabitants were not lawfully extinguished under this arrangement, they were certainly severely restricted:

> [Indians] were admitted to be the rightful occupants of the soil, with a legal as well as a just claim to retain possession

of it, and to use it to their own discretion, but their rights to complete sovereignty as independent nations were necessarily diminished, and their power to dispose of the soil at their own will, to whomsoever they pleased, was denied by the original fundamental principle that discovery gave exclusive title to those who made it.[11]

Among the cultural baggage the Europeans brought with them to North America, Africa and other colonies was an ingrained belief in their race's superiority, which may explain how ordinary men and women could have gone about the task of dispossession and even genocide without apparently questioning the morality of their actions. Alexander Sutherland, a nineteenth-century historian, saw the killing of indigenous peoples not as an ethical issue but as part of a divine plan:

As to the ethics of the question, there can be no final conclusion. Whether the European has the right to dispossess these immemorial occupants of the soil ... is a problem incapable of absolute determination.... It is a question of temperament; to the sentimental it is undoubtedly an iniquity; to the practical it represents a distinct step in human progress, involving the sacrifice of a few thousand of an inferior race.... If it is a divine law that Anglo-Saxon people must double themselves every half century, it must be divine law that they are to emigrate and form new homes for themselves in waste lands. Yet there will ever cling a pathos around the story of a vanishing race.[12]

Not everyone agreed with him. In 1830, S. Bannister wrote a treatise appealing for the more humane treatment of indigenous peoples. Finding no logical explanation for the practice of "destroying everywhere those whose only crime is that they precede us in the possession of lands which we desire to enjoy to their exclusion," Bannister recognized that European notions of "racial superiority" played a significant part in their destruction.[13] Thus racial prejudice came to represent one of the most lethal weapons to be used against the indigenous populations of the colonized territories of Africa and North America.

THE CLEARING OF LANDS AND LANGUAGES

Many indigenous peoples who were colonized by European powers over the past four hundred years suffered the double loss of ancestral lands and cultural identity. The loss of indigenous languages – an intrinsic part of human identity – has had profound and far-reaching consequences for the colonized peoples of South Africa and Canada.

The close relationship between the languages of indigenous peoples and their ancestral land is eloquently described by South African historian Noël Mostert. African languages, Mostert writes, are among the most beautiful in the world, they "seem to resound always with the very nature, the poetic character of the lands where they were used. The sand and dry heat and empty distance of the semi-desert lands where the Khoikhoi originated are embedded in their speech. But so is softness, greenness. They run together like the very passage of their olden days."[14] Yet the Europeans who came to settle on their lands dismissed the complex diction of local languages as closer to animal sounds than human speech.[15] The psychological and social impact of this dehumanization of African people endures to this day.

In post-apartheid South Africa, the voices of aboriginal minorities like the Khoikhoi and San are still struggling to be heard. The Nama (Khoikhoi) people of the Richtersveld, who were driven from their ancestral lands by colonial settlers, are clinging to the last vestiges of their land and language. For generations, Afrikaans replaced Nama as the home language of most Nama families. Parents stopped using *Khoekhoegowap* (the Nama language) because they perceived it as a burden rather than a medium of advancement in their lives. Even in the new South Africa, Nama is not one of the eleven official languages. There is no institutional support for it to be used on radio, television, in the print media or to correctly name and spell places that are derived from Nama words. In this way, the Nama have suffered the dual loss of ancestral lands and their cultural identity.

The San, whom the colonists named Bushmen, met with a similar fate to the Khoikhoi.[16] For most of the twentieth century, the tiny remnant of San still to be found in South Africa were depicted by educators and museum curators as less than human, as part of South Africa's indigenous fauna. Western media have portrayed them as humorous relics of a bygone age, untouched by the modern world. The movie *The Gods Must be Crazy* tells nothing of the reality of a people dispossessed of their land and humanity by waves of intruders. In the 1970s, hundreds of San men were recruited by the South African army to serve in ethnic-based units in the war against SWAPO (South West Africa People's Organization) in Namibia. In 1996, after apartheid had crumbled, the Truth and Reconciliation Commission heard evidence of atrocities committed against San soldiers by their white comrades. The allegations were that San trackers who stepped out of line would be summarily executed.[17]

The impact of this dehumanization of South Africa's first peoples is starkly apparent in a desolate settlement called Schmidtsdrift, an hour's drive west of Kimberley (where diamonds were discovered in the 1860s) in the northern Cape. This is home to the largest community of San people in South Africa of more than 4,300 people. Schmidtsdrift, a former South African Defence Force camp, consists of rows of military tents set on an open, windswept and stony slope leading down to the Vaal River. Many of the former soldiers continue to draw pensions and there are two schools (Afrikaans is the medium of instruction) and a clinic. But the rampant use of alcohol and dagga (marijuana) is a sign of the dislocation and loss that afflict so many indigenous communities worldwide. According to the army doctor at Schmidtsdrift, children as young as twelve are addicted to alcohol. Staff Sergeant Mario Mahonga, the leader of the !Xhu Traditional Council, points out one of the primary causes for the social dissolution:

A lot of our culture is lost in our lives … like the old stories that were told by mothers and fathers who would go into the bush and then return to tell the others what they had seen. The problem now is that no one goes out and does anything, so we have no stories to tell our children. We have nothing to pass on. In the old days we had to make a musical instrument and sing along to it. Now we just go to town and buy a tape and listen to that.[18]

The clearing of lands and languages has been experienced differently by South Africa's black majority whose vernacular languages withstood the assault of colonization. But language – or rather the use or manipulation of language – has nevertheless played an important role in the relationship between white and black South Africans, especially during the apartheid era. Despite their overwhelming numerical presence, Africans were rendered "invisible" by their treatment as units of labour in white-owned mines, farms and factories. White employers (who referred to themselves as "Baas" or "Master") seldom called their employees by their African names or spoke their languages. Domestic servants were typically referred to as "boys" and "girls" by white adults and children alike. Thus language became a psychological tool that was used to subjugate and deprive African workers of their human dignity.

The language used by white farmers when addressing their black workers was notoriously demeaning. While farm workers were frequently maltreated physically, verbal abuse was also commonly used to undermine the dignity and independence of Africans. The life story of

Kas Maine, who worked as a sharecropper (tenant farmer) on a white farm between 1895 and 1985, reveals how the pain of losing ownership of his ancestral land was compounded by the ignorance and brutality of his white Afrikaner landlord. After many years of longing for the birth of a son "to help him coax a living out of the dry Transvaal soil," Kas Maine went to his landlord's house to announce the arrival of his newborn son as tradition required. This is how Maine recounted the incident to historian Charles Van Onselen sixty years later:

> That was the rule on the farms. When a child was born you went to the landlord and said, "We have had a baby boy." The landlord would be pleased and say, "Oh, you have had a little monkey, have you cut off its tail?" Then we would say, *"Nee baas, ek het die stertjie afgesny, is nou 'n mens, is nie meer 'n bobbejaan nie."* (Yes master, I have cut off the tail, it's a person now, no longer a baboon.) That was how the white farmers used to put it.[19]

These words, spoken with such mocking cruelty, were made even more unpalatable by the meanness of the Maine family's illiterate landlord, who prided himself on his inability to read the finer print in the countryside's code of race relations. As Van Onselen explains, "[n]ormally, a price was attached to such joking relationships, since the white landlord, having 'won' a verbal joust that affirmed the Darwinian-cum-social order in his own mind, was expected to give his 'defeated' vassal a sheep to celebrate the arrival of another potential male labourer on the property. This embarrassing exchange was therefore left without its customary conclusion, and Kas departed feeling humiliated."

Kas Maine, who died in 1985 at the age of ninety-one, did not live to see the birth of the new South Africa. However, his unwavering dignity and innate sense of pride provided a model for his children and grandchildren to follow. Canadian anthropologist Hugh Brody argues that where languages survive – as they have for black South Africans – the experience of loss is less absolute. As a nation Africans have lost their lands and endured unspeakable humiliation but their sense of identity and pride in who they are and have been has remained intact.[20]

In Canada, the clearing of indigenous land and languages took place in different ways. Less than a century after the first fur-trading mission in Haida Gwaii (or Queen Charlotte Islands, an archipelago of more than 150 islands off the coast of British Columbia), the sea otter has vanished, and the migratory populations of various other species of fish are greatly reduced. Over the decades, the lakes and forests of Haida Gwaii have

Clearcut forests, Moresby Island, Queen Charlottes, British Columbia.

been damaged almost irreparably by over-hunting, over-fishing, and clear-cut logging. But according to Robert Bringhurst, "the single most abused and heavily damaged ecosystem in Haida Gwaii to date has been the fragile, half-tangible ecosystem of language, thought, memory and behaviour: the ecosystem of culture."[21] Few totem poles, distinctive symbols of west coast cultures, remain on the islands.[22] Many of these imposing structures now grace the hallways of the Smithsonian Institution in Washington, D.C., and museums in Vancouver and Ottawa.

In the perception of many Western people, aboriginal oral traditions epitomize what is different and "other" to their own written histories and traditions. Missionaries who came to North America in the seventeenth and eighteenth centuries tried to capture the mystical quality of oral literature by devising orthographies for the North American languages. But their purpose was not to preserve the culture: it was to create tools for proselytizing the Christian faith and thereby subvert the influence of the shamans and traditional storytellers. It was an effort to render aboriginal cultures invisible. The results have been little short of catastrophic. With the exception of Cree, Ojibwa and Inuktitut, most aboriginal languages have been lost or are on the brink of extinction.

For societies steeped in oral traditions and the transfer of knowledge through legends and stories, language is as critical to their survival as their ancestral lands. In North American aboriginal tradition, language has a spiritual value; through their languages, the people are able to

Totem poles at the University of British Columbia's Museum of Anthropology, Vancouver, British Columbia.

communicate with the spirits of the animal world. According to one legend, there was a time when all animals and humans spoke the same language: the language of Mother Earth. But human beings abused the animals and provoked them into taking new voices and new languages. Since that time, human beings have found it difficult to understand beings who are different from themselves. The moral of this legend is: "to live well on the earth, one must learn its languages."[23]

Stories played a central role in the language of Indian diplomacy. There were stories told through songs and dances, stories of sorrow and shared sufferings, stories of burying the hatchet and rejoicing, stories about connections made, broken and renewed, and stories that envisioned all humankind as one people united under a Great Tree of Peace.[24] However, as the diversity of peoples in North America increased, Indian diplomats had to supplement this language and learn to communicate in different ways. The records of treaty councils and negotiations in the seventeenth and eighteenth centuries describe the remarkable creativity of Indian diplomats. In the twentieth and twenty-first centuries, negotiating treaties with Canadian federal and provincial governments requires special skills to reach settlements that are meaningful to Indian communities and respectful of the common good.

John Snow, Chief of the Stoney Nation in the foothills of the Rocky Mountains, recounts in his memories of childhood that storytelling was an ongoing educational process. Aboriginal children learned the his-

Haida totem pole at Old Masset, Queen Charlotte Islands, British Columbia.

tory of their people and all they needed to know about life from their parents, grandparents and elders around the campfires, in the teepees, on the hillsides, in the forests, and at a variety of special gatherings.[25] When residential schools were introduced in Upper Canada in the 1850s this treasured way of life came to an abrupt end for thousands of Indian children. As a key program in the process of assimilation, the schools were seen as an effective way to "stamp out" Indian languages and cultures.

The purpose was to remove children from the "uncivilized" influence of their parents and communities, a major source of the "Indian problem." By 1894 attendance at school became compulsory under Canadian law for all aboriginal children, and parents were liable for imprisonment for failing to send their children to school. In the testimony given at the Mackenzie Valley Pipeline hearings in the 1970s, people told how they were treated like criminals for preventing their children from attending school. The priests came down in barges, they said, and seized children from each village. The parents would hide them in the bush until the priests had gone.[26]

One of the first things that happened to the thousands of Indian children who attended these schools was that they were forbidden to use their own names. Many received only a number; others were given a "Christian" name. By insisting that only English be spoken, the Indian children were deprived of their self-esteem, their culture, their knowledge of who they were and where they came from. The impact of this loss of language on former students now has a direct bearing on the ability of aboriginal communities to reclaim their land and resources. As Hugh Brody expressed it, "they must first reconcile themselves to a profound loss at the centre of their being and then move forward to assert their rights to land and resources in the language of the settlers."[27]

Canada's residential schools for Indian children cannot be equated to the British educational system of the day, nor can the church authorities claim they were unaware of the conditions in the schools. This letter written in 1899 by Elizabeth Shaw, a matron at a Presbyterian Church home for Indian boys in Port Simpson, B.C., is one of many outraged complaints from former teachers and staff to be found in church archives.[28] The conditions she witnessed were clearly extraordinary even to her Victorian eyes:

The slightest mistake on the part of the boys brought down the wrath of authorities and the severe flogging, which were the almost inevitable consequences of wrong-doing, seemed to me in many cases to be out of all proportion to the gravity of the offence. I know that children need to be corrected and Indian children are probably no exception to this rule, but to keep them in a state of chronic fear, as these children were, seems to me wrong and unnatural ... I was compelled to set meat before the boys that my brothers would not set before their dogs ... this, when there was an abundance of good wholesome food in the house seemed to me inexcusable.[29]

Contrary to the expectations of the church leaders and government officials who established the residential schools, instead of producing invisibility and integration, the schools have produced generations of aboriginal people determined to maintain their cultural roots and to reclaim their ancestral land. A high proportion of the leadership in aboriginal political organizations came through the residential school system. Elijah Harper, John Tootoosis, Phil Fontaine and Matthew Coon Come are among the current leaders who were educated in residential schools. But on the other end of the spectrum are generations of people gravely damaged by the experience. As one Peigan woman explains, "They took away our brains, because they brainwashed us in residential school. They took away our languages. They took away our songs.... They just whipped our spirits. It's the emotional part and the spiritual part that hit us so hard."[30]

The term "land claim" is itself a barrier to aboriginal justice in Canada. It implies that in order to claim their homes the burden of proof lies with the original inhabitants to make their "claim" for its return. Moreover, European-based courts set the criteria for making these claims. If the claim is based on aboriginal rights, then the claimants must prove that they use and occupy the territory to the exclusion of other people; that they have lived there from time immemorial; and that they are an organized society. Aboriginal Australians face these same challenges (See Appendix).

The language of the Canadian court system presents an additional obstacle for aboriginal people. The Reverend Stan McKay, a Fisher Lake Cree from Manitoba and the first aboriginal Moderator of the United Church of Canada, sees the current land claim process as a continuation of colonial domination and dispossession. The very language of land claims runs counter to aboriginal values and relationship with the land. To participate, "our statements and language are forced to become sterile and technical ... the legal jargon contains concepts of ownership that contradict our spiritual understanding of life.... As marginalized people, forced to live on tiny plots of land, we encounter the world view of the wealthy and powerful in the land claim process and are forced to compromise or die."[31]

Despite the impact of missionaries and government interference, story telling and oral traditions remain a distinctive part of North American Indian culture. In his recent book about Canada's northern peoples, Hugh Brody describes how the Nisga'a, like many other west coast societies, have celebrated and institutionalized the power of the word. The young are still trained in public speaking. In the potlatch, the famous

The Right Reverend Stan McKay, Moderator of the United Church of Canada (1992–94).

west coast event at which inheritance, territory, names and disputes are adjudicated, to be able to talk with authority is part of *having* authority.[32] The Inuit of Canada's northern regions share this tradition. Despite an educational system seeking to replace Inuktitut with English, Inuit isolation from mainstream society has worked in their favour. Many northern families still speak their own language, and the elders continue to gather the children around them and tell their stories.[33]

When the Gitxsan and Wet'suwet'en brought their case to the Supreme Court of British Columbia in May 1987, they refused to be silenced by standard court protocol and conventions. In addition to the evidence brought forward by their legal team and expert witnesses, their testimony included traditional stories and songs in accordance with the rules of their own society. At one point, Chief Mary Johnson of the Gitxsan people proceeded to tell the history of her territory through a traditional story. As with many stories, this one included a song. Justice McEachern told the leading council, "I have a tin ear … It's not going to do any good to sing to me." But Mary Johnson sang her song anyway. As Brody, who attended the trial, writes:

> Her voice was strong, and the sadness of the lament was clear, anguished and startling … It did not belong in this court, against the opposition of the judge, resounding in his tin ear. Yet it was somehow perfect, a complete expression of Gitxsan language, in all its senses, with all its meanings…. The history of the region and of the nation, of the encounter between colonists and indigenous cultures, the story of whites and Indians, the deaths by smallpox, the losses of life, of land, of hope.[34]

For the Gitxsan people in court, the song evoked memories of loss and starvation. But not everyone was moved. The judge, whose indignation was conveyed in his hunched shoulders, expressed his displeasure and non-comprehension by ruling the oral testimony of the claimants inadmissible. Judge McEachern concluded that the Gitxsan and Wet'suwet'en could not claim aboriginal title to their territories because their societies "lacked all the badges of civilization, [since they had] no written language, no horses, or wheeled vehicles." But the response of the hereditary chiefs showed their case was not to be dismissed so easily:

> Aboriginal people will protect their rights and will force this agenda. The actuality, or threat of violent force by the state cannot keep people down. It has not worked in South Africa and it did not work last summer in Oka. Justice will be served in the end and this province may expect considerable unrest, protest and direct political action if the government attempts to use this small, silly judgement to inform policy. An appeal can be expected.[35]

A decade later, the Supreme Court of Canada overturned McEachern's ruling. In 1997, Chief Justice Antonio Lamer ruled that the lower court had erred in its rejection of the Gitxsan and Wet'suwet'en case and ordered a retrial. The most striking part of his ruling was his assertion that courts should recognize oral history as evidence in aboriginal land claim cases; that stories matter.

Part One

Dispossession

Chapter One
The Land and the People

The Day we die
A soft wind will blow away our footprints in the sand.
When the wind has gone,
Who will tell the timelessness
that once we walked this way in the dawn of time?

From an old song of the /Xam (San)[1]

THE FIRST PEOPLES OF THE CAPE OF GOOD HOPE

The San – known to the colonists as Bushmen – are believed to be the earliest inhabitants of Africa's southern-most region. For thousands of years this diminutive people lived in small communities as hunters and gatherers, medicine men and women, painters and engravers, and story-tellers. The rock paintings found in caves and sites scattered across South Africa (some dating back 26,000 years) testify to their spiritual and physical oneness with the land and the wildlife that sustained them.

Around two thousand years ago, the hegemony of the San was challenged first by the Khoikhoi, cattle herders from the northwest, and then from the east by Bantu-speaking tribes. The Khoikhoi numbered at least a hundred thousand people when the Dutch arrived at the Cape in 1652. They lived mainly along the Orange River and on the coastal belt stretching from present-day Namibia to the Transkei. The Khoikhoi (named Hottentots by the settlers in imitation of their speech) had a more elaborate social organization than the San and were distributed in large patrilineal tribes of up to twenty-five thousand members. Khoikhoi herders were probably the first indigenous group to greet the European ships on their way to India.

According to the journals of European explorers who stopped for fresh provisions on the southwestern shores of Africa, the local people seemed eager to trade with them. Portuguese sailors rounding the treacherous "Cabo de Boa Esperance" describe how they obtained fresh meat

Mural at Bartolomeu Dias Museum in Mossel Bay, Cape.

in exchange for copper and iron from the local people.[2] As Vasco da Gama, one of the earliest navigators to reach the Cape, recorded in his journal in 1497:

> On Sunday there came about forty or fifty of them … and with *çeitis* (knives) we bartered for shells that they wore in their ears, which looked as if they had been silvered over; and for fox-tails, which they fastened on to sticks and with which they fan their faces. Here I bartered a sheath, which one of them wore on his member, for a *çeitis* … and a black ox for three bracelets.… We dined off this on Sunday; and it was very fat and the flesh as savoury as that of [meat in] Portugal.[3]

Referring to the local herdsmen as "kafirs" (meaning infidel or heathen), the French explorer Jean-Baptiste Tavernier noted in his journal in 1649 the remarkable healing skills of the local people and the way they tended members of his crew.[4]

> These kafirs, however beastly they are, yet have a special knowledge of herbs, which they know how to use against the sicknesses they suffer.… Of nineteen sick that were in the ship, fifteen were put into the hands of these kafirs to tend and bandage them because they suffered from ulcers on the legs and from wounds received in battle; and in less than fifteen days they were all completely cured.[5]

The Dutch explorer Laendert Janz made a similar entry in his ship's log-book when the crew of the *Haarlem* received friendly assistance from the local Khoikhoi people. Not only did they "come daily to the fort to trade with perfect amity and brought cattle and sheep in quantity," but they also brought fire wood when the chief mate Jacob Claas lay sick for several weeks. While the language of the Khoikhoi (with its four click sounds) seemed to confound the Europeans, Janz claimed that the natives had no difficulty learning Dutch: [They] learnt to say "hout halen" (fetch wood) and call almost all the people of the *Haarlem* by name.[6]

Initially, trade helped maintain a good relationship with the local in-habitants. As Janz and Proot wrote in their report persuading the Dutch East India Company to establish a refreshment station at the Cape, "good correspondence with the natives" would not only save hundreds of sail-ors from dying of scurvy, but would benefit the Company in a number of ways:

> By maintaining good correspondence with the natives, we shall
> be able in time to employ some of their children as boys and
> servants, and to educate them in the Christian religion ... so
> that the formation of the fort and garden will not only tend
> to the gain and profit of the Honorable Company but to the
> preservation and saving of many men's lives and, what is more,
> to magnifying God's Holy Name and to the propagation of the
> gospel whereby, beyond all doubt, your Honor's trade over all
> India will be more and more blessed.[7]

But the marriage of Christianity and profit was not easy to sustain. The cordial trading relationship between travelers and local people soured rapidly when the Dutch East India Company, under the leadership of Jan Van Riebeeck, established a provisioning station at the Cape of Good Hope in 1652. Trading a few head of cattle with passing ships was one thing; but provisioning hundreds of ships en route to India each month required large quantities of meat. As long as they had surplus stocks, Khoikhoi herdsmen were not averse to trading them for European goods. Initially, they brought cattle to the Company fortress (known as the castle) for trade. But as their stocks became depleted, and competition for the remaining healthy herds grew, Khoikoi herders began raiding Company stocks.

The Company then dropped all pretence of friendly relations. The hedge of *Erkelbosch* (hooked thorns) that Van Riebeeck had been in-structed to plant around the castle to seal off the new settlement from "marauding natives" was both slow-growing and ineffective. Open conflict ensued when the Company ordered armed commandos to simply seize cattle allegedly stolen from the castle. Thousands of local people were killed in these raids. As historians Richard Elphick and Hermann Giliomee describe it, the slaughter was immense. Between 1786 and 1795, 2,840 indigenous people were killed, according to records which were almost certainly incomplete.[8]

Forced labour was one of the by-products of these raids. It was common practice to take survivors as war booty at that time – in most cases, women and children. The commando raids thus had the dual purpose of clearing the land for settlement and gaining a captive labour force. British traveler John Barrow observed that Company farmers had their work done for them by Khoikhoi men and women who cost them "nothing but meat, tobacco and skins."[9] Egbertus Bergh, a Company servant who was born in the Cape Colony, makes a similar observation in his memoirs, published in 1802:

> The Hottentots and other original inhabitants of this country
> were brought to a state of completely slavish subjection; these
> people, freeborn and rightful possessors of the land, do not
> now own even an inch of land as their property.... They are not
> even tolerated, unless it be for them to keep their wives and
> children on a piece of land situated at some remote corner where
> they had erected a miserable hut, while they themselves, for a
> trivial wage, suffering the most inconceivable maltreatment, are
> obliged to do the most difficult and despicable work as serfs of
> the farmers and other inhabitants.[10]

Thus, the loss of their cattle – part of their cultural identity as well as their primary source of food – became the first significant loss sustained by the Khoikhoi people, who had inhabited this vast southerly region of Africa for generations.

Land – particularly well-watered land – became the second flash point of the conflict between the local Cape people and European settlers. In 1657, the Company began granting land to Dutch settlers at the Cape of Good Hope, with the laying out of farms for the first "free burghers" (Company servants who were permitted to become farmers) on the lower eastern slopes of Table Mountain.[11] At first, burghers were given freehold title to as much land as they could farm in three years. This was to remain "their property for ever," with the right to sell, lease or alienate, and with a respite from taxation thrown in. The only condition was that they had to sell all their produce to the Dutch East India Company – hardly a concession, since the Company needed as much fresh produce as possible to supply the passing ships.[12]

As the colony expanded, more and more land was taken for the use of farmers. The Company gave Dutch settlers access to the traditional Khoikoi land as if it had been unoccupied. Very little if any acknowledgment was made to the prior rights of the inhabitants, and compensation was rarely considered. O.F. Mentzel, a German in the employ of the Dutch East India Company in 1741, described how the Khoikhoi were sometimes tricked into parting with their land by Dutch settlers in this way:

> The Hottentots are, as it were, the bloodhounds who smell out the most fertile lands. When their kraals are discovered in such places several Europeans or Afrikanders (Dutch) soon appear and, by gifts, flattery and other forms of cajolery, wheedle the Hottentots into granting permission for them to settle alongside. But as soon as the pasture land becomes too scanty for the cattle of these newcomers and the Hottentots, the latter are induced by trifling gifts to withdraw and travel further inland.[13]

As the best land passed into the hands of the Europeans, the independence of indigenous peoples diminished. Had they been farmers instead of pastoralists, the Khoikhoi may have been harder to drive from their lands and fountains. But as it was, their numbers greatly reduced by a sequence of smallpox epidemics, the few surviving Khoikhoi herders depended on white farmers for grazing rights. Thus, by the middle of the eighteenth century, the process of land dispossession was well under way.

When the freeburghers (or Boers, as they became known in this period) began to move further inland, they had to confront the San hunters who inhabited the semi-desert Karoo region. Although the San stole cattle and occasionally drove colonists from their farms, the Boers used their guns and horses to gain the upper hand. In 1863, the San pleaded for a "Bushman Reserve" – a small piece of their lands – to save the surviving community of 500 from the threat of starvation. The Company denied the request. As a result, the San who survived withdrew into the interior (primarily to Namibia and Botswana) or assimilated into the Khoikoi and so-called Coloured (Euro-African) populations. Some fled east and found temporary sanctuary in the Drakensberg Mountains between Lesotho and Natal. These fleeing groups left a poignant but

Rock paintings, Giant's Castle (Drakensberg), KwaZulu-Natal.

powerful record of their final battles against colonial aggression. Painted on the walls of caves and overhanging shelters are images of their own destruction: ox-wagons bringing Dutch settlers and British soldiers on horseback firing their rifles. Here and there on the rock face are the white-bodied figures of shamans transmitting the spiritual power of their ancestors that sustained them throughout their ordeal.

As the Boers moved further into the interior of the country, they encountered large groups of Nguni-speaking Africans. The largest and most powerful of these tribal nations were the Xhosa and the Zulu. When Europeans first arrived in South Africa, the Xhosa were distributed from around the Kei River all the way to what became known as southern Natal. The Zulu nation predominated further north along the coast and into the interior of Natal. The land throughout this region was ideally suited for subsistence farming and the raising of cattle, the focus of cultural identity of both groups of people. Although there was a hierarchical structure to Xhosa society, it was essentially democratic in nature. Over the years, the Zulus lost their former tradition of democratic control over royal prerogatives to become subjects of a centralized royal despotism. This was the essential difference between the two otherwise similar nations upon whom the burden of resistance to white penetration of the South African interior was to fall.

How North American Indians first arrived on the continent and how long they have been here remains open to speculation. The theory generally accepted by anthropologists and archeologists is that the first North Americans crossed the frozen Bering Strait from Siberia on foot between fifteen thousand and forty thousand years ago. There were several periods during the late Pleistocene geological age when a land bridge called Beringia emerged across the Bering Strait, the first identifiable one dating back to about seventy-five thousand years ago, and the last one ending about fourteen thousand years ago. This may have been the route they took. However, as Olive Dickason observes, there is no reason to conclude that because the land bridge offered a convenient passage for herders and large animals alike, that this was the only route available or used. The sea offered many options for travel as well. The Japanese Current sweeping from the Asiatic coast eastwards to the Americas provided a natural aquatic highway.[14] Recent research suggests that the Indians arrived in North America by more than one route and describes complex patterns of transoceanic migration in the North Pacific.

The first North Americans spread out and established themselves in widely diverse communities across what is now the United States and Canada. Some lived in villages, while others had mobile seasonal camps. While Indians in warmer climates built cities, the most northerly being Cahokia in Illinois, no cities were built in Canada. The social organization of North American Indians was quite diverse. Some societies were organized under matriarchal or patriarchal clans, while others had no clan system at all. Societies on the northwest coast became hierarchical, with clearly marked divisions between chiefs, nobles, and commoners based on wealth and heredity. In some west coast villages, slaves made up one-third of the population.[15] Of the historic Plains people, the Algonkian-speaking Blackfoot were probably the earliest to arrive on the vast open prairies of present-day Alberta, Manitoba and Saskatchewan. The most recent arrivals in this northwestern region, with the exception of the Plains Ojibwa (Saulteaux, Bungi) who reached Saskatchewan in the late eighteenth century, were the Plains Cree. Further to the east, in the Northeastern Midland Woodlands of North America, horticultural communities thrived. Huronian and Iroquian settlements in southern Ontario and Quebec and on the southern margins of the Canadian Shield were known for their cultivation of corn, beans and squash (the "three sisters"), evidence that they had traded with cultures in Mexico and Peru, where these crops had originally developed. Oral traditions and the rock paintings on the cliff faces of the Shield date back over two thousand years show the ancient home of the Algonkian-speaking Cree and Ojibway, whose roots may extend back to the beginning of human occupancy in the region almost ten thousand years ago.[16] The pictographs portray everyday life – canoes, animals, peoples – but also reveal the artists' connectedness with the spiritual world, the healing powers of the *manitous*, and Mother Earth.

Before the arrival of the Europeans, Canadian indigenous populations varied in size across the continent. On the east coast, the Mi'kmaq and Maliseet nations reportedly numbered thirty-five thousand people in 1534, according to the French explorer, Jacques Cartier. Also well populated was the fertile area around the Great Lakes in Southern Ontario and upstate New York, home of the Iroquois nation, who are estimated to have numbered about sixty thousand. But in contrast to scattered populations in the plains and river valleys, the west coast indigenous population was largest of all. The Gitxsan, Wet'suwet'en, Nisga'a, Haida, Nuu-chah-nulth, Kwagiulth, Tsimshian and many other nations developed sophisticated technologies to exploit the rich natural resources of fish (especially salmon) and game. The population of the northwest coast before European contact has been estimated at about two hundred thousand people, making it one of the most densely populated non-agricultural regions in the world.[17]

When Europeans arrived on the continent of North America in the sixteenth century, they encountered well-established societies fully engaged in highly competitive trading operations. In his study of Tsimshian culture, Jay Miller describes the fierce conflicts that took place between coastal communities before the arrival of Europeans. Far from living peacefully together, these communities were frequently at war with each other, guarding their territories and fishing grounds from rival groups.[18] In her seminal work on the history of Canada's First Nations, Olive Dickason notes that although intertribal hostilities were endemic in the Americas, Indians did not fight for the acquisition of land as such (although conflicts on the west coast often centred on resources) but for blood revenge, individual prestige, and, above all, for the possession of prisoners, either for adoption or sacrifice.[19]

As happened in southern Africa, North American Indians at first welcomed the Europeans as potential trading and military partners. According to the accounts of early explorers on Canada's east coast, two fleets of Mi'kmaq canoes (some forty or fifty of them) greeted French explorer Jacques Cartier in 1535 in Chaleur Bay, eager for fresh opportunities to trade. According to one eyewitness account, "some of these savages

"Passage by Sail" plaque, near Campbell River, Vancouver Island, British Columbia.

came to the point at the mouth of the cove, where we lay anchored with our ships … they made frequent signals to us to come ashore, holding up to us some furs on sticks." Once Cartier's men had come ashore, trading became so vigorous that the Indians finally withdrew naked, having bartered even the skins they wore as clothing.[20]

Similar stories are told about the reception of Europeans on Canada's west coast. After Captain James Cook visited the west coast of North America in 1778, his ship had scarcely any brass left on board, so eager were the Indians to acquire iron of any kind – and the sailors to part with it in exchange for furs. Some years later, in July 1787, Captain George Dixon's ship *The Queen Charlotte* was approached by a group of Haida who were "falling over each other to trade their cloaks and furs." According to Dixon's journal, when his vessel left the islands he had named the Queen Charlottes, it had almost two thousand furs on board.[21] Encouraged by the reception they received, British navigators continued to visit the western shores of North America in quest of the elusive Northwest Passage to India.

North American Indians on both sides of the continent were generous with the strangers who visited their shores, evidently perceiving no threat from them. Probably the best-known account of North American hospitality is contained in Jacques Cartier's journal. Having already lost twenty-five members of his crew to scurvy during the winter of 1535–36, Cartier describes how he and his men were rescued from complete extinction by Donnacona and his Huron people, who showed them how to create Vitamin C from cedar boughs and survive the brutal cold.[22] The French explorers and traders who followed Cartier learned from the Indians how to hunt, travel, and farm in the harsh Canadian environment. Inuit women in the Arctic made heavy parkas for the European whalers who wintered with their communities. Attracted by the prospect of European trade, the Montagnais, Innu-Naskapi, Mi'kmaq and Maliseet established conciliatory and mutually rewarding relationships as participants in the fur trade.

But not all North Americans were eager to trade with the newcomers from Europe. Like the aboriginal people of Van Diemen's Land (Tasmania), who fiercely resisted European encroachment on their island home, the Beothuk of Newfoundland, an island off the east coast of North America, refused to accommodate European interests in their land (see Appendix). The first Europeans the Beothuk encountered were the Vikings, who settled briefly on the northern tip of Newfoundland in AD 1000 and appeared to have little contact with the local people. In the 1500s, Basque fishermen exploited the rich fishing grounds off Canada's eastern seaboard. The Beothuk gave them a wide berth at first, leaving the Basque fishing gear and boats (left in the whale ports each winter) untouched until the fishermen returned from Spain the following spring. However, when the Basque began developing fish-drying operations onshore, the atmosphere changed. The Beothuk had developed special sites for summer fishing; when the Basque erected their drying racks on these favoured sites, the conflict began.[23]

The British, who eventually colonized the island, were left in no doubt about the hostility of the local people. Early in the seventeenth century, Sir Richard Whitbourne, one of the "fishing admirals" of the Grand Banks, reported that operations were being thwarted because the "Savages of that country.... Secretly every year come into Trinity Bay and Harbor, in the nighttime, purposely to steale Sailes, Lines, Hookes, Knives, Hatchets and such like...."[24] Meanwhile British immigration to the region grew. In 1814–15 alone, eleven thousand Irish immigrants arrived in Newfoundland. The Beothuk gradually retreated further into the interior until they were confined to a small area close to Red Indian Lake at the centre of the island. As settlement increased, the conflict intensified. The European settlers sent out so-called reprisal expeditions, very like those conducted by the Dutch East India Company at the Cape of Good Hope, to punish and subdue the Beothuk. In his 1842 treatise about the situation in Newfoundland, Sir Richard Bonnycastle wrote: "It has been the disgraceful practice of the ruder hunters, furriers, and settlers

Fishing village on west coast of Newfoundland (2004).

in Newfoundland, to hunt, fire at, and slaughter [Indians] wherever they could find them, treating these rightful lords of the soil as they would the bears and wolves, and with just as little remorse."[25]

In addition to the deliberate killing by hunters and fishermen, many Beothuk lost their lives to diseases like smallpox, venereal disease and tuberculosis, introduced into the country by Europeans. Hundreds perished from starvation, their livelihood destroyed by furriers' traplines and the consequent disruption of the caribou hunt. Less than two hundred years later, Newfoundland's charming fishing villages reveal nothing of their tragic history. The Beothuk are rarely mentioned in Newfoundland's museums. Their "disappearance," when referred to at all, is attributed to their vulnerability as a "primitive race."

The Arctic region (north of the sixtieth parallel), which is now home to the Inuit and other indigenous peoples, notably the Dene and the Métis, has a long history of European intrusion. First the Vikings, then, between 1530 and 1740, a number of European whalers and later traders and settlers came to the Arctic. Sir Martin Frobisher made several journeys in the 1500s, followed by Henry Hudson in 1610. Sixty years later, the Hudson's Bay Company was granted its charter over Rupert's Land. The fur trade and whaling operations in the northeastern Arctic (Davis Strait) were followed by missionary activity. The first mission of the Moravian Church was established in 1770 on the coast of Labrador. Later, the Franklin Expedition (1845–48) brought international attention to the High Arctic.

But apart from these activities, the people of the north were left largely undisturbed until the latter half of the twentieth century.

SLAVERY IN CANADA AND SOUTH AFRICA

Like their counterparts in other French and Dutch colonies, both New France and the Cape colony were slave-holding societies. France's involvement in the slave trade in its West Indian colonies played an important role in the introduction of slavery in New France. The practice of enslaving Indians taken in war was widespread in both North and South America. In the French colonies, enslaved Indians were called *panis*.[26] By the early seventeenth century, there were more *panis* than enslaved Africans in New France. But although the institution of slavery received royal sanction in 1689 and lasted for seventy-four years in New France, its legal footing was never very secure. Moreover, the captive population of New France was never very large and certainly never exceeded the settler population. When the colony came under the administration of Louis XIV in 1663, the importation of enslaved Africans was seen as both a means of increasing the colony's population and providing the necessary manpower to develop it. However, some scholars claim that slaveholding was primarily a symbol of status in New France, since there was little use for a captive labour force on the small family farms that supported the needs of the small colony.

In the Cape of Good Hope, the institution of slavery had a much more extensive history than it had in Canada. Because the Dutch were already heavily involved in the slave trade in the East and West Indies, they automatically expanded the trade to the Cape settlement. Chattel slavery started under Dutch East India Company rule and remained in place for nearly two hundred years. Although domestic slave policy took shape more gradually, the experience of the Dutch in the East Indies meant that slavery came to the Cape fully developed, governed by laws already in force and overseen by experienced Company officials in the East Indies.[27] The first shipments of captive Africans from Dahomey and Angola arrived in 1658, six years after Jan Van Riebeeck took over as Commander of the settlement. By the early 1700s, the slave population, drawn from Africa as well as Indonesia, exceeded that of the settlers. According to Davenport and Saunders, it was "the abundance of apparently free land and the scarcity of suitable labour" that predisposed the Cape settlement (as with other similar societies) to import slaves.[28]

The unquestioned association of labour with skin colour in the minds of white South Africans has traditionally been blamed on slavery – although it could be argued that it was the notion of racial superiority that gave rise to slavery in the first place.[29] Certainly, both slavery and the racial ideology that supported it were major factors in creating South Africa's peculiar racial labour order. Historians Elphick and Giliomee describe the three-tiered social structure that emerged from the slave era as a pyramid with the slave population at the base, a second servant class comprised of Khoikhoi and San people and "free" blacks (emancipated slaves) at the centre, and the European masters on the top – who did not themselves produce labour but depended on slave and indigenous labour.[30] Apart from attitudes relating to labour, slavery seems to have laid the foundations of a hierarchy of rights in South Africa where only the civil rights of white people were respected. To quote Rodney Davenport, "Cape society developed along caste lines, an almost unbridgeable legal and social divide separating the free men who possessed civil rights – the right to marry, to own property, to provide for their children, to bring or defend an action in court – and the slaves who, as Roman Law … made clear, possessed only the natural right to eat and sleep, and to cohabit, and not to be deprived of life without sufficient cause."[31]

Despite the enormous impact of slavery on South Africa's highly race-conscious society, it is only in the last few decades that scholars have paid it much attention. Nigel Worden and Kelly Ward note that for several generations, former slaves and their descendants used to celebrate the anniversary of the emancipation of slaves in the Cape of Good Hope (December 1, 1834) as a public holiday. But this practice stopped by the early twentieth century, as those born in slavery died out. Then, as the effects of racial laws eroded their desire to commemorate the painful past, a state of collective amnesia set in. Images and representations of slavery have been firmly submerged in the Cape for a century, in striking contrast to African American cultures in the United States and the Caribbean, where slave descendants still identify strongly with their slave heritage. Until 1994, and the end of the apartheid era, school curricula and museums were silent on the subject, and even slave descendants themselves (Euro-Africans who were often referred to as "Cape Malay" or "Coloureds") repressed their slave ancestry in order to improve their economic and political status. As Africans became increasingly marginalized under apartheid, people of mixed heritage had more to gain by identifying themselves with their white ancestry than with their slave or black heritage.[32]

Slavery and the notion of racial superiority that underpinned it has penetrated Canadian culture in more subtle ways. Robin Blackburn points out that the very presence of black slaves in colonial societies contributed to the denigration of indigenous peoples and a sense of equality and "leveling up" among whites.[33] The experiences of maltreatment of the so-called Refugee and Maroon Negroes who flooded into Nova Scotia (also a slave society) after the War of 1812 shows the racial attitudes of the colonials. Like many Indian communities across the country, these refugee African men and women lost their self-sufficiency through displacement. Their failure to flourish on the poor land they were given and adapt to their new life and environment fed the scorn of the white colonists, who regarded them as "neither prosperous nor useful."[34]

When the British Parliament abolished slavery throughout the Empire in 1833, the terms of liberation were spelled out for the almost 1,800 slaves still in captivity in the Cape of Good Hope, the Caribbean, Bermuda and Mauritius. British North America was not considered to be among the slave-owning nations, although fifty slaves were freed under the Act.[35] It is interesting to note that while slave-owners were compensated for their loss, albeit at a rate considered inadequate by many colonists, compensation for those who had spent their lives in captivity was never considered. No provision was made for land or capital for the freed men and women of the British colonies.

BRITISH NORTH AMERICA

In 1760, the capitulation of the French to British forces on the Plains of Abraham (New France) brought a sudden shift in the relationship between aboriginal and settler societies in North America. During the conflict, Indian nations had made military alliances with the European powers on the understanding that the Europeans would have use (not ownership) of the land in return for annual "presents" (mainly provisions and ammunition) and other conditions. However, once the French had capitulated, the British lost no time in withdrawing the "presents" which they viewed as no longer necessary. But the Indians regarded the agreements differently. To them, the gifts were not only symbols of their renewed allegiance with the English but also an agreed-upon price for occupation and use of their lands. With the French defeated, rumours quickly spread that the British were going to seize Indian lands for settlement. The Indians were well aware of the danger they faced. In 1760, Ojibway Chief Minweweh sent this message to the British Colonial Office:

> Although you have conquered the French, you have not
> conquered us. We are not your slaves. These lakes, these woods
> and mountains were left us by our ancestors. They are our
> inheritance, and we will not part with them to none.[36]

But Minweweh's message was apparently ignored and the alienation of Indian lands continued.

Over the next few years, the British forces faced fierce resistance from Indian nations determined to protect their homelands from foreign invasion. But British generals were willing to go to great lengths to achieve their objectives, many of which would offend modern codes of international ethics, even in wartime. One of the most notorious incidents in Canadian history took place during this period. In 1763, Ottawa war chief Pontiac and the combined forces of northern tribes came close to driving the British forces from the Great Lakes. When the Indians launched a series of successful attacks against the British, destroying a number of their forts, British Commander-in-Chief Jeffrey Amherst ordered that every method should be used to "extirpate this inexorable race." Included in his instructions to Colonel Henry Bouquet was the directive to distribute smallpox-infected blankets to Indian camps.[37] Although there is no proof that Colonel Bouquet carried out these orders, many Indians fell victim to this disease at about this time. One by one, the Indian leaders decided to sue for peace. In 1764, each of the nineteen chiefs involved in the war signed separate agreements at a peace conference at Fort Niagara. Pontiac was not among them, but seeing no alternative, he too signed an agreement the following year. This agreement allowed the British to reoccupy their forts with only one condition: that Indian hunting grounds remained undisturbed. Thus, the Indians were able to keep partial control over their lands; but the capitulation to the British and alienation of large swaths of their land was a serious blow to Indian independence.

An important outcome of the Pontiac war was the Royal Proclamation of 1763, which set a boundary line between white and native America along the Appalachian chain. The Proclamation, signed by King George III, has been hailed as a "Magna Carta" for North American Indians. However, it is evident from the wording of the document that the primary motivation on the part of the Europeans was essentially self-interest:

[It is] just and reasonable, and essential to our interests, and the security of our colonies, that the several Nations or tribes of Indians with whom we are connected, and who live under our protection, should not be molested or disturbed in the possession of such parts of our Dominion and Territories as, not having been ceded or purchased by us, are reserved to them or any of them as their hunting ground.[38]

While the British were motivated at least in part by genuine fear of re-prisals from the powerful Indian nations that surrounded them, the Royal Proclamation clearly recognized the inherent rights of aboriginal peoples to their ancestral territories. As such, it remains the legal basis for many Indian reserves, land claims, and aboriginal rights issues in the United States and Canada.

During the next phase of European conflict – between Great Britain and the rebellious Thirteen Colonies – Indian military alliances came under the greatest pressure. The outcome was the weakening of Indian power and the loss of Indian land. Although the Iroquois Confederacy had been very successful in serving its own agenda before 1760, it was divided by the American war against Britain. The Mohawks and the Cayugas were pro-British, while the Oneidas and Tuskaroras sided with the Americans. The Seneca and Onondaga were split between the two warring factions. Yet despite the price the Iroquois Confederacy paid in lives and unity, the Peace of Paris (1783) concluded the American War of Independence without mentioning the Indian nations at all. Under the terms of the Treaty, their lands were simply divided up between the two European nations without reference to the inhabitants, allies or otherwise. However, in an effort to placate their Iroquois allies (and provide a resting place for the thousands of refugees displaced by the war), the British purchased land from the Mississauga (Ojibwa) on the north shore of Lake Ontario, along the Grand River in Upper Canada. Although the original grant of 1784 has been much reduced in size, this is still Iroquois territory.

With an eye to securing the strategically important region of what is now southwestern Ontario as a buffer against possible American en-croachment, the British government began to negotiate for the purchase of Indian land and actively encourage the settlement of British immi-grants. Over the next decade, the Ojibwa and closely related Odawa nations relinquished large tracts of land between Lake Erie and the Thames River in Upper Canada for European settlement. A hallmark of these treaties was the use of totemic signatures by the Indian chiefs involved, statements of their distinctive identity as aboriginal peoples.[39] Among these is Upper Canada Treaty 5 for the purchase of lands in the Penetanguishene area signed in 1798.

In the early 1800s, a new Indian leader emerged to fight for the American Indians' rightful ownership of ancestral lands. Part Shawnee, part Cree, Tecumseh set out to rally the indigenous peoples of North America in this cause. Like Pontiac, he was connected to a pan-American

Treaty No. 5, Penetanguishene Area, Upper Canada, 22 May 1798.
Source: Library and Archives Canada, c15390.

religious movement that promoted the notion that land did not belong to any one tribal nation but to North American Indians as a whole. His crusade met with considerable opposition from chiefs who believed his proposed intertribal council would undermine their own authority. At the same time, conflict between the colonies of British North America and the United States was heating up at the turn of the nineteenth century. So the British began wooing Tecumseh and other chiefs with the re-introduction of "gifts." When the War of 1812 broke out on the border of Upper Canada, Tecumseh became one of Britain's most valued allies. The fall of Michilimackinac on 17 July 1812, to British and Indian forces, due in part to Tecumseh's ingenious surprise strategy, was among the many decisive victories of the war. But the Treaty of Ghent, which formally ended the war in 1814, did not restore any of the Indian lands lost before the American War of Independence. Tecumseh died in battle, and his dream of a united Indian front died with him.

The War of 1812 marked the end of an era for the Indians of British North America. In 1830, the British government shifted Indian administration from the military to a new civilian arm of government. At the same time, the demise of the fur trade (due to over-hunting and the subsequent decline of the beaver population) brought an end to the period of accommodation and cooperation that characterized Indian-European relations in the early years. If the fur trade was the glue which bound the people of the Old and New Worlds together, its conclusion emphasized the deep gulf between the two societies. The cleavages became even more distinct after the 1820s, when major colonial priorities shifted from trade and military alliances with Indians to land for settlement. By this time, the British were accustomed to thinking of the land as theirs and were acting accordingly.

THE CAPE UNDER BRITISH RULE

Similar patterns of land alienation developed in the Cape of Good Hope. For the indigenous inhabitants, the end of Dutch rule in 1806 and the advent of British rule was a significant landmark. When the British abolished the slave trade in 1807, the Khoikhoi became increasingly important as a labour force. The slave-like status of the Khoikhoi was confirmed by the Hottentot Proclamation of 1809, which made it a crime for them to be in a "white area" unless employed there.

The difference between the Hottentot Proclamation and North America's Royal Proclamation of 1763 is striking. Despite both being instruments of British colonial administration, the North American proclamation recognized the inherent rights of indigenous inhabitants to their land while the Khoikhoi were denied even the freedom to move from one part of their country to another. Under the terms of the Proclamation, the rule that slaves had to carry passes (identity documents) was extended to the Khoikhoi and later to the so-called "Basters" (descendants of European and Khoikhoi parents).[40] As landless wanderers, the Khoikhoi were subject to yet another piece of legislation. When the draft Vagrancy Act was published in 1834 (it never became law, being superseded by the Master and Servant Act of 1842), field cornets (frontier police) were permitted to issue passes and arrest any Khoikhoi they considered to be a "vagrant."

However, in 1828, the Colonial government revised its Cape policy, partly to appease missionary sensibilities. The promulgation of the 49th and 50th Ordinances gave the Khoikhoi some degree of legal status, but only temporarily. Claiming to afford the Khoikhoi people full legal equality with European colonists, these two pieces of legislation were touted by the British as the "Hottentot's Magna Carta." Under the terms of Ordinance 50 (1828), passes were abolished, and "Hottentots and other free persons of colour" were declared fully eligible to purchase or possess land in the colony. By that time, however, all the best land had been taken over by Dutch settlers. Moreover, colonial authorities were very reluctant to grant land to Khoikhoi in the vicinity of towns or villages.[41] The freedoms described in the Ordinances (if they were indeed such, since there were no mechanisms in place to enforce them) were short-lived. In 1842, the Ordinances were repealed, and the legal status of the Cape Khoikhoi reverted once again to near-slavery.

FRONTIER SOCIETIES

As the tentacles of colonial rule extended across the frontiers of British North America and the Cape Colony, confrontations over land increased. Competition for land affected not only the indigenous populations but also the people of mixed descent who sought new homes for their communities in these remote areas. The cultural blending that took place during the fur trade era in North America, and in the multicultural milieu of the Cape Colony, resulted in the formation of distinct societies, each of which developed their own identity, languages and political structures. Although the circumstances of their origins were different, the story of the Métis (people of Indian-French descent) and the Griqua (people of Euro-African descent) have much in common. Both went out in search of independence and a territory of their own. Both gained some success as frontier societies under charismatic leadership, despite British challenges to their quest for territorial and political independence.

While people of mixed European and indigenous descent are scattered across Canada, it was only in the North-West that a dominant group emerged with an identifiable history and culture. Initially, the term "Métis" applied to people of French and aboriginal parentage, but later it referred to anyone with aboriginal ancestry who considered themselves to be Métis. The unique Métis culture that developed was neither Indian nor European but shaped by the special conditions of the fur trade and the highly organized buffalo hunt on the prairies.

The sense of political identity that emerged within the Métis community had its genesis in the 1860s when it appealed to the newly founded Canadian government for recognition of its sovereignty as an independent nation. The government's response was to send out a military contingent to assert its own sovereignty over the claimed territory. In 1869, under the leadership of Louis Riel, the Métis launched their first uprising against government forces and formed a provisional government in what was to become the province of Manitoba. When this rebellion was crushed, many Métis migrated to what is now Saskatchewan, where they launched a second rebellion in 1885, in which the Métis were militarily and politically defeated. Riel was later hanged as a "traitor," and the Métis people were further dispersed north and west. According to historian D.N. Sprague, although the aboriginal rights of the Métis had been recognized in the Manitoba Act of 1870, the promises of special land rights have never been fully honoured.[42] Olive Dickason adds that the question of Métis land rights is complicated by the fact that after all the confrontations over land, the vast majority of Métis took a cash settlement rather than "scrip" land that was unsuitable for farming. The Métis who took scrip often sold their land for a song to prospectors. Fortunes were made at the expense of the Métis, creating a class of "half-breed scrip millionaires."[43] Today, the Métis nation is urging the federal government to deal with its land claims on a nation-to-nation basis. Moreover, the Métis demand that their constitutional rights as one of Canada's aboriginal peoples be recognized through modern treaties which would specify the extent of their land bases and compensation for past injustices.

The history of South Africa's Griqua people is similar to that of the Métis in a number of ways. Originally known as "Basters" or "Bastaards" until renamed by the missionaries, the Griqua were the descendants of Dutch settlers (or soldiers or sailors from visiting ships) and slave or Khoikhoi women. The Griqua who settled on the eastern frontier of the Cape Colony developed as both pastoral farmers and game hunters – primarily of elephant – and established a lucrative trade in ivory. As with the Métis, their decline as a people resulted from a shortage of game and competition with white settlers for land and resources.

Like the Métis, the Griqua enjoyed a brief period of political autonomy as a frontier society. Under the leadership of Adam Kok I, a former slave, one branch of Griqua society formed a republic known as Griqualand West, with its own legal code, courts and coinage. A second Griqua state was formed at the former missionary station at Philippolis, where the community became successful sheep farmers. Both communities received protection (as well as arms and ammunition) from the Cape colonial government for their services in driving out their Khoikhoi kinsmen to make way for white settlement. But in 1854, when the Boer colony, the Orange Free Sovereignty was granted independence, the Griqua's land and political rights were undermined. Intimidated by the Boer authorities, Griqua farmers began to sell off their land in panic sales, much as the Métis did in Manitoba. After an epic trek across the mountains, they established a third Griqua state just south of modern Lesotho, which they called Griqualand East. However, once again, settlers encroached on their territory. In 1878, the Griqua rebelled; but the Cape Colony eventually took over their territory. South African historian Rodney Davenport ascribes the failure of the Griqua to sustain their hard-won independence and territorial integrity to "white racialism" (the Griqua were perceived as inferior because of their African heritage) and the shortage of arable land.[44] The discovery of vast deposits of diamonds in the Griqua's former territories in the 1860s was probably the most important factor of all.

Other groups of Afro-Europeans settled in different areas. Among these were the Nama people who traveled north along the Atlantic seaboard and settled south of the Orange River in what became known as Namaqualand. Mission stations at places like the Richtersveld, Komaggas, Steinkopf, Leliefontein and Pella were established in the nineteenth century. In 1868, a group of Nama people trekked across the Orange River under the leadership of a Rhenish Missionary, Hermanus van Wyk, and established a new home for themselves at Rehoboth in present-day Namibia. They are called the Rehoboth Basters, who have maintained their identity into the twenty-first century as a distinct close-knit community.[45] Yet another group of Khoikhoi descendants settled on the Orange River in the region of its confluence with the Vaal River. These people were known as the Kora (or Korana). Finally, there were the

Khoikhoi and San who blended with the surviving community of Free Blacks and former slaves (many of whom were Muslims) after Britain's emancipation legislation of 1828–33. All of these distinct communities were classified as "Coloured" by European governments.

CONCLUSION

The indigenous peoples of North America and southern Africa faced similar colonial forces – wars, diseases, enslavement, miscegenation, and land appropriation – and defended their right to control the lands they had occupied for thousands of years. Indigenous North Americans (with the exception of the Beothuk) were more successful in retaining some autonomy and control over their lands and resources than the original people of the Cape. Using their fur trade knowledge and diplomatic skills, they were able to play one European power against the other and force the recognition of their inherent aboriginal rights.

But when colonization spread across the colonial frontiers of British North America and the British Cape Colony, and European settlement took on a more permanent nature, the power relationship on both continents shifted away from the indigenous inhabitants. The wars, rebellions, leadership strategies and alliances of both North American and African indigenous groups show that they regarded themselves as landowners and sovereign people, not squatters or slaves. It took deliberate and often cunning strategies on the part of European settlers to wrest control of the land from the North American and African peoples. Underlying these strategies were notions of imperial right, European legal process and racial superiority. But nowhere did North American Indians or Métis or Africans, Khoikhoi, San or Griqua willingly give their land to the invaders.

Chapter Two
Land Rights and Treaties

We have both outraged the natural sense of right and the feelings of
independence, always remarkably strong in wild people, by taking
their all without attempting a compensation; and, after this violent
exclusion of the rightful owner, we have almost exclusively re-
appointed every acre to white people.

> *Report of the Select Committee on Aborigines*
> *(British Settlements), Vol. 16, 1836.*

INTRODUCTION

In the early 1830s, British colonialism came under the critical scrutiny
of a group of British reformers. The British humanitarian movement
had just won a significant victory against slavery and now saw ominous
parallels between the wholesale slaughter and dispossession of indigenous peoples and slavery. As Sir Thomas Buxton of the Aborigines
Protection Society declared, "I hate shooting savages worse than slavery
itself."[1] The re-direction of the passion and zeal which had achieved the
abolition of slavery was clearly expressed in the Society's first Annual
Report in 1838:

The abhorred and nefarious slave traffic, which has engaged
for so long a period the indefatigable labours of a noble band
of British philanthropists for its suppression and annihilation,
can scarcely be regarded as less atrocious in its character, or
destructive in its consequences, than the system of modern
colonization as hitherto pursued.[2]

Under pressure from the Aborigines Protection Society, the British government established an inquiry: the Select Committee on Aborigines
(British Settlements) which published its report in several volumes between 1836 and 1838. The conclusion the Select Committee reached was

that, rather than being the blessing many had hoped for, colonialism had been a dreadful blight on the history of the British Empire and on the lives of the so-called uncivilized nations of the world. In their testimony to the Committee, missionaries, traders and military officers warned that if the destructive trends continued, indigenous populations would "melt like snow before the advancement of European settlement."

However, the reformers were not against colonization *per se* – far from it. They believed it was the Christian duty to "civilize the dark corners of the earth." What seemed to be required was some form of protection for the " Inferior Races" against unrestrained colonial aggression. The recommendation of the Select Committee was that local authorities in the colonies make an effort to negotiate treaties with the indigenous inhabitants for the alienation of their lands and to set aside "reserved lands" for their sole use and benefit. The idea of treaties was not new. Hundreds of peace and friendship treaties had already been signed between indigenous chiefs and British consuls and agents in colonies throughout the Empire, but these were largely related to securing military allies (or trading partners in the case of North America) and seldom involved the acquisition of native lands.

Thus the idea of negotiating with aboriginal peoples for the alienation of their land through legal treaties became accepted policy in most parts of the British Empire. These agreements came within the accepted definition of a nation-to-nation treaty and were taken seriously by the British Colonial Office. Between 1820 and 1924, the Librarian and Keeper of the Archives of the Foreign Office in London compiled and published a series of thirty volumes of treaties known as *Hertslet's Commercial Treaties*.

CANADIAN TREATIES

The earliest treaties in North America between European powers and Indian nations were primarily concerned with peace and friendship; land was secondary, if mentioned at all. In New France, land never became an issue because the fur-trading French were more interested in preserving good relations with their Indian allies than acquiring land for settlement. In British North America, on the other hand, land was a factor because the colonized territories were occupied by aboriginal farmers who were less likely to allow even usufructuary rights (the use but not ownership of land) to the Europeans without adequate compensation. The Treaty of Halifax (1752) with the Mi'kmaqs of Nova Scotia was among the most important of the early peace treaties negotiated by the British. Not only did the treaty terminate the war which the Mi'kmaq had initiated against the British, but it also guaranteed hunting and fishing rights for the

Indians and regular gift distributions, which would later be transformed into annuity payments for surrendered lands.[3]

After defeating France in 1760, the British took possession of vast territories of North America previously under French control, including Acadia (Nova Scotia). The assumption seemed to be that, having defeated France, Britain had not only acquired sovereignty over New France but was also released from the obligation to compensate local people for their land. When New Brunswick was separated from Nova Scotia and became a colony in its own right in 1784, the British colonial authorities refused to recognize the only land grant that had been made to King John Julian of the Mi'kmaq by the previous administration, twenty thousand acres (8,094 hectares) along the Mirimachi River.

By the turn of the nineteenth century, the leverage the aboriginal peoples had gained through trade and military alliances had declined dramatically. A hundred years after the signing of the Treaty of Halifax (1752), the Mi'kmaq complained about the miserly compensation the British had paid them for the "lands, forests and fisheries, long since taken from them." Moreover, the "permanent plots" promised to them when they "laid down their arms and smoked the pipe of peace" had never materialized.[4] Maritime Indians had been greatly reduced in number and had suffered drastic losses of political leverage as well as land since the early years of colonization. Their needs had been pushed aside to accommodate those of the new immigrants, especially the United Empire Loyalists fleeing the American Revolution.[5] In 1848, the Commissioner for Indian Affairs for New Brunswick reviewed the unhappy history of the Mi'kmaq and the Maliseet of the colony in these words:

Both tribes were very numerous and powerful when New Brunswick was first entered upon as a British colony after the taking of Québec by General Wolfe. At the outset, whole districts of country were assigned to the Indians and treaties were made by which English settlers were restricted to certain areas. As settlement advanced, the Indians were driven back and tracts of land, called Indian Reserves, were set apart for their use and occupation which were gradually reduced in extent.... Land grants were made to Loyalists without treaties or surrenders being attained from the Indians.[6]

The situation of indigenous communities on Cape Breton Island in Nova Scotia was very similar. In 1845, a report to the Nova Scotia Legislative Assembly stated that

These lands [Cape Breton Island] are eagerly coveted by the
Scotch [*sic*] Presbyterian settlers. That the Micmac's fathers were
sole possessor's [*sic*] of these regions is a matter of no weight
with the Scottish emigrants. They are by no means disposed
to leave the aboriginals a resting place on the Island of Cape
Breton.[7]

By the turn of the nineteenth century, the purpose of treaties in North
America had changed. The shifting ground of international law during
the course of the nineteenth century – away from notions of equality to
the rights of "discovery" – had a profound impact on the role and nature
of treaties in North America. With declining aboriginal populations (resulting from disease, wars and above all, displacement from their ancestral lands), treaties of peace and friendship were no longer essential to the
safety of colonists. The objective of negotiating agreements with Indian
nations was now to clear the path for European settlement. During the
period of colonial expansion just prior to and following Confederation in
1867, treaties provided a veneer of legitimacy to the wholesale alienation
of Indian lands for European settlement.

In 1850, William B. Robinson, a former fur trader, entered into the first
of a series of so-called numbered treaties on behalf of Upper Canada.
Treaties One and Two, which encompassed vast areas on the north shores
of Lake Huron and Lake Superior, set the pattern for future treaties by
including hunting and fishing rights as part of the compensation package. After Confederation in 1867, the policy of treaty-making became a
source of national pride, since it removed the necessity of entering into
wars against Indian landholders, as was occurring in the United States.[8]
In 1871, the Nova Scotian politician Joseph Howe stated to an approv-
ing House of Commons that "it was impossible to deny that the policy
of the British North Americans has been not only just and generous but
successful."[9]

Land alienation in Canada's west coast region of British Columbia,
which joined Confederation in 1871, began with a set of treaties signed
by Governor James Douglas on Vancouver Island in the 1850s. Unlike
the Robinson treaties, which were at least nominally founded on the
notion of aboriginal rights, the Douglas Treaties on Vancouver Island
were based on a British legal precedent established in New Zealand. The
Waitangi Treaty (1840) in New Zealand had effectively dispossessed the
Māori of their land by designating all uncultivated land as "waste land"
and making it available to colonists (see Appendix). Thus, in fourteen
land sale agreements with the First Nations of Vancouver Island between

1850 and 1854, the Indians retained ownership only of their village sites and enclosed fields (land under cultivation). Their only right in the surrounding areas was a usufructuary right: the right to hunt and fish as before. The agreements were sealed with "payment" of blankets and promises of money.

Although Governor Douglas' Indian policy is often portrayed as sensitive to Indian needs, it was strongly influenced by the positivist theory that the rights of "civilized" nations take precedence over those of aboriginal nations. Vastly outnumbered by the indigenous inhabitants of the west coast, the colonists used considerable force and intimidation to obtain the agreement of local people. The final Douglas Treaty was made with the Saalequun people, who were occupying the site of the Hudson's Bay Company's coal mining operation at Colvilletown, later named Nanaimo. The signing of that treaty was preceded by "random displays of gunnery" from a two-storey bastion Douglas had built close to the coal shaft. In his description of the land sale agreement with the Saalequun chiefs, Chris Arnett includes the testimony of a Saalequun elder, Quen-es-then, who was present at the signing as a boy:

The Hudson's Bay Company men talked to the Indians: This coal is no good to you, but we would like it; but we want to be friends, so, if you will let us come and take as much of this black rock as we want, we will be good to you.... The Good Queen, our great white chief, far over the water, will look after your people for all time, and they will be given much money, so that they will never be poor.... Then they gave each chief a bale of HBC blankets and a lot of shirts and tobacco ... these presents are for you and your people, to show we are your good friends.[10]

However, the promised payment never came. As another Saalequun witness stated, "We think there was some mistake at that meeting, or, maybe, our people did not fully understand what was said. Later when our people asked for some of the money for their coal, the HBC men said to them 'Oh, we paid you when we gave you those good blankets!' But those two chiefs knew that the men had said, 'The Queen will give you money.'"[11]

Because of their traditional dependency on the land for survival, many Indian communities entered into agreements because they saw few other options. This was especially the case with the Plains Indians. With the gradual disappearance of the bison, the mainstay of their traditional lifestyle, Indians entered into treaties in the hope of salvaging at least a portion of their territory and independence. An example is the 1874 deal between Commissioner Morris and the gathered chiefs at Qu'Appelle, Saskatchewan. In this case, the chiefs were able to negotiate both reserves and the right to hunt and fish on land that was not yet settled. Even the terminology and patronizing tone used by the government officials when addressing the Chiefs could be interpreted as bargaining language tolerated by the Indians in order to gain the most favourable terms possible.

> The Queen knows that her red children often find it hard to live. She knows that her red children, their wives and children, are often hungry, and that the buffalo will not last for ever and that she desires to do something for them.... The Queen has to think of what will come along after to-day. Therefore, the promises we have to make to you are not for today only but for to-morrow, not only for you but for your children born and unborn, and the promises we make will be carried out as long as the sun shines above and water flows in the ocean. When you are ready to plant seeds the Queen's men will lay off Reserves ... and you will have the right of hunting and fishing just as you have now until the land is actually taken up.[12]

The offer of seeds for planting and government assistance to train them in agriculture was a further incentive to sign treaties. However, as an Indian Affairs official observed in 1946: "While these treaties or agreements were bilateral in form, actually, of course, the Indians had to accept the conditions offered or lose their interest in the lands anyway."[13] The last numbered treaty to be signed in western Canada was Treaty Eleven in 1921.

Even though Canadian treaties tacitly acknowledged aboriginal rights, reserved lands were gradually whittled away by Orders in Council. New legislation frequently overruled treaty promises of annuities and other forms of compensation. For example, after the signing of Treaty Eight following the Klondike gold strike in 1898, the federal government introduced new legislation to restrict native hunting and trapping. Both the treaty and the provision of hunting and fishing rights had been insisted upon by the Yukon Indians. Thus, there was strong resistance when the Northwest Territories Games Act and Migratory Birds Convention Act were passed in 1918, restricting the hunting of caribou, moose and certain other animals essential to the economy of native people. Northern Indian groups regarded these laws as breaches of their treaties.

Treaty Number Eleven

Articles of a Treaty

made and concluded on the several dates mentioned therein, in the year of Our Lord One thousand Nine hundred and Twenty-One, between His Most Gracious Majesty George V, King of Great Britain and Ireland and of the British Dominions beyond the Seas, by His Commissioner, Henry Anthony Conroy, Esquire, of the City of Ottawa, of the One Part, and the Slave, Dogrib, Loucheux, Hare and other Indians, inhabitants of the territory within the limits hereinafter defined and described, by their Chiefs and Headmen, hereunto subscribed, of the other part:—

Whereas, the Indians inhabiting the territory hereinafter defined have been convened to meet a Commissioner representing His

Western Treaty Number Eleven, 1921. Source: Library and Archives Canada, c107634.

TREATIES IN COLONIAL SOUTH AFRICA

The indigenous peoples in South Africa involved in treaty negotiations with their European invaders fared even worse than the first peoples of North America. Despite the seventeenth-century arguments concerning the illegality of foreign occupation, colonial policy at the Cape of Good Hope was established under the dictum that might was right. Under

Dutch East India Company rule, land was regarded as the legitimate "reward" of conquest, although "presents" were sometimes offered to chiefs who still posed a threat. This account from the journals of Jan Van Riebeeck is a typical example of early peace treaties in the Cape Colony:

> They [the Khoikhoi] dwelt long upon our taking every day for our own use more of the land, which had belonged to them from all ages.... They also asked whether, if they were to come to Holland, they would be permitted to act in a similar manner ... I replied that the country had now been justly won by the sword in defensive warfare, and that it was our intention to retain it. But we concluded the peace by giving them presents, as well as a party, where the brandy flowed so freely that they were all well fuddled, and, if we had chosen, we could have easily kept them in our power.[14]

In 1780, the Company Directors in Amsterdam sent this directive to the Commandants of the Eastern Country:

> Should the kafirs not be disposed to adhere to and fulfill the treaty which the governor made with them regarding the boundary, and not be induced to comply thereto by arguments, you will at once assemble a respectable and well-armed commando and thus forcibly compel them to go to the further side of the Fish River and remain there.[15]

As white settlement spread into the interior, the colonists were faced with the powerful resistance of two well-organized and well-populated Nguni-speaking peoples – the Xhosa and the Zulu. Treaties were used by both the Voortrekkers (the Dutch farmers who migrated from the Cape in what became known as the Great Trek) and the British colonists, as well as African chiefs determined to protect their lands from foreign invasion. However, most of the competition for land was largely resolved through military conflict. Where treaties failed (and they usually did), well-armed commandos were the colonial solution.

Initially, the purpose of commandos was to retrieve cattle allegedly stolen from the colonists by the Africans. The issue was complicated by the different approaches to land ownership of the contending parties. The colonists believed that when they obtained permission from the Cape to stake out a farm, it was theirs absolutely and beyond challenge. The

Xhosa had no such tradition or belief: the idea of fixed title and exclusive private possession was unknown to them. The land belonged to the chief, but the use of it was communal. Nevertheless, the chiefs preferred to wage war against the colonists than to relinquish control over more and more of their land. Chief Congo (Chungwa) of the Gqunukhwebe tribe expressed this view succinctly: "For our children have increased and our cattle have increased, and we must have that land, as it was formerly our country. We are determined to fight for it, sooner than be without it any longer."[16]

Military aggression against the Xhosa people began in the early 1800s, as small, independent Xhosa groups began to cross the Fish River boundary and settle in the Zuurveld and the eastern Cape. As one British officer reported in 1811:

> The country is on every side overrun with Kaffres, and there never was a period when such numerous parties of them were known to have advanced so far in every direction before; the depredations of late committed by them exceed all precedent … unless some decisive and hostile measures are immediately adopted … I apprehend considerable and most serious consequences.[17]

Outright war against the Xhosa was delayed temporarily by the Napoleonic wars in Europe, but the colonists were determined to drive them out. Soon after his arrival as Governor of the Cape in 1811, Sir John Cradock, gave orders to expel the Xhosa people from across the Fish River. On Christmas Day 1811, the colonists launched the first of nine frontier wars on the Xhosa people. Armed with rifles and assisted by the newly formed (Khoikhoi) Cape Regiment, the combined British and Boer forces confronted the impressive Xhosa army united under the leadership of Chief Ndlambe. Two months later, the colonists had accomplished their objective. This was the first great removal in South African history. Twenty military posts were established across the Zuurveld to secure the Fish River border as well as two settler villages, Grahamstown and Cradock. (Map 2, *xvii.*)

After their expulsion from the Zuurveld, the Xhosa suffered acute hardship. A severe drought had set in and the Xhosa people, whose cattle had been taken and crops and gardens burned by the colonial forces, were severely affected. Not surprisingly, relations with the colonists deteriorated as the dispossessed Xhosa raided farms and stole cattle to sustain their people. Despite the clamour of the settlers for reprisals,

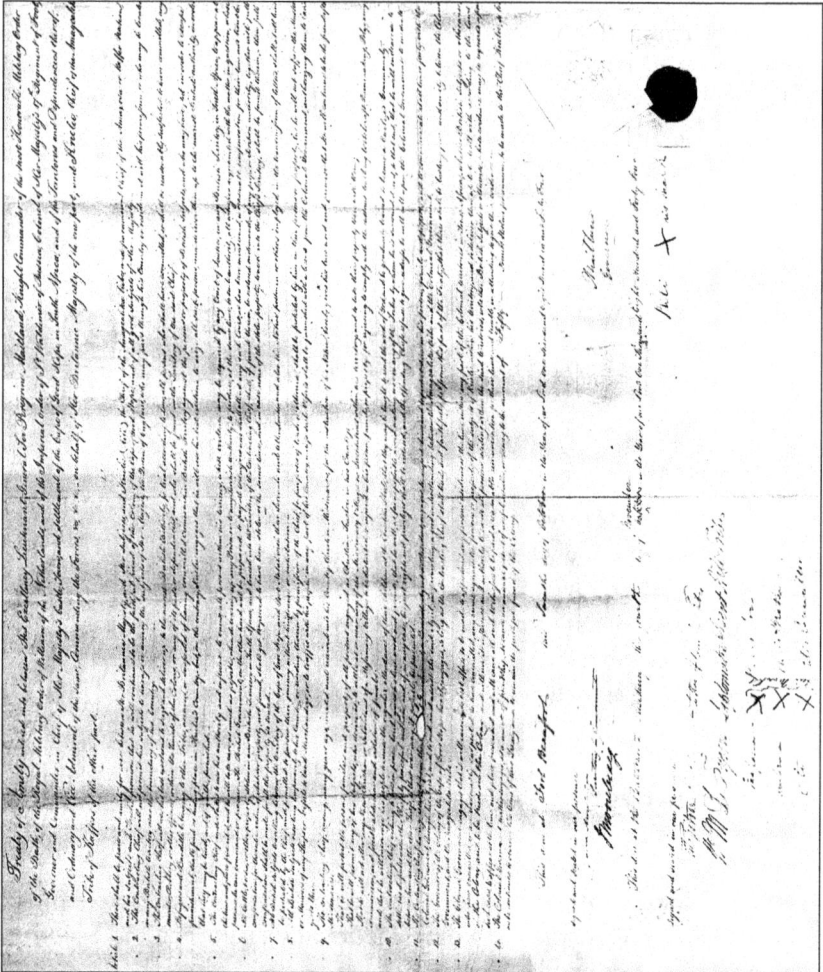

Treaty of Amity between Chief Kreli of the Amagcalike and the British, 1834.
Courtesy RSA State Archives, Cape Town.

the new Cape governor, Sir George Napier was determined to avoid war at any costs. It was cheaper in his view to compensate farmers for their losses than incur the bloodshed and expense of war. In this he had the total support of the British government and of the British humanitarian movement.

In 1834, when Sir Benjamin D'Urban was sent out as Governor of the Cape Colony, his instructions were to preserve the peace by establishing a system of alliances with the principal chiefs. The peace treaties with Xhosa tribes made by Andries Stockenstrom, Commissioner General and Lieutenant Governor of the Eastern Cape in the mid-1830s were an attempt to satisfy the grievances of the colonists and create a just solution to the frontier problem. Historian George McCall Theal lists at least twenty treaties between colonial officials and African chiefs negotiated between 1834 and 1866. However, the Stockenstrom treaties appear to have satisfied neither the colonists nor the Xhosa. Through these agreements, the British pushed back the boundaries between colonial and tribal territories and created buffer zones between the warring factions. Traditional law was retained in the tribal territories; but the presence of a diplomatic agent near the residence of the chief was effective in establishing Colonial control. The intention of these peace treaties with loyal chiefs was to separate them from rival tribesmen and thus break the solidarity of the Xhosa front.

When Sir Peregrine Maitland arrived at the Cape as its new governor in September 1844, his first priority was to pacify the colonists. They were demanding to be given back the power of armed reprisals (for cattle thefts) and to adjust the frontier territories to allow them access to more land. In other words, to abrogate the Stockenstrom treaties altogether. The new system of treaties introduced during Maitland's tenure gave the colonists exactly what they wanted. Stockenstrom's policy had been that the Xhosa should be treated as independent peoples and dealt with through his diplomatic agents. Maitland, on the other hand, simply dictated treaties as though to a subject people and tore up the standing agreements without prior notice or consultation.

One example is the Treaty of Amity with Xhosa Chief Kreli of the Amagcalike signed by Maitland on 4 November 1844. Under the terms of this treaty, Kreli was required not only to give free access to British subjects wishing to travel through his territory "without hindrance or molestation" but also to return or compensate them for any animals they claimed to have tracked inside his territory.

The cattle, horses, or other property stolen in any British
Territory in South Africa, and traced into the territory of the
contracting chief, shall, if found therein, be restored on demand
of any proper British authority, together with full compensation
for the entire value of whatever property, not found, shall yet
be proved to have been stolen at the same time, and in case
none of the stolen property traced into the chief's territory shall
be found therein, full compensation shall be paid for all the
property so traced.[18]

As happened in British North America, the Colonial Government promised an annual present of useful items or fifty pounds sterling per annum "to be paid to the chief as long as he continued to observe the terms of this Treaty and to remain a faithful friend of the colony." But as the Xhosa people lost their capacity to resist the colonizers, treaties disappeared accordingly. Like Governor Douglas on Vancouver Island, the colonial authorities at the Cape were not above a display of intimidation to achieve their objectives. In 1848, the newly appointed Cape Governor, Sir Harry Smith, brought the short-lived treaty policy to an end. After the Seventh Xhosa War ended in 1848, Smith gathered the Xhosa chiefs and announced the annexation of British Kaffraria to the Crown: "I make no more treaty. I say this land is mine!" To make his point, he exploded a wagon load of dynamite. As historian William MacMillan put it, "with a stroke of a pen (and a spectacular show of Sir Harry's fireworks) treaties were finally swept aside."[19]

Existing treaties, such as the agreement with Kreli, were soon abandoned to make way for white settlement. One of the first things Harry Smith's successor Lieutenant-General George Cathcart did on his arrival at the Cape was to call on the settlers to raise a force to "chastise" Kreli for pretending to be at peace while "plundering the colony." The settlers were prompt in their response: Kreli's principal village was burned to the ground and his cattle seized.[20] Other tribes met a similar fate. The chiefs were told that their locations (reserved lands) would be where they were sent. In return for the land, they had to solemnly pledge to repudiate witchcraft and the "sin of buying wives" (the Xhosa custom of *lobolo* involved the transfer of several head of cattle to the bride's father). They were also required to acknowledge no chief but the Queen of England. Thus the end of treaties in the Cape dealt a serious blow to African land power and self-determination.

The pattern of conquest and subordination took a slightly different form in the Boer republics. By the 1830s, the Boers had abandoned their isolated and precarious existence as farmers in the Cape hinterland and had trekked into the unknown interior intent on establishing their own independent states. While black land tenure was forbidden in both Boer republics, in the Zuid Afrikaansche Republiek (ZAR) every (white) man who had taken part in the Great Trek was entitled to two farms. As in the Orange River Sovereignty, white land ownership covered areas already settled by African communities. ZAR President M.W. Pretorius demonstrated this ownership when he repudiated the Keate Award of 1871. Pretorius had pledged to accept arbitration on whether the territory of the Bataplin and Baralong tribes should be part of the republic.

But when R. W. Keate, the Lieutenant-Governor, ruled that the African lands did not belong in the ZAR republic, Pretorius refused to be bound by his decision. The ZAR subsequently occupied the territory outside its boundaries and regarded the African owners as their subjects.[21]

Like the early Voortrekkers who followed the Khoikhoi (as if they were bloodhounds) to well-watered areas, the ZAR settlers knew there were advantages to claiming ownership of African-owned lands. Not only were these lands likely to be cultivated but they also offered the possibility of a labour supply. For example, the Kopa people were expected to pay rent in cash, kind and labour to the new owners of the land. When the Ndebele ruler, Mabhogo, denied the validity of the Boer claims to the land and refused to recognize their right to rent or tribute, armed conflicts ensued. In the early 1870s, only the chiefdoms within the Pedi domain remained unbowed. But this was not the case throughout the republic. In the more densely settled and controlled heartland of the ZAR a different picture emerged. A missionary who arrived in the Rustenburg area in 1866, for example, found that Africans were "living on Boer farms in kraals and had not an inch of ground they could call their own."[22]

The British colonial role in the alienation of African lands was not negligible. Before the Bloemfontein Convention of 1852 (which created the Orange River republic), a Royal Proclamation renounced British sovereignty over the Orange River Territory (including by necessary implication the territories of the chiefs). In granting unconditional independence to the new Orange Free State, Britain also backed down on its treaty promises of protection to the Griquas and undertook not to make further treaties prejudicial to the interests of the Orange River government. The land rights of Africans in the ZAR were similarly ignored. Under the terms of the Pretoria Convention of 1881 (which created an independent Transvaal state), a Native Location Commission was authorized to set aside African reserves. The 1881 Proclamation stated that "all paramount chiefs, chiefs and natives of the Transvaal" were permitted to buy land or acquire it in any manner, "but the transfer will be registered on their behalf in the name of the Native Location Commission."[23]

This breakup of tribal authority and power coincided with the industrialization of the country. After the unearthing of diamonds (in Griqualand West in 1867) and gold (on the Witwatersrand in 1886), African settlements or reserves were required in order to provide an essential reservoir of cheap labour for white-owned mines and industries. Pass Laws, effective in both the Cape and Boer republics in the late nineteenth century, provided the mechanism to control the influx of labourers and maintain low wages. Failure to carry a pass in 1873 in the ZAR carried a penalty varying from one to ten pounds, and to a severe flogging.[24]

By negotiating treaties with African chiefs, the colonial authorities (both British and Boer) did initially acknowledge the inherent rights of African chiefs to the territories they occupied. It was only later, after the wars had finally crushed tribal power, that African rights to the land were denied by right of conquest. When Colonial magistrates were imposed on the defeated tribes in the 1870s, the Honorable William Ayliff, then Secretary of Native Affairs, toured the territory explaining the new system to the people and obtaining their consent to its introduction. However, as Theal observes, although the chiefs all thanked the Secretary, according to African custom, and gave their consent to the payment of a hut tax, this was not done willingly.[25]

The notion that the Boer republics were established on "empty land" provided further legitimacy to white occupation.[26] Once densely populated by Sotho-Tswana pastoralists and farmers, the region experienced major disruptions during the 1820s. The word Mfecane (a Zulu term meaning "the crushing") is used by historians to describe the period of destructive and violent upheaval caused by the rise of the Zulu kingdom under Shaka. Although the actual causes and extent of the disturbance remain in dispute, the apparent depopulation of many parts of the interior made it easier for the migrant white farmers of the Great Trek to appropriate the areas that became the Transvaal and Orange Free State republics.[27] Speaking in 1962, Dr Dönges, Minister of Finance in the apartheid government, claimed that it was "history" that had drawn the boundaries between black and white South Africans, not the government, and therefore Africans had no moral claim to more land than they already occupied.[28]

STRATEGIES OF LAND ALIENATION IN CANADA AND SOUTH AFRICA

Treaties had a much briefer history in the South African colonies than they did in Canada for a number of reasons. First of all, the abundance of land in Canada and the diminishing indigenous population (due to smallpox epidemics and the erosion of traditional lands and lifestyles) may have made treaties more appealing or practical than military conquest. Secondly, the treaty system of protecting hunting grounds proved highly successful in avoiding the costs of warfare and in bringing indigenous groups under British authority. After the War of 1812, the colony recognized that it needed to protect the lives of its colonists from Indian attacks and at the same time give the native population a sense of permanency on their lands. Treaties made it possible to accomplish all these objectives.

The reverse happened in southern Africa. Vastly outnumbered by African inhabitants, British and Boer colonists saw military action (with the aid of rival tribal forces and superior weaponry) as their only recourse. The brutal measures used against African peoples (such as the burning of villages and crops) is explained at least in part by the growing paranoia of the white minority in the face of what Sir Theophilus Shepstone called the encroachment of "barbarism and inhumanity."[29] The power and sheer numbers of Africans and fear of swamping can be seen as a powerful incentive to crush rather than negotiate a compromise with African chiefs.

Probably the most significant factor of all in explaining why treaties found favour in Canada but not in southern Africa was that aboriginal North Americans themselves regarded these formal ceremonial agreements as an essential part of their dealings with Europeans. The Aborigines Protection Society acknowledged the Indian treaty skills in a letter to the Secretary of State in 1858:

The Indians, being a strikingly acute and intelligent race of men, are keenly sensitive in regard to their own rights as the aborigines of the country, and are equally alive to the value of the gold discoveries ... the English government should be prepared to deal with their claims in a broad spirit of justice and liberality. It is certain that the Indians regard their rights as natives as giving them a greater title to enjoy the riches of the country than can possibly be possessed either by the English Government or by foreign adventurers.[30]

Robert A. Williams Jr. observes that European colonists could neither avoid dealing with Indians nor disregard Indian conceptions of justice. Indian treaties in this early period affirmed the sovereign capacity of Indian nations and tribes to engage in bilateral governmental relations, to exercise power and control over their lands and resources, and to maintain their internal forms of self-government free from outside interference.[31]

In her study of Prairie Indians and government policy in the nineteenth century, Sarah Carter points out that Indians were anxious to negotiate treaties as a way of ensuring their economic security in the face of a very uncertain future. In 1871, the Cree chief Sweetgrass sent this message to Adam Archibald, lieutenant-governor of Manitoba and the North-West Territories: "We have heard our lands were sold and we did not like it; we do not want to sell our lands; it is our property and no one has the right to sell them."[32]

The revisions that were made to Treaty One in response to the protests of the Saulteaux (Ojibwa), the Swampy Cree, and other signatories is another example. Five years after the signing of Treaties One and Two, several Indian chiefs insisted that many of the verbal agreements (or "outside promises") be written up in a Memorandum to be part of the original treaties. Treaty One and the Memorandum attached to it then became a model for future negotiations. As D.J. Hall observes, this renegotiation demonstrated the participation of the Indians as aggressive negotiators.[33] John Tobias argues that the government at that time had no clear Indian policy (beyond a policy of expediency and the desire to avoid costly conflict) and that negotiating treaties with the Ojibwa of North West Angle and the Saulteaux of Manitoba would not have taken place at all had it not been for the insistence of the Indians concerned.[34]

In South Africa, treaties had a short and unsuccessful history. In the Cape Colony, African chiefs regarded the treaties with colonizing Europeans with a high degree of suspicion. The British practice of rewarding loyal chiefs with land taken from other chiefs did little to create confidence or trust between the colonial authorities and African chiefs. Moreover, the treaty terms were miserly at best, offering the Africans few incentives to negotiate treaties. As Captain Robert Scott Aitcheson admitted to the Select Committee in 1835, the lands assigned to Gaika's people in place of the fertile areas they were forced to vacate were appalling.

> I assure you there was not a blade of grass upon it any more
> than there is in this room, it was as bare as a parade ground....
> But the chiefs had no choice.... We being the stronger party, did
> not give that latitude to the objections on the part of the native
> tribes. From first to last, Gaika's concession was an unwilling one
> ... there seemed to be a general agreement that right to land be
> controlled by the Colonial government.[35]

Although Davenport and Hunt argue that paper treaties were among the most potent instruments of European expansion on the African continent, they admit that these agreements, through cession or concession, depended heavily on the way they were interpreted. The process was further complicated by the fact that the colonists found it difficult to determine whether the chief who signed the treaty held undisputed authority over the territory in question.³⁶ Another difficulty was the African approach to land ownership. South African historian Peter Delius writes that when tribal leaders agreed to peace treaties, they did so on the understanding that they were granting settlers the right to use their land (usufructuary rights), not to take ownership of it. In exchange, the chiefs hoped to gain welcome allies against rival tribes and at the same time entrench their own authority over their people.³⁷

The fact that four separate treaties are known to have been negotiated with the Zulus for the same territory in Port Natal supports this understanding that private ownership of land was an imported invention. The terms of these alleged treaties (two with Zulu Chief Shaka and two with his successor, Dingane) also reveal the extent to which written agreements served the colonial agenda to take control over vast swaths of land. For example, Shaka's "grant of land" to F.G. Farewell and Company included not only Port Natal and an extensive surrounding area of twenty thousand square miles but also the promise of "cattle and corn, as required" as a reward for Farewell's "kind attention to me in my illness from a wound:"

The whole of the neck of the peninsula in the south-west entrance, and all the country ten miles to the southern side of Port Natal ... and extending along the sea coast to the northward and eastward as far as the river known as by the name "Gumgelote" and now called "Farewell's River" ... together with all the country inland ... one hundred miles backward from the seashore with all rights to rivers, woods, mines and articles of all denominations contained therein....³⁸

The terms of Dingane's legendary treaty with Voortrekker leader Piet Retief in 1838 are equally generous to the settlers. According to the document retrieved from the site of Piet Retief's murder at the hands of Dingane's *impis* (army), the Zulu chief ceded Port Natal, together with all the land annexed to it, in exchange for a few head of stolen cattle:

KNOW ALL MEN BY THIS That whereas Pieter Retief, Gouvenor of the Dutch emigrant South Afrikans, has retaken my Cattle, which Sinkonyella had stolen; which Cattle he, the said Retief, now deliver unto me; I, DINGAAN, King of the Zoolas, do hereby certify and declare that I thought fit to resign unto him, Retief, and his countrymen (on reward of the case hereabove mentioned) the Place called "Port Natal," together with all the land annexed, that is to say, from Dogela to the Omsoboebo River westward; and from the sea to the north, as far as the land may be usefull and in my possession. Which I did by this, and give unto them for their everlasting property.

[Signed] De merk + can Koning Dingaan.[39]

Piet Retief apparently entered into a number of land agreements with Zulu chiefs before his fateful meeting with Dingane. Although, according to historian J.A.I. Agar-Hamilton, no trace of these treaties remain, the Voortrekkers established their first republic on lands "ceded" to them by Dingane.[40] The Voortrekker Republic of Natalia had a short history, however. When the British annexed Natalia in 1843, most of the trekkers decided to emigrate to the highveld; they were replaced by a large influx of British immigrants. By the mid-1850s there were ten thousand whites in the British colony of Natal and the African population (who outnumbered them by ten to one) were placed in reserves.

The abandonment of South African treaties for outright military conquest and annexation of tribal lands had far-reaching consequences for the African population. Delius describes the dramatic rise and fall of the powerful Pedi (northern Sotho) nation who, like the Zulus after them, were "bludgeoned into submission" by British-led armies. In contrast to the promises of annuities and benefits of North American treaties, the British imposed taxes on African people to induce compliance and bring them under white control and domination. The custom of forcing Africans to kneel when paying their taxes is one of the methods the white minority used to reinforce their position of power.[41] When a hut tax of ten shillings per annum was first levied in the Cape Colony in the late nineteenth century, most Africans tried to come up with the money by selling their crops or cattle rather than their labour. However, once their lands were taken, increasing numbers of them were forced to seek wage labour in the white-owned mines, industries and farms.

CONCLUSION

The status of Canadian treaties under international law is still a matter of debate among Canada's (non-aboriginal) legal and academic community. Some legal analysts claim that the colonial powers clearly recognized aboriginal rights when they made the majority of the treaties in the mid-1800s. As evidence, they cite the decisions of Chief Justice John Marshall of the United States Supreme Court in *Johnson v. McIntosh* and

Worcester v. Georgia which upheld the view that Indian title was absolute, subject only to the preemption right of purchase acquired by the United States as the successor of Great Britain. For this reason, Government land grants could not become operative until the Indian title had been extinguished in accordance with common law principles, that is, with the Indians' consent and on the payment of compensation. Chief Justice Marshall's rulings paved the way for recognition of aboriginal rights in Canada. His approach to aboriginal title was formally adopted by the Canadian government in 1880 on the approval of the British Privy Council in Westminster. While treaties were considered to be legally binding by the British and Canadian governments and the Indian nations involved, it was the European courts which decided exactly what these rights entailed. The verdict in *Attorney General of Canada vs Attorney General of Ontario* (1897), for example, shows the bias in the court's perspective:

> Their Lordships have had no difficulty in coming to the conclusion that, under the treaties, the Indians obtained no rights to their annuities, whether original or augmented beyond a promise and agreement, which was nothing more than a personal obligation by its governor, as representing the old province ... that the Indians obtained no right which gave them any interest in the territory they surrendered.[42]

In 1965, Pierre Trudeau (as Minister of Justice in the Pearson administration), declared: "The way we propose it, we say we won't recognize aboriginal rights. We will recognize treaty rights. We will recognize forms of contracts which have been made with the Indian people by the Crown and we will try to bring justice to that area and this will mean that perhaps the treaties shouldn't go on forever. It's inconceivable, I think, that in any given society one section of the society have a treaty with another section of the society."[43] These views were later restated in the Liberal Party government's White Paper of 1969 when the problem of the language in treaties was raised. From the government's point of view, the treaties were honoured: annuities were paid, reserve lands set aside, and benefits provided, apart from a few exceptions where Indians had failed to select the reserve lands they wanted.[44]

However, Treaty Indians regard the legality of treaties differently. As Harold Cardinal wrote in his response to the White Paper in 1970, not only the words but also the spirit of the treaties have to be respected: "To us who are Treaty Indians there is nothing more important than our

Treaties, our lands and the well-being of our future generations.... The intent and spirit of our treaties must be our guide, not the precise letter of a foreign language. Treaties that run forever must have room for the changes in the conditions of life."[45] In 1973, a case in the Northwest Territories, *Paulette et al. v. The Queen* raised for the first time the fundamental question of whether the literal words of treaties represent the understanding of Indian signatories.[46] Legal historian Bruce Wildsmith agrees that the intention of both parties in treaty negotiations was to make a legal obligation of a permanent nature that neither side could evade unilaterally. In his view, Indian treaties constitute a legally enforceable obligation, although the extent of appropriate compensation when breaches of treaty obligations occur remains to be determined.[47] Historians Peter Cumming and Neil Mickenberg concur with this view. Native rights have a four-hundred-year history in international law and have been part of the common and statutory law of British North America and of Canada for well over two centuries. Rights which originated in such a rich history, in their view, cannot be easily ignored.[48]

Chapter Three
Sovereignty and Segregation

> The position we strongly hold is that Indians are citizens plus: that
> in addition to the normal rights and duties of citizenship they
> also possess certain rights as charter members of the Canadian
> community.
>
> *Report of the Hawthorn Commission, 1967*[1]

INTRODUCTION

When European settlers arrived on the shores of North America and
southern Africa, they adopted the view that people who appeared to have
no recognizable system of government or legal codes could legitimately
be ruled by their colonizers. It was a case of supplying sovereignty (or
supreme authority) where none existed. As competition for colonies
intensified, the rights of Europeans to carve out spheres of influence for
themselves were strongly asserted by international lawyers in the late
nineteenth and early twentieth centuries. In 1904, J. Westlake argued
in his book *International Law* that because indigenous societies were
"unable to supply a government suited to white men" they could not be
"credited" with sovereignty.[2]

One of the ways the European powers maintained sovereignty over
indigenous peoples was to segregate them physically and socially from
mainstream (non-aboriginal) society. Canada and South Africa used
segregation to achieve different objectives; but in both countries, the
policy had a largely negative impact on indigenous communities.

SOVEREIGNTY AND CONSTITUTIONAL RIGHTS IN CANADA

The sporadic recognition of treaty rights in Canada during the first
century after Confederation can best be understood in the context of
Canada's constitutional history. The principle of separate and "protected"
Indian lands as articulated in the Royal Proclamation of 1763 and in the
British North America Act (BNA) of 1867 continued alongside the con-
tradictory policy of assimilation which became the official policy of the

new Canadian government in 1867. The provisions of the BNA Act of 1867 that "lands reserved for Indians" could only be alienated by the Crown is a double-edged sword. On one side, by adopting the Westminster style of parliamentary government, Canada continued British conventions and practices, which included recognition of colonial-era treaties. However, under the BNA Act, the state had fiduciary responsibility for the welfare of aboriginal peoples. The new government created special legislation and a special government department to administer this responsibility. The Indian Act (1876) consolidated pre-Confederation legislation on Indian affairs into a nationwide framework that is still fundamentally in place today. Although the Act has been amended several times, it has never been abolished.

The Indian reserve lands are at the centre of the Indian Act. However, they were not given any consideration in the acts of Confederation. Treaty boundaries were ignored in the territorial arrangement of provinces of the new country. Many Indian territories spanned more than one province – and even international boundaries with the United States, as in the case of the Akwasasne Reserve in Quebec. Thus, from the outset, aboriginal reserves were excluded from the new country's framework and remain an awkward anomaly in the system. The Indian Act purported only to protect reserve lands from immigrant acquisition. Through most of its history, the Indian Act defined reserves as:

> any tract of land set apart by treaty or otherwise for the use and benefit of or granted to a particular band of Indians, of which the legal title is in the Crown, but which is unsurrendered and includes all trees, wood, timber, soil, stone, minerals, metals or other valuables thereon or therein.[3]

Moreover, the extent of Indian reserves in Canada has never been firmly established by law. Richard Bartlett points out that the reserves were all created at different times under different legislation: some by Crown grants of land to religious communities and missionaries (mainly in Quebec in the eighteenth century); some by treaties and modern agreements (mainly in the Prairie Provinces and Ontario); and some by federal purchase of land or executive action (mainly in British Columbia and the Maritime Provinces). Thus, each reserve has its own history, with distinct legal consequences for provincial jurisdiction and Indian interest in the land. Since each reserve is unique, there is no single way of dealing with them effectively, either for the government or for the Indians seeking sovereignty.

Under the Indian Act, Status Indians (members of registered bands) became "wards" of the federal government. Thus the government assumed control over all aspects of the lives of Indians living on reserves through a federally appointed resident Indian Agent. As a further indication of their loss of autonomy, Indian tribal systems were replaced with an elective band structure (the band council) under the direct authority of the Superintendent General. Traditional chiefs and leaders were no longer recognized as representatives of their people: the Indian Superintendent designated elected officials (always male at that time) as band spokesmen. Men were even selected for this role in Iroquois country and other territories where clan mothers had always held the most influential positions of power.

Shortly after Confederation, the Ottawa bureaucracy began to impose assimilation measures on the reserves. In 1884, the elaborate gift-giving feasts of the west coast nations, known under the general label of "potlatch," were banned along with other traditional rituals. Dickason explains that the "give-away" aspect of potlatches was held to be "incompatible with Western economic practices and inimical to the concept of private property." The prairie thirst dances (Sun Dance) were also banned for supposedly "interfer[ing] with the planting season." In addition, revisions to the Indian Act in 1914 imposed the penalty of a fine or imprisonment on any Indian who "participated in any Indian dance outside the bounds of his own reserve."[4] So although the Indians retained portions of land, they did not have sovereignty over it.

As surprising as it may seem with hindsight, nineteenth-century Canadian governments did not regard the establishment of reserves and Canada's subsequent policy of assimilation as incompatible. After Confederation, the government's stated objective was to make Indians over in its own (European) image. As Canada's first prime minister, Sir John A. Macdonald, announced to Parliament in 1880, the policy was "to wean [the indigenous people] by slow degrees, from their nomadic habits, which have become an instinct, and by slow degrees absorb them or settle them on the land. Meantime they must be fairly protected."[5] Thus, the reserves, allocated through treaties or by orders-in-council to registered bands, were seen merely as a staging area before total assimilation could take place: the government had never considered them to be permanent lands.

Official practice echoed these priorities. Edgar Dewdney, Lieutenant Governor of the North-West Territories (the western prairies) from 1881 to 1888, endorsed the reserve scheme on the grounds that it would "strike at the heart of tribalism" and foster self-reliance among the Indians and emulation of white society. Dewdney's successor, Hayter Reed, had a different set of objectives. He arranged to have the reserves surveyed in order to promote private ownership of reserve lands. Frank Oliver, in charge of Indian Affairs in the early 1900s, also favoured the sale of reserve land. In 1906, the Indian Act was amended to permit the sale of reserve land, but with the Indian residents retaining only 50 per cent of the purchase price. By selling their land, Indians were assured of sizable annuities (mostly in lump sum payments), and many bands were pressured to give up hundreds of thousands of acres. In 1911, the Oliver Act allowed the removal of Indians from any reserve situated next to a town of eight thousand or more residents.[6] Thus, the government's policy of assimilating Indians into the general population started to take effect.

Missionaries and teachers in Canada helped hasten the assimilation process. Describing the work of the Presbyterian Church in North America in the nineteenth century – which he dubs the "Great Century of Protestant Missions" – Michael C. Coleman writes that missionaries were regarded by their contemporaries as "cultural revolutionaries" whose objective was the transformation of Indian life. Although missionaries had not consciously set out to weaken Indian resistance to the encroachment on lands, they had no qualms about harmonizing their religious fervour with the "civilizing" goals of their governments. They offered Indians what they saw as superior ways of life, a way of compensating for the wrongs that had been perpetrated against them.[7]

In his biography of Kahkewaquonaby (Peter Jones), a Mississauga-Welsh Métis who became an influential Methodist missionary, Donald Smith observes that powerful linkages were made between Christian conversion and the material values of European society.[8] Britain's Select Committee on Aborigines frequently heard evidence of the "transformation" that took place as a result of missionary endeavours among the Mohawk and Chippeway Indians of Upper Canada, in particular the Credit Reserve on Grand River. Quoting a letter written by the Canadian educator and Methodist minister, the Reverend Egerton Ryerson of Upper Canada, one witness told the Committee:

> [The Indians] were proverbially savage and revengeful, as well as
> shrewd; so as often to be the terror of their white neighbors....
> But a few years ago (1825) when the Gospel was preached to
> these Mohawk Indians, as well as to several tribes of Chippeway
> Indians, a large portion of them embraced it.[9]

Chippeway Chief Kahkewaquonaby himself, in a written submission to the Committee, describes the changes wrought by Christian conversion in the lives of women in his community. Many women wore cloaks instead of blankets and have a shawl around their necks "exactly like the English ladies:"

In their heathen state, [women] were looked upon by the men as inferior beings, and were treated as such. The women were doomed to do all the drudgeries of life, such as making of the wigwam; the carrying of materials for the wigwams in their wanderings; the bringing in of the deer and bear, killed by the men; dressing the skin, cooking, and taking care of the children; planting the Indian corn ... I rejoice to say, since the introduction of Christianity among us, nearly all these heavy burthens have been removed from the backs of our afflicted women. The men now make the houses, plant the fields, provide fuel and provisions for the house.[10]

In the process of inculcating European values, Indian languages were seen as obstructions to advancement in the "white man's world." Like many of his contemporaries, the Methodist missionary John MacLean recognized the richness and sophistication of Indian languages; yet he actively supported the government policy to prohibit the use of native languages in schools. Writing in 1896, MacLean declared:

Our Canadian Indians have beautiful languages, accurate and full in their grammatical structure, euphonious and expressive.... There can be no legitimate method of stamping out the native language except by the wise policy of teaching English in the schools and allowing the Indian languages to die out.[11]

The collusion of church and state, so powerfully exemplified in the residential school system, continued well into the twentieth century. The 1920 Annual Report of the Department of Indian Affairs applauded the successful incorporation of Indians into the fabric of Canadian society:

This informal union between church and state still exists, and all Canadian Indian schools are conducted upon a joint agreement between the Government and the denominations as to finance and system. The method has proved successful, and the Indians of Ontario and Quebec, in the older regions of the provinces, are every day entering more and more into the general life of the country. They are farmers, clerks, artisans, teachers, and lumbermen. Some few have qualified as doctors, and surveyors; an increasing number are accepting enfranchisement and taking up the responsibilities of citizenship. Although there are reactionary elements among the best-educated tribes, and stubborn paganism on the most progressive reserves, the irresistible movement is towards the goal of complete citizenship.[12]

Thus, until the 1970s, the government objective was to gradually dismantle the reserve system and to assimilate the Indian population into the non-aboriginal society.

ASSIMILATION IN TWENTIETH-CENTURY CANADA

After World War I, pragmatic national concerns further encroached on Indian land claims. The Greater Production Program to increase food production on the Prairies had an adverse effect on the Plains Cree. Contrary to treaty promises, Superintendents of Indian Affairs were given the power to lease Indian lands without their consent and to charge the costs of stock, machinery material and labour against any fund held by the government on the Indians' behalf. Indian reserves were declared to be "much too large," and "idle lands" were seized and handed over to immigrant farmers to be worked more profitably. The Cree were given alternative land, which they themselves called *iskonikum*, meaning "scraps" or "leftovers." Much of this land was ill-suited for agriculture and had long since become unsuitable for trapping and hunting as well.[13] Thus, formerly self-supporting Cree bands were forced to work on their own lands for wages and abandon their traditional way of life.

After World War II, the spiralling costs of maintaining separate structures and special programs spurred governments to draw indigenous people into the mainstream society, both economically and socially. Moreover, new organizations, such as the United Nations and the International Labour Organization (ILO), considered the well-being of dependent aboriginal communities to be a matter of concern in promoting economic, social and political stability throughout the world. In 1952, the ILO invited Canada to become a member of the Committee on Indigenous Labour and to demonstrate that Canadian Indian policy was above reproach. Membership in the ILO acted as an important impetus to maintaining more constructive relations with indigenous Canadians.

Concerns about national security during the Cold War era were another factor in determining Indian policy. One British Columbian petitioner, C. Wilmott Maddison, Vice President of the Army, Navy and Air Force Veterans' Association in Canada, Vancouver Unit, asked for revisions to the Indian Act because of the vulnerability of Canada's Pacific Rim:

> If war came Indians would be very useful on account of their knowledge of the Northern hinterland. Unless we give them a "square deal" … we may find them disgruntled on such account.[14]

Maddison emphasized his point by adding that "certain interests, actual and positive enemies of our Great British Empire and Commonwealth, have already intruded tentacles among Canadian Indians." Thus, a combination of fear and international scrutiny forced Canada to re-examine its relationship with aboriginal people.

The fact that other governments were also reviewing their policies regarding aboriginal populations influenced the direction Canada was to take over the next decades. The United States, like Canada, had adopted assimilation as the stated cornerstone of its Indian policy, while isolating its Indian population on reserves. The American experiment, however, also managed to accommodate some Indian aspirations by restoring many aspects of Indian self-government and removing restrictions which had seriously hampered Indian economic development.[15] According to David Fulton, a Progressive Conservative Member of Parliament in 1951, it was important to at least appear to match the American sense of fair play and justice:

> In the United States, which has an Indian problem at least similar to ours … they have accepted the principle that Indians should vote without giving up these privileges which we gave in perpetuity in compensation [for Indian land] … I hope that we are not behind the United States in our ideals of citizenship. We have not the Fifteenth Amendment or anything like it … [but these rights] are inherent in our constitution and in our way of life.[16]

Fulton also recognized that the conditional franchise under the Indian Act was contrary to the Canadian constitution, an unusual observation for someone of his time period. Indians did not have the right to vote unless they left the reservation system and became part of the "white" culture. Although there was some interest in reforms to this law, Canadian policy makers were not in favour of creating a second tier of citizenship for aboriginal Canadians. For example, New Zealand's system of having four aboriginal members of parliament represent the interests of the aboriginal population was not regarded as an acceptable solution. As Member of Parliament D.F. Brown declared in the House of Commons: "We certainly do not want to have any one section of our country stand as a festering sore; we want the people to be assimilated so that they will join us as one."[17]

The 1951 revisions to the Indian Act changed very little in the lives of most Indian people. The only perceptible change in the wording of the Act was one of semantics. Indians were now to be "integrated" rather than "assimilated" into mainstream society. The term "integration," implied economic and political integration and the recognition of cultural identity, rather than wholesale absorption of aboriginal peoples into the dominant society. Even the amendments to lift the prohibition on the potlatch and to make fund-raising for political organizations legal were regarded as largely cosmetic. As the Leader of the Opposition and future prime minister John Diefenbaker declared in Parliament, far from being an improvement the 1951 revisions to the Indian Act were "a perpetuation of bureaucracy and a denial of the rights of Indians."[18]

During the 1960s, the contradictions between segregation and integration continued. On the one hand, Diefenbaker's Conservative Party government changed Canada's Elections Act to allow Indians the right to vote without the penalty of losing their Indian status. Thus Indians were encouraged to stay on the reserves. Yet in the mid-1960s, the government was also offering subsidies to Indian families to relocate into cities. In 1963, the Hawthorn Commission on Indian affairs stressed the special status of Indian citizens. "Differentiation on ethnic grounds has become synonymous with discrimination, apartheid, second-class citizenship, and generally a host of emotive words," the Commission's report declared, showing its awareness of international scrutiny. The key premise of the report recognized that indigenous peoples should be treated not only as citizens of Canada, but also as "citizens plus."

In the late 1960s, the Liberal administration of Prime Minister Pierre Trudeau rejected the Hawthorn Commission's notion of "citizens plus." Instead, his government pursued its objective of integration. The 1969 White Paper proposed the abolition of the Indian Act and the current system of Indian administration, including the fiduciary responsibilities of the federal government in both the Royal Proclamation and the

BNA Act. Like public services to all Canadians, services to Indian people would now be provided by the provinces. In his statement proposing the White Paper in Parliament in 1969, Jean Chrétien, Minister of Indian Affairs and future prime minister, stressed the equality of all Canadians as the basic principle of the policy:

> The government does not wish to perpetuate policies which carry with them the seeds of disharmony and disunity, policies which prevent Canadians from fulfilling themselves and contributing to their society.... It is no longer acceptable that the Indian people should be outside and apart.... Services should not flow from separate agencies established to serve particular groups, especially not to groups identified ethnically.[19]

Among the White Paper's proposals was the dissolution of treaties and the eventual removal of all references to Indians in the BNA Act: any vestige of special rights, including aboriginal title was to be removed from the statute books, and an Indian Claims Commissioner was to be appointed to take care of residual treaty obligations. The White Paper did not become law because of Indian protests, but it showed the government's plan for full integration.

In 1982, Canada adopted a Constitution, which changed the sovereignty-segregation argument considerably. The new Constitution tilted power away from governments (both federal and provincial) and towards individual citizens. By strengthening individual rights, it weakened the acceptability of collective rights, including those of aboriginal bands and nations. Any tendency to privilege one group over another was seen as contrary to the spirit of the Constitution and the Charter of Rights and Freedoms. As a further contradiction, aboriginal rights were included in the new Constitution, but without details on how they should be upheld.

More recently, the Canadian liberal democratic ethos has spawned both an integration ethic and a self-determination ethic. These ethics may prove impossible to reconcile. Reconciliation entails accepting an un-level playing field that promotes the flawed notion that "separate and equal" can co-exist. As Bruce Clark puts it, "We have in Canada *de facto* separateness of Indian communities and to deny them *de jure* rights to manipulate their own destinies may be little short of tyranny."[20] The ambiguities of the legal status of Canada's aboriginal population have made the issue of aboriginal justice and the restoration of land rights extremely difficult to resolve.

From the Indian perspective, the issue of overlapping sovereign rights does not exist, since most aboriginal nations have never accepted the assertion that their sovereignty has been extinguished by the mere presence of Europeans on their territory. The Gitxsan and Wet'suwet'en proclaimed this strongly in the Delgamuukw case. For them, the case was not about regaining sovereignty – they already had that. Gitxsan and Wet'suwet'en sovereignty was never in question: they would continue to live as they had always done with or without the recognition of European courts. This is true for every aboriginal group claiming the right to ancestral lands and the right to manage and conserve it as their people had done for thousands of years.

The Iroquois nation has been making this claim to uninterrupted sovereignty since the time of Tecumseh in 1812 and long before that. For the Iroquois, the relationship between European colonizers and themselves is most clearly symbolized in the two-row treaty belt, which embodies the right to aboriginal self-determination and self-government. The belt, made of wampum, depicts the aboriginal and non-aboriginal peoples of Canada traveling the river of life together, side by side, but each in their own boat, neither steering the other's vessel. Tribal visions of law like those symbolized by the two-row treaty belt (Gus-Wen-Tah) have sought to establish paradigms for behaviour in the relations between indigenous peoples and the settler societies of North America.

SOVEREIGNTY IN SOUTH AFRICA

Sovereignty issues in South Africa are much less ambiguous than they are in Canada. Despite the different histories of the four colonies that made up South Africa (two Boer and two British), their policies on the status of the indigenous population merged into one very clear policy when the Union of South Africa was formed in 1910.

The Cape Colony, influenced by British "liberalism," was the only former colony with a colour-blind franchise and rule of law for all. The other British colony, Natal, was openly protective of white interests. It had only a very limited franchise (based on land ownership) for its non-white population.[21] In the two former Boer republics, the Orange Free State and the Zuid Afrikaansche Republiek (ZAR), racial equality and the inclusive rule of law had never been practised. The Orange Free State's Constitution of 1854 was blatantly pro-white. The sovereignty of "the people" was recognized and certain rights guaranteed (such as the right to peaceful assembly, equality before the law, and right to property), but the term "equality" had to be read within the mores of the white Afrikaners (as the Boers were beginning to call themselves).[22]

The franchise was granted to "citizens only," and white pigmentation was required for citizenship. The ZAR (later named the Transvaal) was even less welcoming to non-Afrikaners, especially Africans. The initial ZAR's Grondwet (Constitution) of 1858 was frankly racist. It expressly stated that "the People desire to permit no equality between coloured people and white inhabitants, either in church or state." The legislature (Volksraad) was both sovereign and non-representative: neither Uitlanders (non-Afrikaner Europeans) nor Africans had the vote. Thus the lawmakers could (and did) manipulate the law to ensure Afrikaner hegemony.

But Cape liberalism did not survive the 1910 union of the four colonies. In its eagerness to placate and win the support of Afrikanerdom after the Anglo-Boer War, Britain granted responsible government to both ex-republics in 1906-7 on their own terms, including the absence of a black franchise. The Treaty of Vereeniging, which brought an end to the war in 1902, was deeply resented by the African people. In his study on early political protest, André Odendaal describes their outrage at the fact that Boers who had shown themselves to be "the enemies of the king" should be favoured, while Africans who had shown their loyalty to the British "in heart and deeds" were ignored.[23]

However, racial inclusiveness was not a high priority for either the Boers or the British. Lord Alfred Milner, High Commissioner for South Africa after the war, stated the prevailing British imperial mindset in his usual forthright style: "The ultimate end is a self-governing white community supported by well-treated and justly governed black labour from Cape Town to the Zambezi."[24] Speaking in 1908, Jan Christiaan Smuts, a Boer general in the Anglo-Boer War and later prime minister of South Africa (1919-24, 1939-48), was distinctly hostile to the idea of an African franchise:

Every white man, however poor and ignorant is born into a community with a long civilized past behind it with training and tradition which constitute a strong presumption in favour of his being able to exercise his franchise properly. But in favour of the Native there is no such historical and cultural presumption. The *onus probandi* is distinctly on him; he has to prove his fitness before he is admitted into the charmed circle.[25]

Predictably, a compromise was reached over the thorny issue of an African franchise. The final decision was to allow the Cape to retain its qualified franchise while the northern provinces retained their whites-only policy. The terms of Union were seen as a way of compensating the Boers for British excesses during the war and ensuring access to the lucrative gold and diamond mines. Ignoring the petitions of Africans and their white supporters, the British Parliament gave approval to the draft Constitution. The Union of South Africa came into being on May 31, 1910.

Over the following decades, the Cape franchise was gradually whittled away. In 1930 white women were enfranchised, which bolstered the white vote, and in 1936, Africans were removed from the common voters' role. After World War II, Africans in the Cape requested increased representation (by white Members of Parliament) from three to ten members but were refused by the Smuts government. The irony here was that had Smuts granted the increase, he would probably have won the 1948 election.[26] However, the Afrikaner National Party, under the leadership of D.F. Malan, won the 1948 election by a majority of five seats on the platform of "apartheid." A decade after the apartheid government came into power, Smuts' "charmed circle" was sealed off completely. The last tiny wedge of African representation (the right to elect four white representatives to the Senate through a system of electoral colleges) was removed in 1959, under the misnamed Promotion of Bantu Self-Government Act.

PRAGMATIC SEGREGATION IN SOUTH AFRICA

The reality of being outnumbered in population has always determined a great deal of European policy in southern Africa. Even after their lands had been taken and the power of their chiefdoms had been reduced, the overwhelming number of Africans presented a particular challenge to the early colonial authorities. But the colonies also needed a supply of cheap labour. Thus the policy of segregation became a useful tool for simultaneously controlling and exploiting the large African population.

In 1847, a Locations Commission was set up in Natal to devise a scheme for settling the land and administering the colony's reserve system. In wording reminiscent of Canadian Indian policy, the Commission was mandated to look into the "gradual improvement" of Africans.[27] One of the commissioners was Theophilus Shepstone, who had been appointed diplomatic agent of Natal in 1845. Shepstone was to play a critical role in developing the colony's native policy; but it was in the locations of Natal that his policy of paternal government, one of the earliest variants of "indirect rule," came to be applied. In a very short space of time, Shepstone created a structure of Zulu leadership under the framework of European control, with himself as "paramount chief." Like the Canadian band council system, Shepstone's system replaced indigenous authority structures with European-designated authorities. He was unpopular with Natal's white farmers for setting aside such large locations that African workers were disinclined to work on the farms; and yet labour was at the root of Shepstonian policy. While traditional Zulu laws were maintained under Shepstone's policy, restrictions were placed on celebrations such as the "dance of the first fruits," a ritual which involved the parade of armed warriors and emphasized both the solidarity and strength of Zulu chiefs. In the words of African historian Mzala, Shepstone "set out to dismantle the Zulu military structure and transform its thirty thousand warriors into labourers working for wages."[28]

Although early South African policy was also geared towards "civilizing" Africans, the underlying objective was to turn them into "useful servants and consumers" to serve the interests of the white economy. As the Governor of the Cape in the 1850s, Sir George Grey, expressed it, Africans should be "made part of ourselves, useful servants, consumers of our goods, contributors to our revenue."[29] Furthermore, by insisting that European dress be worn, legislators and missionaries helped to create a dependency on European goods which would boost the economy. The economic motive for requiring Africans to "go decently dressed" was clearly articulated by Natal's Kafir Commission, which published its report in 1853:

All kafirs should be ordered to go decently clothed. This measure would at once tend to increase the number of labourers, because many would be obliged to work to procure the means of buying clothing; it would also add to the general revenue of the colony through customs dues.[30]

The Report added that "it is cheaper and infinitely preferable to train the young kafir in industry than to exterminate him; and one or other must be done." Arguing from the premise that Natal was a "white settlement" whose black inhabitants were foreigners "living under British protection," the Commission recommended that the colony drastically reduce the number and size of its African reserves.[31]

As in Canada, Christian missionaries to South Africa contributed to the "civilizing" process by blending spiritual and materialist values. Turning Africans into good Christians meshed well with government policy to create good consumers. The goal of Methodist missionaries, writes church historian Daryl Balia, was to "domesticate" the indigenous population: "In converting the Africans and casting them adrift from their cultural and moral codes, the missionaries were indirectly responding to the needs of capital to create labourers and consumers of British manufactured products."[32]

Their efforts were only partially successful. In 1893, Fitz E.C. Bell, Chief Magistrate of the Kentani District, reported on the painfully slow "advancement" of Africans under his jurisdiction:

> There has been no visible sign of advancement by the natives towards a higher civilization. The Gaicas and Gcalekas alike are not as progressive as the Fingo are. They are indifferent whether their children are educated or not and dislike European clothing. The men will only wear it when at service or traveling on the more main roads or attending courts. The women, on returning from service in the colony, resume their red garments and revel in the freedom and licence allowed by their customs and style of living.[33]

The strength of African culture and traditions seemed surprising to their colonizers, who regarded them as vastly inferior to their own. However, another important factor in the pace of "civilizing" Africans was the size of the white population in relation to Africans in the region – Kentani had a population of twenty-nine thousand Africans and two hundred Europeans at the time the report was written.

While Christian missionaries had little regard for indigenous religions and did their best to stamp out traditional customs like ancestor worship, they recognized the potential for conversion in their work among Africans. Frequent interference in traditional structures (*e.g.*, the customs of lobolo and circumcision as part of initiation rites) undermined the traditional foundations of African life as it had been lived for centuries. Polygamy was another tradition that came under persistent attack. However, the motive behind the cultural attacks was not the eventual assimilation of Africans into white society (as it was in Canada), but rather to weaken their traditional economies and entice them to enter the labour market.

Cheap labour was also the motivation behind policies in British Kaffraria (later named Ciskei), which was incorporated into the Cape Colony in 1880. In 1894, Cecil John Rhodes (Prime Minister of the Cape and mining magnate with a vested interest in creating a cheap black labour force) introduced his "Bill for Africa" – the Glen Grey Act. The Act set a pattern for African land tenure throughout the continent, replaced traditional tenure (wherein chiefs held land on behalf of their people) with perpetual rents for individuals, and limited the size of plots to four morgen (a Dutch land measurement equal to about two acres). It also imposed a labour tax on non-titleholders to discourage squatting. As Monica Wilson points out, the land tenure provisions were designed with the specific intention of ensuring that only a limited number of African men would remain on the reserve as farmers. No provision was made for the natural increase of the population; so once the land became impossibly overcrowded, the surplus (the other nine-tenths) would be forced to leave and find work elsewhere.[34] This is clearly what Rhodes had in mind when he explained his policy to Parliament:

> Every black man cannot have three acres and a cow, or four morgen and a commonage right … It must be brought home to them that in the future nine tenths of them will have to spend their lives in daily labour, in physical work, in manual labour.[35]

European governments provided moral justification for this policy of exploitation by depicting Africans as inherently lazy and lacking in intelligence. Rhodes himself complained at great length about the way rural Africans existed on the "great preserves" living in sloth and idleness: "The average Kaffir is a highly odorous and dirty savage with less intelligence than it is possible to conceive and whose only ambition is to make enough money with as little exertion as possible, to buy one or more wives to work for him for the rest of his useless life."[36]

In 1905, leading up to the 1910 union, the South African Native Affairs Commission (SANAC) devised a reserve policy to satisfy both British and Boer demands. The Commission formalized the idea of racial segregation by envisaging reserves as a mandatory and permanent principle of land allocation. Under the terms of the South Africa Act (1909), lands set aside for the occupation of the natives could not be alienated except by an Act of Parliament.[37] The labour reserve rationale behind the establishment of reserves was clearly stated by Sir Godfrey Lagden, the Commissioner of SANAC (also known as the Lagden Commission), in 1909:

> A man cannot go with his wife and children and his goods and chattels on to the labour market. He must have a dumping ground. Every rabbit must have a warren where he can live and burrow and breed, and every native must have a warren too.[38]

The reserve system developed as a method of both keeping Africans separate from white communities and making them available as labour. The size of reserves was among the first contentious issue addressed by the Boers and the British after the Anglo-Boer War (1899–1902). Industrialists (mainly English-speaking) wanted reserves to be maintained as reservoirs of cheap black labour for the mines and industries. The idea was that the reserves would support subsistence agriculture, operated by "surplus labour" (mainly women), to supplement the low "single man's" wages in the mines and factories. Boer farmers, on the other hand, wanted the size of reserves restricted in order to increase their own holdings and force landless Africans to work as farm labourers. Furthermore, the white farmers wanted to protect themselves from competition from black farmers.

Colin Bundy refers to this conflict as the competing needs of "gold" and "maize." In his study of African peasantry, he points out that black farmers flourished in the period after the Anglo-Boer War as hundreds of Afrikaners abandoned their farms for military service. The conventional wisdom that Africans were failed farmers (like Indians in the Canadian prairies at the turn of the twentieth century) was a convenient justification for taking their lands away from them.[39] Unlike the Canadian prairies, where Indian farmers were forbidden to sell their produce or purchase goods without a permit issued by the Indian Agent, African farmers were simply evicted from their flourishing farms and forced to either become sharecroppers on white-owned farms or find wage labour in the cities.[40] As Bundy and others have argued, the emergence and decline of the African peasant was a crucial element in the transformation of farmer-pastoralists into a reservoir of cheap, right-less and largely migrant labourers.[41] Monica Wilson has also drawn attention to the fact that the reserve areas of South Africa (and in the territories that are today Botswana, Lesotho and Swaziland) were initially very prosperous.[42]

Sharecropping became a common practice after the war. Many white farmers without capital or access to labour turned to sharecropping with black tenants as a way to keep their land productive. Through these verbal agreements, African farmers (and often their entire family) contributed their skills, labour and equipment in order to keep a share of the harvest. In many sharecropping relationships, Africans retained a certain amount of power. But these arrangements were outlawed by the Native Land Act of 1913.[43] The perception arose that African farmers were growing richer and more independent while an increasing number of whites (mainly Afrikaners) were becoming poor. The so-called "poor white" problem was the basis of a populist mobilization against African competition leading up to the Native Land Act.[44]

Based on the recommendations of the Lagden Commission, the Native Land Act formally reserved the lands which had been set apart for Africans and barred them from purchasing lands outside these "Scheduled Native areas." Under this Act, all previous land agreements (including sharecropping agreements) with Africans were terminated, and Africans were summarily evicted unless their labour was required. The Boer republican law prohibiting Africans from living on farms except as servants was thus extended to the whole Union. The more successful the black sharecropper, the more likely conflicts were to occur when Africans refused to pay increased rents, to deliver the labour of wives and children, or to hand over their ploughs or wagons to their white landlord.

In essence, the Native Land Act was a precursor of apartheid because it made Africans homeless in their own country. Under the Native Trust and Land Act (1936), additional land was added to the "scheduled" areas, and a Native Trust was established to administer all reserve lands. The additional "released" land (which extended the "Native reserves" from 7 percent to a little under 13 percent of the country) was presented as a major "gift" to the African population. When the Report of the South African Lands Commission was published in 1916, recommending that additional land be allocated for African settlement, Sol Plaatje, Secretary of the South African Native National Congress, described the offer and its misleading presentation of the facts with some bitterness:

There are pages upon pages of columns of figures running into four, five or six noughts. They will dazzle the eye until the reader imagines himself witnessing the redistribution of the whole subcontinent and its transfer to the native tribes.... They talk of having "doubled" the native areas. They found us in occupation of 143 million morgen [of land] and propose to squeeze us into 18 million. If this means doubling it, then our teachers must have taught us the wrong arithmetic.[45]

For all their destructive impact, the land acts were more a statement of ideals than a practical legal code. As a policy of social engineering, they were not practicable at the time because thousands of white farmers depended on the work of black tenants on their lands. White farmers had neither the skill nor the capital to replace the role played by black labourers. State subsidization of white farmers through such agencies as the Union Land Bank was still in its infancy in 1913, and the coercive power of the state was very limited. Although there was displacement of hundreds of people from farms immediately after the passage of the Act, it was only in the 1960s and 1970s that the principles of the Land Act were implemented with the forced removal of people from black-owned areas (officially termed "black spots") and from urban areas to the bantustans. These delayed effects of the land acts were explained by Laurine Platzky and Cherryl Walker in their 1985 publication about the Surplus People Project:

> Large numbers of isolated, African-owned farms as well as extensive tracts of state-owned land long settled by Africans were not approved for release [under the Native Trust and Land Act of 1936]. The freehold areas were thus isolated as "black spots," whose continued existence ran counter to the reserve policy, while those Africans living on state land became classified as illegal squatters. The Act thus pointed to the eventual relocation of these people at some stage in the future.[46]

The predominant feature of South African reserves was the migrant labour system; the lynchpins that held the system in place were the Pass Laws. Often brutally enforced, these laws and regulations monitored and controlled every movement of the black population. Not only did the hated "pass book" record and confine movements from one area of the country to another, the pass laws also determined and restricted the kinds of work for which any given worker was eligible. The options facing pass offenders were stark: a fine which most were unable to pay; eviction from the urban area where they were currently working; or a prison sentence which usually included hard manual labour, usually on a farm. As Allen Cook observes, "the words 'farm labourer' stamped on a pass was the stamp of doom. Isolated on remote farms, prisoners were habitually subjected to maltreatment by their employers."[47] The pass laws and apartheid were inextricably intertwined. Philip Frankel observed in 1979, "[t]oday, both locally and nationally, the notions of apartheid and pass laws are considered as virtually inseparable."[48]

IDEOLOGICAL SEGREGATION AND SOVEREIGNTY: APARTHEID SOUTH AFRICA

In the 1930s, Afrikaner intellectuals returning home with doctoral degrees from German universities produced pamphlets, tracts and articles glorifying Nazi ideals. Notions of "racial purity" became a central theme of Afrikaner discourse. In the words of one pamphleteer, "The preservation of the pure race tradition of the Boerevolk (Afrikaner nation) must be protected at all costs in all possible ways as a holy pledge to us by our ancestors, as part of God's plan for our people."[49] African integration was anathema to the goals of white supremacy. The policy of racial segregation was clearly articulated by the Afrikaner National Party, which gained power in 1948. Their election manifesto stated, "The Bantu in the urban areas should be regarded as migratory citizens not entitled to political or social rights equal to those of whites."[50] The Transvaal leader of the National Party, J.G. Strydom (later to succeed D.F. Malan as Prime Minister), appealed to genuine fears about the survival of the Afrikaner people as a separate and distinct entity in white South African society:

Our policy is that the European must stand their ground and must remain baas (master) in South Africa. If we reject the herrenvolk (master race) idea … if the franchise is to be extended to non-Europeans, and if the non-Europeans are given representation and the vote and the non-Europeans are developed on the same basis as the Europeans, how can the European remain baas? … Our view is that in every sphere the European must retain the right to rule the country and to keep it a white man's country.[51]

With apartheid, a new level of white supremacy was reached in South Africa. The word apartheid (Afrikaans for "separateness") represents much more than the mere segregation of the races: it was both an ideology and a political system that permeated every aspect of the political, social and economic life of South African society. Under apartheid laws, which numbered in the hundreds, racial segregation was institutionalized. The key laws (the so-called pillars of apartheid) were the Population Registration Act of 1950, which classified the South African population into four main groups (white, Coloured, Asian and African); the Group Areas Act of 1950, which regulated how and where they were allowed to live and work; and the Prohibition of Mixed Marriages Act of 1949 and the Immorality Amendment Act of 1957, both of which prohibited interracial sex and marriage.

The goal of the newly elected National Party government was to stem the tide of Africans streaming into the cities and towns and to keep unwanted "surplus" workers out of the white areas. With this end in view, the Minister of Native Affairs, Hendrik Verwoerd (who later became prime minister), began to conceptualize the reserves as separate "national" entities. The key aspects to his policy were, first of all, to "retribalize" and resettle urban Africans, and secondly, to remove communities living on African-owned land surrounded by so-called white areas (officially labelled "black spots") and relocate them in the so-called Bantu Homelands. The term "bantustan," by which these areas later became known, originated as a satirical term but grew in usage because of the resistance of Africans to the notion of designated "homelands" – places most of them had never seen.

In 1949, the government commissioned Professor Frederik R. Tomlinson, an agricultural economist, to investigate conditions on South Africa's 264 scattered reserves. The facts were already well known. Numerous studies bore witness to the serious soil erosion of vast tracts of land and to the impoverishment of the people to the point at which malnutrition and disease caused a high rate of debilitation and death. After five years examining every aspect of African life on the reserves, the Tomlinson Commission submitted its report in October 1954. The report recommended two interrelated steps: 1) the current evolutionary process of integration of white and black communities should be stopped immediately through a policy of separate development; and 2) massive infusions of state funding should be pumped into the economy of the "Bantu Areas" in order to create economically viable tribal homelands.

While the establishment of "separate communities in their own separate territories" was presented as something that would ultimately benefit the African people, the Report makes no effort to hide its main objective – the protection of white interests:

> The policy of separate development is the only means by which the Europeans can ensure their future unfettered existence, by which increasing race tensions and clashes can be avoided, and by means of which the Europeans will be able to meet their responsibilities as guardians of the Bantu population.[52]

Citing the example of the former British India (which had gained its independence in 1947), Tomlinson expressed fear that failure to stop the evolutionary process towards integration might result in "the European being swamped by the superior numbers of the Bantu" and "intensify racial friction and animosity." As the Report stated,

> The dilemma with which this policy of integration confronts the South African people may be described in the following terms. On the part of the European population, there is an unshakeable

resolve to maintain their right of self-determination as a national and racial entity; while on the part of the Bantu there is a growing conviction that they are entitled to … the fruits of integration, including an even greater share in the control of the country.[53]

The government rejected Tomlinson's recommendations concerning the economic development of the reserves but accepted the principle of transforming them into national "homelands." The concept of making the reserves "the true home or fatherland of the Natives" had been the declared objective of the apartheid government before it gained power; Tomlinson's prescription for securing white supremacy thus became the blueprint for the apartheid government's "homeland" policy.

Under the Promotion of Bantu Self-Government Act (1959), eight African national reserves were recognized. The number was later increased to ten; these were: Transkei, Ciskei, Venda, Bophuthatswana, KwaZulu, KaNgwane, Lebowa, QwaQwa, Ndebele and Gazankulu. By partitioning the reserves along tribal lines, the apartheid government attempted to undo the intermingling of African peoples which had been taking place for many decades. The artificial classifications ignored the reality that Africans had lived peacefully together for generations and that many Africans were intertribal in language and descent. The model of the ethnic "homeland" was thus a government-sponsored version of nationalism imposed on the African population without their will or consent. To add to the impracticality of the scheme, only the Transkei was one contiguous landmass: the other nine consisted of 260 small and separate plots scattered throughout the country. (Map 1, *xvi*.) In his book on the 1960 uprising in Pondoland (Transkei), Govan Mbeki described the "homelands" in these words:

They are South Africa's backwaters, primitive rural slums, soil eroded and under-developed, lacking power resources and without developed communication systems. They have no cities, no factories, and few sources of employment … they are areas drained of their menfolk, for their chief export is labour and while the men work in the white-owned farms and in mines and industry, their women-folk and old people pursue a primitive agriculture incapable of providing even subsistence. The "homelands" are mere reserves of labour, with a population not even self-sustaining, supplying no more than a supplement to the low wages paid on the mines and farms.[54]

A total of 13.9 million people were removed from urban South Africa under the 1959 Act as "surplus people." Between 1960 and 1983, another 3.5 million Africans were forcibly removed to the already overcrowded and impoverished bantustans. The rudimentary towns and rural areas were in fact nothing but dumping grounds for old people, women and children whose labour was not required by the white economy. As Nelson Mandela put it,

> The main object [of forced removals] is to create a huge army of migrant labourers, domiciled in rural locations in the reserves far away from the cities. Through the implementation of the scheme it is hoped that in the course of time the inhabitants of the reserves will be uprooted and completely severed from their land, cattle and sheep, and to depend for their livelihood entirely on wage earnings.[55]

Africans now had a type of citizenship, but only of these designated "homelands" that comprised some of South Africa's least favoured areas in terms of natural resources. Reserve-dwellers were eligible only for what their impoverished local governments could afford (or chose) to pay them. The Deputy Minister of Justice, Mr. S. Froneman, shrugged off any further responsibility for the bantustan people: "The White State has no duty to prepare the homelands for the superfluous Africans because they are actually aliens in the White homelands who only have to be repatriated."[56] Migrant workers were therefore excluded by law from the welfare services available to white South Africans because they were regarded as "foreigners" or "temporary sojourners" in white South Africa. Dr. Connie Mulder, speaking as Minister of Bantu Administration, introduced the 1978 Bantu Homelands Citizenship Amendment Bill by baldly stating: "If our policy is taken to its logical conclusion as far as the Black people are concerned, there will not be one Black man with South African citizenship."[57] Thus, Africans became "aliens" in South Africa: they ceased to qualify for South African passports and could be deported at any time to their assigned "homeland."

The evolution of segregation in South Africa is portrayed by some historians as a natural progression from the bitter almond hedge planted by Jan Van Riebeeck in the 1600s through the slave era to colonial conquests. In their view, apartheid was an inevitable culmination of South Africa's adoption of Nazi ideology on top of a history of racial exploitation and conflict. John Cell argues that the policy of segregation was extended "layer upon layer, dimension on dimension, building on the legacy of racial prejudice that survived from its isolated frontier past."[58] Others believe that segregation was not at all inevitable, that it was a twentieth-century phenomenon deliberately imposed to protect white supremacy.[59] Ray and Jack Simons argue that a multiracial, democratic society could easily have been born in South Africa after the Second World War. Although colour prejudice was deeply ingrained among whites, South Africa's policy of racial discrimination differed in degree rather than in kind from that of other colonized countries.[60]

THE STRUGGLE FOR SOVEREIGNTY IN SOUTH AFRICA

The political awareness of black South Africans began in the late 1800s as missionary-educated Africans took the lead in publishing their dissent in their own languages. Vernacular newspapers, initially produced on mission printing presses, proliferated in this period as a mouthpiece for political activism. Although the circulation of African newspapers was never high, their impact was extensive. Even in the rural areas, illiterate villagers would gather around a teacher, minister or other educated person who would read them the latest news. In this way, interest in politics among Africans was stimulated and the horizons of audiences broadened by discussions and comments in the newspapers on matters affecting their lives.[61] The futility of continuing to oppose white expansion through war and the need to find other avenues of political expression is clearly articulated in a poem by Xhosa poet I.W.W. Citashe. The poem appeared in the newspaper *Isigidimi Sama Xhosa*, published at the London Missionary Society school, Lovedale College in 1887.

> Your cattle are gone, my countrymen!
> Go rescue them! Go rescue them!
> Leave the breechloader alone
> And turn to the pen.
> Take paper and ink,
> For that is your shield,
> Your rights are going!
> So pick up your pen.[62]

In the years following the Anglo-Boer War (1899–1902), the emergence of African protest movements across the country increased. Unlike Canada, where the indigenous peoples formed separate groups to demand political, social and economic rights, South Africans from every racial group were drawn together to confront a common problem. The need for African unity was forcefully brought home by the South

Africa Act of 1909 which provided legal status exclusively to white South Africans. The African National Congress (ANC) was launched in 1912 at a mass rally in Bloemfontein, in the heart of Afrikaner country. Pixley ka Isaka Seme, the first president of the organization, stated the aims of the Congress in these words:

> Chiefs of royal blood and gentlemen of our race, we have gathered here to consider and discuss a theme which my colleagues and I have decided to place before you. We have discovered that in the land of our birth, Africans are treated as hewers of wood and drawers of water. The white people of this country have formed what is known as the Union of South Africa a union in which we have no voice in the making of the laws and no part in their administration. We have called you therefore to this conference so that we can together devise ways and means of forming our national union for the purpose of creating national unity and defending our rights and privileges.[63]

The thrust of African protest in the years following the formation of the African National Congress, was against the removal of thousands of Africans from their land following the Native Land Act of 1913 and the pass laws. Before the outbreak of World War I, the newly formed Congress submitted petitions to the government and sent a delegation to the British government in protest against the Native Land Act. In the 1920s and 1930s, the struggle for land and sovereignty continued. But the 1948 elections and the offensive laws of apartheid provoked renewed resistance from the black majority. In the black rural areas, protest centred around the enforcement of the government's Betterment Schemes, which involved the highly unpopular program of cattle culling. Local people were not necessarily against the reduction of their herds, since grazing land was extremely scarce in these arid and over-populated areas, but resented the high-handed and demeaning way this program was administered. Protests flared into violent confrontations with the police for a variety of reasons. One such incident, involving the suspension of a village teacher, took place on 27 November 1950 on the Orange Free State reserve of Witzieshoek. Two policemen and a number of residents were killed in a protest against the authoritarian behaviour of the Native Commissioner.[64]

In the urban areas, laws discriminating against African people were fiercely protested. In 1952, the African National Congress Youth League launched the "Defiance Campaign Against Unjust Laws." The object of the Campaign was to deliberately violate the colour bar as an act of organized protest. All over the country, African protesters courted arrest by walking in groups through whites only railway entrances, broke the curfew laws, and burned their passes. Thousands of men, women and children went to prison before government legislation finally brought the Campaign to an end. Nelson Mandela was one of twenty leaders charged and convicted under the Suppression of Communism Act for organizing the campaign.

In 1955, a Congress of the People held in Kliptown, near Johannesburg, marked the culmination of the Defiance Campaign. Incorporating a wide spectrum of South Africans, including the ANC, South African Indian Congress, the South African Coloured People's Organization, the (white) Congress of Democrats, and the South African Congress of Trade Unions, the Congress established the blueprint for a new, non-racial society: the Freedom Charter. Drafted by a subcommittee of the National Action Council from contributions submitted by groups, individuals and meetings all over South Africa, the Charter declared that South Africa belongs to all who live in it, black and white, and that no government can justly claim authority unless it is based on the will of the people.[65]

However, the concept of a single, non-racial state was diametrically opposed to the apartheid government's own vision of the country: the partitioning of the country into separate, ethnic states as outlined in the Tomlinson Report released the same year. Prime Minister Dr. Hendrik Verwoerd (a Dutch immigrant to South Africa) moved forward with his creation of African "homelands" as if the Freedom Charter had never existed. In an article entitled "Verwoerd's Tribalism," Nelson Mandela described the unequivocal African response to the homeland scheme. At a widely attended mass rally in Bloemfontein in 1956, organized by the United African clergy, representatives from a broad base of political affiliations (African, Coloured and Indian) unanimously and uncompromisingly rejected the Tomlinson principle on which Verwoerd's bantustan scheme was based, and voted in favour of a single society.[66]

On 21 March 1960, in the African township of Sharpeville, Transvaal an event occurred which had a profound impact on the course of South African history. Following a peaceful march in protest against pass laws, the police opened fire on a crowd that had gathered at the local police station, killing sixty-nine people and injuring one hundred and eighty. Most of the protesters were shot in the back as they tried to get away. Later the same day, a similar tragedy (but on a smaller scale) occurred in the township of Langa, outside Cape Town. The killings, which attracted worldwide attention, outraged the black community but the government's response was to tighten the reins even further. It placed an embargo on all public meetings and banned a number of anti-apartheid organizations, including the African National Congress (ANC) and the Pan Africanist Congress (PAC). Having lost all hope of achieving their objectives through peaceful protests, a new spirit of militancy emerged in the resistance movements. In December 1961, the ANC's military wing, *Umkhonto we Sizwe* (Spear of the Nation), was launched with Mandela as chairman. Mandela was arrested and charged with conspiracy against the state in 1964. With the major liberation organizations banned and most of its leadership (including Nelson Mandela) serving life sentences in prison, the resistance continued with strikes, demonstrations and every form of civil disobedience.

In the 1970s, when the apartheid government pushed forward its plans to make the bantustans "independent states," opposition was quickly crushed. In the Transkei, the State of Emergency regulations in effect since the Pondoland uprising in 1960 prevented any effective opposition from taking place.[67] With the support of his followers, Chief Kaiser Matanzima accepted the government's offer of independence, arguing that Africans now had the opportunity to regain control of their land. But elsewhere the transition to self-government was less peaceful. In Bophuthatswana (comprising a scattering of eight pieces of territory spread over three provinces), the proposed Legislative Assembly in Mafeking was burnt to the ground in a mass demonstration. The response of the South African government was to pass a special security regulation that prohibited meetings of more than five people and allowed bantustan police to arrest and detain people without charge.[68]

Some African leaders (like Transkei Chief Matanzima) chose to accept the homelands scheme despite its limitations. But the majority of rural Africans perceived these leaders as puppets of the apartheid government.[69] Instead of providing a government which would benefit the local people, as the apartheid regime had promised, the homeland system was a mere extension of white supremacist legislation implemented by hand-picked African leaders. As Govan Mbeki observed, the homeland policy was launched at a time when the South African government was under severe international pressure. The killing of protesters by state police in Sharpeville and Langa in March 1960 had incensed international audiences. By advertising its "gift of self-government" to Africans in certain areas, Mbeki notes, it hoped to silence world censure.[70]

In 1983, organized protests against the apartheid state gained momentum and unity when the government introduced a new Constitution providing for a segregated tricameral parliament. Under the new system, separate chambers were created for the Coloured and Asian communities, both under the veto of the white parliament. But the black majority was not included in the new dispensation. Moreover, the revised constitution was shaped in such a way that the majority party of the white House of Assembly (in this case, the Afrikaner National Party) effectively remained in power. As citizens only of the bantustans (and therefore foreigners in South Africa), the African majority remained voteless and without parliamentary representation. The 1983 constitution unleashed a fresh wave of resistance, and thousands of people were detained without trial in violent confrontations with government forces that continued for the next decade.

By the 1990s, the apartheid state's totalitarian-style repression of African resistance had attracted worldwide condemnation, resulting in economic sanctions and boycotts. As a result, the South African government was forced to negotiate with the powerful liberation movement or face civil war. Nelson Mandela's release from prison on 11 February 1990 after twenty-seven years was the first step in the negotiation process, but the following four years were fraught with violence and insecurity. Thousands of people were killed in state-orchestrated violence that erupted between the Inkatha Freedom Party and the ANC.[71] But a compromise agreement was eventually negotiated. With South Africa's first democratic non-racial elections in April 1994, South Africans finally reversed the political exclusion of its indigenous majority and elected a black president to an interim Government of National Unity (GNU). The new government eliminated the enforced territorial segregation (both rural and urban) of the South African population and incorporated the bantustans into the nine newly created provinces of the new South Africa.

Between 1994 and 1996, Africans were active participants in drafting a new Constitution. The South African Constitution approved by the Constitutional Court in October 1996 is the very antithesis of the tricameral Constitution of 1983, which entrenched the National Party policy of separate development. The new Constitution with its Bill of Rights ensures that South Africa belongs to all who live in it. The words of Nelson Mandela left this in no doubt: "Our pledge is: Never, never again shall the laws of our land rend our people apart, or legalize their oppression or repression. Together we shall march, hand in hand to a brighter future."[72]

CHALLENGING THE CONCEPT OF SOVEREIGNTY IN CANADA

The struggle for justice and liberation from colonial and foreign rule has been fought very differently in Canada. The primary objective of

Canadian aboriginal communities has not been the overturning of an oppressive dominant culture, as it was in South Africa, but rather, to be recognized as sovereign independent nations within the Canadian state. Fundamental to this recognition is control over ancestral lands and resources and the honouring of treaty rights.

The 1969 White Paper of the Liberal government was a major catalyst for aboriginal protest. By threatening to terminate both their treaty rights and what protection still existed of their land and resources, the new policy helped to define and clarify native goals and objectives. The Indian Association of Alberta responded to the White Paper with substantive recommendations for a new policy based on this premise. Known as the "Red Paper," authored by Harold Cardinal, the document reasserted the constitutional basis of the federal government's responsibilities towards Canada's first peoples and stressed its legal obligations to fulfill the terms of treaties:

> We say that the federal government is bound by the British North American Act, Section 9k, Head 24, to accept legislative responsibility for "Indians and Indians' lands." Moreover, in exchange for the lands which the Indian people surrendered to the Crown, the treaties ensure the following benefits.[73]

Faced with united and well-organized protests, Trudeau withdrew the proposed White Paper on 17 March 1970. Although the Liberal government remained hostile to the recognition of aboriginal rights, they began initiatives towards a new constitution and bill of rights and freedoms, which indirectly opened the way for native organizations to assert their constitutional rights. By the 1970s, the French separatist cause had moved from the fringes of Quebec politics and terrorist actions into the Parti Québécois, a political party with substantial power in Quebec. Suddenly, the word sovereignty was exclusively associated with French separatism. But through the separatism crisis, Canadians became aware of the need to redefine confederation and rewrite the BNA Act. In 1972, the Molgat-MacGuigan Committee, a joint committee of the Canadian Senate and House of Commons, concluded that the time was right for constitutional change; but it wasn't until the Parti Québécois came into power in Quebec in November 1976 that constitutional reform was pushed ahead. The Committee recommended that no constitutional changes concerning native peoples be made until their own organizations had completed their research. This paternalism stoked the fire of aboriginal assertiveness.[74] Two events in the 1970s gave Canada's aboriginal communities reason to hope that the tide had finally turned. In 1974, the federal government accepted the Berger Inquiry's recommendation to delay the proposed Mackenzie Valley pipeline until outstanding land claims had been settled. A few years later, the Cree of Northern Quebec negotiated an agreement with the federal government: the James Bay and Northern Quebec Agreement which awarded them both compensation for land and the promise of self-government on the remaining territory. (Map 3, *xviii*.)

But the critical event that pushed native rights onto the public agenda came from within the native community itself. Frank Calder, a hereditary chief of the Nisga'a nation in British Columbia, made Canadian legal history by challenging the validity of provincial land legislation which ignored Nisga'a land claims. The case of *Calder v. The Attorney General of British Columbia* (1973) was groundbreaking in that, for the first time in Canadian history, the notion of aboriginal rights was recognized in a court of law. As Justice Thomas Berger commented, the Nisga'a case not only opened up the whole question of aboriginal rights but it also catapulted the issue of aboriginal land title into the political arena.[75] One of the most significant consequences of the decision was the reversal of Prime Minister Trudeau's integration policy and the Liberal government's introduction of a comprehensive land claim policy. The government also made funding available for the research of native claims.

In contrast to the South African apartheid government's constitutional "reforms" in 1983, which sparked massive unrest throughout the country, the exclusion of Canada's indigenous minority from the 1982 Constitution talks went largely unnoticed by the non-aboriginal community. From the early 1970s, when talks about constitutional reform first began in earnest, it was Quebec's far more pressing sovereignty demands that captured the attention of both the media and the federal and provincial leaders. Numerically much weaker and with few viable land bases, the aboriginal peoples were almost completely overshadowed. Not only were aboriginal rights peripheral to the constitutional agenda, but aboriginal leaders were not consulted. It was only after native organizations had launched strong protests in Canada and abroad that the three major aboriginal organizations – the National Indian Brotherhood (NIB), the Native Council of Canada and the Inuit Tapirisat – were permitted observer status to the Constitutional Conferences.

Eventually, the provinces agreed to reinstate Section 35 of the BNA Act into the 1982 Constitution Act, providing for the "existing aboriginal rights and treaty rights" of Canada's aboriginal peoples. Also included in the Constitution Act was the recognition of Métis and Inuit as "aboriginal peoples of Canada." This was a major victory for their organizations which had lobbied hard for constitutional recognition. However, the campaign had taken a severe toll on aboriginal solidarity. Instead of intensifying the cohesion that existed between the various groups, the wording of the Act produced complete disarray among the aboriginal community, and a number of people strongly opposed it. The new Constitution did not address the issue of treaty rights, which some groups asserted could not be transferred to Canada since these treaties had been made with the British Crown. Others claimed that the Constitution could not be patriated without the consent of aboriginal peoples. When the Queen came to Ottawa to give Royal assent to the legislation in April 1982, the National Indian Brotherhood (later renamed the Assembly of First Nations) declared a day of mourning

Despite this disunity within the aboriginal community, the Constitution Act was a landmark event in Canadian history and signalled a new chapter in the struggle for aboriginal rights. Under the terms of the Act, the Prime Minister was committed to hold a series of conferences to define the rights of aboriginal peoples. But after four such conferences, held between 1982 and 1988, aboriginal rights were still not clearly defined.

During the 1980s, a number of protest events kept the issue of native rights and self-government in the public eye and on the political agenda. The Haida, Wet'suwet'en and Gitksan nations of British Columbia constructed barricades in the path of logging company equipment to prevent clear-cutting on their ancestral lands. The Lubicon Cree of Alberta also built roadblocks and lobbied international bodies to prevent oil companies from destroying their lands and traditional economies. The Mi'kmaq and Maliseet of Nova Scotia defied restrictions preventing them from exercising their fishing and hunting rights, rights that had been confirmed by the Supreme Court of Canada but that provincial governments were ignoring. The Innu of Labrador camped out on the runway of the airbase at Goose Bay in protest against low-level test flights conducted by the North American Treaty Organization (NATO), which threatened the animal populations on which they depended for food. The most public protest of all was the 1990 Oka uprising: the Mohawk of Kanesatake built barricades to protect their ancestral lands from being taken over for the extension of a golf course by the municipality of Oka. When the Quebec police failed to storm the barricades successfully, the Canadian Armed Forces were brought in. The stand-off at Kanesatake lasted for seventy-eight days in full television view of the international community, and its impact is still being felt more than a decade later.

CONCLUSION

In both Canada and South Africa, state policy was driven by the dominant society's agenda to maintain sovereignty over the lives and lands of indigenous peoples. In both cases, the indigenous societies have challenged this assumption of sovereignty. The aboriginal peoples of Canada have asserted their own sovereign or aboriginal rights and have refused to become absorbed or assimilated into the dominant society. In South Africa, Africans have regained sovereignty over their country after four hundred years of political, social and economic exclusion.

While Canada's 1982 Constitution recognizes the existing aboriginal rights of its first peoples (Indians, Inuit and Métis), it does not offer protection of Indian lands or solve the problem of sovereign rights. Although the Métis are recognized in the Constitution as an aboriginal people, their aboriginal rights have not been recognized by governments. Unlike other aboriginal groups, they have been refused access to modern treaties or negotiated settlements. The key to change in Canada are: the inclusion of indigenous peoples in policy discussions; access to impartial courts; and an interpretation of aboriginal rights that pays attention to the needs of all aboriginal peoples.

South Africans, on the other hand, have only recently been released from the unjust laws of apartheid – and the fetters of parliamentary supremacy. For the first time in the country's history, South Africa has a democratically elected government and a Constitution and Bill of Rights to safeguard the rights of all its people. Although constitutional rights have yet to be fully tested with respect to land rights, the principle of equality and a just sharing of the country's wealth by all its inhabitants is woven into the fabric of the new democracy.

Part Two
Reclaiming the Land

Chapter Four

Litigation

The fact is that when the settlers came, the Indians were there,
organized in societies and occupying land as their forefathers had
done for centuries. This is what Indian title means.

Justice J. Judson: Calder v. The Attorney General
of British Columbia (1973)[1]

INTRODUCTION

In both Canada and South Africa, indigenous peoples have to prove their
legal rights to ancestral lands through litigation – that is, through an
adversarial legal system established by their colonizers. Like most other
former British colonies, both Canada and South Africa have adopted the
British system of common law (also known as case law), a body of law
that has evolved from decisions made by English royal courts since the
time of Norman conquest in 1066. However, the legal systems of these
two countries reflect their distinctive histories.

Canada inherited three strands of law when it was created in 1867:
the laws and social structures of aboriginal peoples, English common
law, and French Civil Law (based on the Napoleonic Code). The English
common law tradition was imposed first on the aboriginal peoples and
then, less thoroughly, on the French-speaking inhabitants of what became British North America. Each of Canada's provinces and territories has its own court system, including a court of appeal. The Supreme
Court of Canada is the final court of appeal and has the power of ultimate interpretation of the Constitution including the Charter of Rights
and Freedoms. Aboriginal land claims are generally heard in provincial
courts first. If their case is rejected by the lower court, plaintiffs may
take their case to the provincial court of appeal (if deemed eligible) or
directly to the Supreme Court of Canada.

South Africa's legal system, like the rest of its political system, was
radically transformed after the collapse of apartheid. However, the principles embodied in its legal system before 1994 (which were derived from

both Roman Dutch law and English law) remain in place. The only differences lie in the abolition of parliamentary supremacy and the creation of a Constitutional Court as the highest court of the land. Unlike other lower courts in the South African system, the Land Claims Court is on the same level as, but independent of, the High Court of South Africa (formerly the Supreme Court of South Africa in the apartheid era). Cases not involving the Constitution are taken to the Supreme Court of Appeal; those that involve constitutional rights can be taken to the Constitutional Court. The role of the Constitutional Court is to safeguard the human rights of all South Africans and to review and abolish racially discriminatory legislation inconsistent with the Constitution.

ABORIGINAL COURT CASES IN CANADA

Canada's land claim history began with the first Indians who were persuaded to relinquish their land for European settlement through treaties or other agreements. In British Columbia, where First Nations began campaigning for land rights in the 1880s, the notion of aboriginal rights was dismissed as nonsense. In 1887, when a delegation of Nisga'a and Tsimshian chiefs met with Premier William Smithe, he refused to even discuss the issue of land rights or self-government, claiming that aboriginal people had no more right to land than the birds or the bears. In 1916, the Allied Tribes of British Columbia appealed again to the provincial government to hear their case but were immediately rebuffed. These actions must have created some fears about possible litigation, because in 1927, the Federal government passed an amendment to the Indian Act making it illegal for First Nations to raise funds for legal action. The law remained in effect until 1951.

The turning point in the recognition of aboriginal land rights came in 1969, when Frank Calder, a hereditary Chief of the Nisga'a Tribal Council (now the Nisga'a nation), challenged the validity of provincial land legislation which ignored Nisga'a land claims. In *Calder v. The Attorney General of British Columbia* (1973), the Nisga'a argued that they had never signed a treaty nor had their sovereignty over their ancient tribal lands ever been lawfully extinguished. The British Columbia Supreme Court ruled against the Nisga'a, on the grounds that whatever rights Indians might have possessed at the time of contact had been extinguished when British Columbia joined Confederation in 1871. On 30 January 1973, the Supreme Court of Canada upheld the ruling (on a vote of four to three) against the Nisga'a. But the case also made legal history by recognizing the existence of aboriginal title in Canada. In his ruling, Justice J. Judson deviated from previous court decisions by defining aboriginal title as a right grounded in original occupancy. As a result of the Calder ruling, Prime Minister Pierre Trudeau conceded that First Nations had more rights than he had recognized in the 1969 White Paper. These existing rights were subsequently entrenched in the Constitution of 1982, despite strong opposition from the provincial premiers.

However, this partial constitutional victory for aboriginal rights has not always received the unequivocal acceptance of the courts. For example, in *Attorney General of Ontario v. Bear Island Foundation (1984)*, the legal nature of the rights of the Teme-agama Anishnabay (Bear Island people) to their ancestral lands in and around Lake Temagami was pitched against those of the provincial government, which wanted to open up the area for resource and tourist development. Justice Donald Steele of the Ontario Supreme Court ruled against the Bear Island people, arguing that the primitive level of Indian social organization meant that "the Indian occupation could not be considered true and legal, and that Europeans were lawfully entitled to take possession of the land and settle it with colonies."[2] But clearly, there is a conflict of interest when the province's responsibilities are decided by the province's own courts. That same year, 1984, the Supreme Court of Canada took an important step towards recognizing aboriginal title as an established legal right in another British Columbia case, *Guerin v. The Queen (1984)*. Unlike the Bear Island decision, which argued that whatever rights Indians possess stem from the Royal Proclamation of 1763, the Court's majority ruled in *Guerin* that aboriginal title in Canada was derived from the historic occupation and possession of the aboriginal people of their tribal lands. Consequently, the Court ruled that pre-existing aboriginal title remained a valid legal right on reserve lands in British Columbia and on traditional tribal lands not alienated in treaties with the Crown.[3]

A third case that made a significant contribution towards the recognition of aboriginal title in Canadian law was *R. v. Van Der Peet (1996)*. Reiterating the words of Justice J. Judson in the 1973 *Calder* case in British Columbia, Justice Antonio Lamer wrote in *Van Der Peet* that the doctrine of aboriginal rights (one aspect of which is aboriginal title) arises from one simple fact that "when the Europeans arrived in North America aboriginal people *were already here*, living in communities on the land, and participating in distinctive cultures, as they had done for centuries." (emphasis in original).[4]

THE GITXSAN AND WET'SUWET'EN OF BRITISH COLUMBIA

The struggle for recognition of aboriginal rights by the west coast Gitxsan and Wet'suwet'en goes back at least a hundred years. In 1884, the Gitxsan

Chiefs of Gitwangak protested against the intrusion of miners to Lorne Creek without their consent. As they told the provincial government,

> From time immemorial the limits of the district in which our hunting grounds are have been well defined. This district extends from a rocky point called "Andemane," some two and a half or three miles above our village on the Skeena River to a creek called "She-quin-khaat," which empties into the Skeena about two miles below Lorne Creek. We claim the ground on both sides of the river, as well as the river within these limits, and as all our hunting, fruit gathering and fishing operations are carried on in this district, we can truly say we are occupying it.[5]

Until 1984, when they brought their case before the British Columbia Supreme Court, the Gitxsan and Wet'suwet'en had tried every avenue at their disposal to protest against their dispossession. For example, in 1909, when Wet'suwet'en lands were given as "South African scrip" for Canadian war veterans who fought in the Anglo-Boer War of 1899–1902, the Wet'suwet'en appealed to the Federal government. In his letter to the Department of Indian Affairs, Chief James Yami described the brutal effects of his peoples' eviction from their traditional territory and the subsequent destruction of their homes:

> The Bulkley River is our river and we get our living therefrom. On the lakes are located some of our houses. They are small and crude of pattern but we cannot do without them. In those houses we have many articles such as hunting, trapping and fishing implements. A white man comes along and sets fire to the houses, and on remonstration we are told by the settler, "You get away from here. I bought this land and if I catch you here again I will have you jailed."[6]

In almost every case, the key issues at stake were the territories' natural resources (mining, logging and fisheries) and the question of sovereignty. Large parts of Gitxsan and Wet'suwet'en territories were being taken over by logging operations. Extensive areas of forested lands were stripped bare as large corporations built faster and more sophisticated, computer-operated sawmills to process the trees into lumber for export. Fishing sites and spawning grounds were also affected, threatening valuable salmon stocks. The Gisksan-Carrier Declaration in 1977 was adamant on the sovereignty issue, insisting that the government "recognize our sovereignty, recognize our rights, so that we might fully recognize yours."[7] However, their appeal fell on deaf ears. The federal and provincial governments refused to recognize the authority of the hereditary Chiefs or to negotiate as equal partners in the management of the fisheries. Their only recourse was to take the matter to court.

In 1984, the Gitxsan and Wet'suwet'en people (who together numbered around 10,000 people) filed a claim to separate portions of fifty-eight thousand square kilometres of land along the Skeena, Nass, Babine and Bulkley waterways in British Columbia in the landmark case *Delgamuukw v. British Columbia*. (Map 3, *xviii*.) The appellants in the case were fifty-one hereditary Chiefs, suing on their own behalf and on behalf of thirty-eight Gitxsan Houses and twelve Wet'suwet'en Houses. Delgamuukw, the hereditary Chief of the Houses of Delgamuukw and Haaxw, was the first appellant listed: hence the name of the case.[8] Meanwhile, despite injunctions to keep logging companies away from Gitxsan and Wet'suwet'en land until the court had made its decision, the clearcut logging continued.

Three years after filing their claim, the case came to trial under Justice Allan McEachern of the British Columbia Supreme Court. The opening sessions of the trial were held in Smithers, B.C., on 11 May 1987, a sawmill town in the heart of the appellants' territory and also a government service centre.[9] Over sixty witnesses gave evidence over the four-year period of the trial. What was exceptional about the trial was that the Gitxsan and Wet'suwet'en claimants chose to lead off with their oral histories told in traditional ways. Expert witnesses in genealogy, linguistics, archaeology, anthropology and geography were called in to support their claim of occupancy on the claimed land prior to 1871, when the colony of British Columbia became part of Confederation. In his introduction, Chief Delgamuukw explained the spiritual and symbolic significance of ancestral lands in Gitxsan and Wet'suwet'en culture:

> For us, the ownership of territory is a marriage of the Chief
> and the land. Each Chief has an ancestor who encountered
> and acknowledged the life of the land. From such encounters
> came power. The land, the plants, the animals and the people
> all have spirit – they all must be shown respect. That is the
> basis of our law.... My power is carried in my House's histories,
> songs, dances and crests. It is created at the Feast when the
> histories are told, the songs and dances performed, and the
> crests displayed.... By following the law, the power flows from
> the land to the people through the Chiefs; by using the wealth of

the territory, the House feasts its Chief so he can properly fulfil the law. This cycle has been repeated on my land for thousands of years. Through the witnessing of all our history, century after century, we have exercised our jurisdiction.[10]

Traditional crests, an integral part of Gitxsan and Wet'suwet'en culture, were presented to the court as visual representations of the history of the House and its people and territories. As one witness testified, "the Gitxsan crests and totem poles are memory devices which are like a map. Their existence on the blankets, house fronts and totem poles call up the history and the rights and authority of the Chief and his or her House. They are evidence, metaphorical and physical, of the root title of the House."[11] In her testimony, Chief Joan Ryan (also known as Hanamuxw) said: "It's like a history book of your House, it's evidence that Hanamuxw's House did exist, does exist and will continue to exist."

In seeking recognition of their ownership and jurisdiction over the land, the appellants' first concern was for the integrity of the land.

> We ask that the court not only acknowledge our ownership and jurisdiction over the land, but also to restore it to a form adequate for nature to heal in terms of restoration. We would like to see clear cuts and plantations returned to forests, contaminated rivers and lakes returned to their original pristine state, reservoirs of drowned forests returned to living lakes, and life-sustaining flows to diverted rivers.[12]

In order to fulfill their sacred obligation to take care of the land as their ancestors had done before them, the hereditary Chiefs explained the specific areas in which the federal and provincial governments would need to "pull back." First, the Chiefs needed to have the power to manage all human activity that affected changes to the land, air and water on all their territories. Secondly, they needed to have control over the economy by managing local resource allocations within the territories – including licensing, leasing and permitting. Also, they insisted that royalties and taxation payments from resource use be paid to the tribes. The Chiefs foresaw that the "layering of responsibilities" among the Gitxsan and Wet'suwet'en and the provincial and federal governments would be resolved through ongoing negotiations. As the Chiefs pointed out, "this case is about learning from the past so we can repair the present and pass on a healthier land to our grandchildren. It is not about retrieving frozen rights from a nineteenth century ice-box."[13]

The judgment passed down by Justice McEachern on 8 March 1991 was a bitter disappointment to the Gitxsan and Wet'suwet'en plaintiffs and indeed to the entire Indian community. While conceding that, at the date of British sovereignty the appellants' ancestors were living in their villages on the great rivers as they had testified, McEachern was not prepared to concede that they owned the territory in its entirety in any sense that would be recognized by Canadian law. The fact that there had been numerous intrusions into the area of other peoples over the years, and that there were overlapping claims to the territory, contributed to his rejection of the Gitxsan and Wet'suwet'en claim. Despite allowing the plaintiffs the right to submit non-written evidence (or "hearsay"), Justice McEachern refused to give full weight to the oral evidence presented to the court. In his view, the oral histories, totem poles and crests were not sufficiently reliable or site specific to discharge the plaintiff's burden of proof.

The Gitxsan and Wet'suwet'en claim to joint sovereignty was similarly rejected. Having heard the Chiefs' arguments and the detailed evidence of the devastating effects of government resource management on the forests and fisheries of Gitxsan and Wet'suwet'en lands, McEachern still maintained that, under Common Law, there was only one kind of sovereignty, and that sovereignty rested solely in the Crown. According to his judgment, when British Columbia joined Confederation in 1871, legislative jurisdiction was divided between Canada and the province, "and there was no room for aboriginal jurisdiction or sovereignty which would be recognized by the law or the courts." In making this judgment, he further dismissed the legal system of the Gitxsan and Wet'suwet'en as "a most uncertain and highly flexible set of customs which are frequently not followed by the Indians themselves."[14]

DELGAMUUKW V. BRITISH COLUMBIA:
THE SUPREME COURT DECISION (1997)

In 1997, the Gitxsan and Wet'suwet'en took their appeal to the Supreme Court of Canada. They decided to drop the claim for joint sovereignty and concentrate on the issue of title. The decision reached by Chief Justice Antonio Lamer, with Justices Cory and Major agreeing, effectively reversed the ruling of the British Columbia Supreme Court and called for a retrial. The judgment was a landmark case in affirming that Canada's first people had a unique claim to their traditional lands and must receive "fair compensation"; that provinces do not have the power to extinguish aboriginal title; and that, in future, oral history ought to carry equal weight with written Canadian history in proving such claims. Finally,

Lamer made a strong plea for the use of negotiation rather than litigation in the resolution of land claims: "Ultimately, it is through negotiated settlements, with good faith and give and take on all sides, reinforced by the judgements of this Court, that we will achieve ... 'the reconciliation of the pre-existence of aboriginal societies with the sovereignty of the Crown.' Let us face it, we are all here to stay."[15]

One of the most far-reaching elements of Chief Justice Lamer's ruling related to his remarks about the specific content of aboriginal title, a question which had received very little previous attention. Insisting that aboriginal title is *sui generis*, or "in a class of its own," Lamer argued that it involved much more than the right to engage in specific activities related to the distinctive cultures of aboriginal societies. "The practices and customs that are included in the exercise of aboriginal title are, to put it colloquially, a lot more than singing, dancing, hunting and hanging out. They may well include considerable rights to the resources of the territory covered by title."[16]

Another important element of the Supreme Court's decision was that oral testimony must be given significant weight in any subsequent legal proceedings by aboriginal claimants: that "stories matter." In his statement, Lamer argued that "unless oral evidence was placed on an equal footing" with the types of evidence courts are familiar with (which largely consist of historical documents), an "impossible burden of proof" would be put on aboriginal peoples who did not have written records. Furthermore, this would "render nugatory" any rights that they might have.[17] First Nations groups and legal commentators recognized this ruling as a major breakthrough for aboriginal justice. As Stan Persky points out, the Court's decision on oral history is a "profound effort to reconcile how different peoples with different cultural traditions see the world."[18]

After the decision was handed down in December 1997, the Gitxsan and Wet'suwet'en tried to re-enter the negotiation process with the B.C. government. Some progress was made in bilateral agreements with the province in 1999. However, soon after the province returned to the treaty table in 2001, there was a change in government. The new Liberal government held a referendum on treaty rights – the results of which have yet to be published – which brought the entire treaty process in British Columbia to a standstill. A breakthrough occurred in June 2003 when the Gitxsan and B.C.'s Forestry Minister signed a short-term agreement that included sharing up to $2.6 million in annual forestry revenues. Gitxsan chief negotiator, Elmer Derrick commented that although the framework agreement was "not a perfect document," it finally "gets our people into the game." But Geoff Plant, the minister responsible for treaty negotiations, was delighted: "Interim measures with First Nations create certainty over the land base and provide long-term benefits for the provincial economy."[19] Thus, as with most negotiated settlements with aboriginal peoples, native justice was a secondary consideration to the province's primary objective: to improve British Columbia's investment climate.

ABORIGINAL LITIGATION IN SOUTH AFRICA

In South Africa, the people of the Richtersveld reserve in Namaqualand, primarily of Nama ancestry, made a land claim similar to that of the Gitxsan and Wet'suwet'en. Like the British Columbian case, a long-established community claimed aboriginal title over territories that had sustained their people for hundreds if not thousands of years. Both were seeking not only the right to some measure of self-government but also a role in the management of the wealth-producing resources of their region (lumber, minerals and fisheries in British Columbia, and minerals and grazing lands in the Northern Cape) and an equitable share in the profits. Their adversaries were the governments and corporations that controlled the management and extraction of resources.

However, the legal contexts in which Delgamuukw and the Richtersveld cases were fought were very different. While the assertion of aboriginal rights has a long history in Canada, the concept of aboriginal title and rights has almost no history in South African jurisprudence and law. In post-apartheid South Africa (where the Constitution of 1996 ensures all South Africans the right to own land), only those individuals and communities whose lands were taken from them between 1913 (when the Native Land Act was enforced) and 1994 (when the laws of apartheid were annulled) were eligible to apply to the Land Claims Commission for land restitution. The Richtersveld community in Namaqualand (Northern Cape), who were initially dispossessed in the colonial era, was the first to reclaim ancestral land on the basis of aboriginal rights as well as racial discrimination.

THE RICHTERSVELD CASE: BACKGROUND

In 2000, the Richtersveld was the largest of the so-called Coloured Reserves in Namaqualand, extending over half a million hectares.[20] The population of about three thousand people was concentrated mainly around the settlements of Lekkersing and Eksteenfontein in the south and Kuboes and Sanddrif in the north. Located in the vast semi-desert area on the west coast of Southern Africa, the Richtersveld has been home to the Nama people for at least two thousand years. As in other parts of Namaqualand, the people were primarily pastoralists (mainly of goats and sheep) and fishermen. They were a nomadic community with shared norms, culture and political system. Village settlements were established close to secure water sources and were often close knit tribal units governed under the leadership of a headman or Chief. The function of the Chief was to manage the community's grazing rights and extract grazing fees from outsiders. Land was communally owned and held in trust for the community by the Chief. There was a clear understanding that land could neither be owned individually (even by the Chief) nor be alienated from the community. The members of each village had the right to all natural resources within the territory it owned, including water, grazing, firewood, game, fruit and medicinal plants.

As the indigenous people of the Cape were driven from their hunting grounds and pasturelands by the colonists further south, the population of Namaqualand increased and became more cosmopolitan. In the late 1700s, the Dutch East India Company granted loan farms in Namaqualand to registered Dutch farmers (known as trekboers) for 24 Riksdollars a year. The extent of the land grants was determined by the distance covered in a half-hour walk in any direction from a specified point. A few farms were registered by Basters (a kindred group to the Griquas), but much of the well-watered land was allocated to the trekboers. Although their territorial base decreased as a result of these allocations, the Richtersveld people maintained control of a large portion of their lands and refused to permit the settlement of outsiders without their permission.

When the Rhenish Mission Society established itself among the Nama-speaking herders and Basters in the nineteenth century, they found a cohesive community led by the Orlams leader Paul (Bierkaptein) Links. The leader, Paul Links and his Raad (council) made the laws, enforced them and took judiciary action against offenders as required. The allocation and enforcement of grazing rights were among their most important functions. Links and the Raad provided internal cohesion within the community and represented the community to the outside world. Even after the Cape Colony expanded its boundaries to the Orange River under British rule in 1847, and Namaqualand was formally regarded as Crown land, the Richtersveld people functioned as an autonomous community under the Links family dynasty. When Paul Links, the council leader, was offered the position of field cornet by the Cape authorities in 1857 in an effort to incorporate the community, he refused, saying he would not become a "paid officer of the government."[21]

When the region came under British control, the missionaries at Richtersveld did not initially claim formal allocation of their station from the authorities in Cape Town. It was only when high grade copper was found in the region that this omission became significant.[22] When a survey was undertaken in 1889, the Richtersveld community decided the time had come to apply for a reserve. However, their application was turned down. According to the surveyor's report, the area of around seven hundred thousand morgen claimed by the community was "much too large" – and also much too valuable – to be left under local control.[23] In 1909, just prior to Union, Coloured reserves were secularized under the Mission Station and Reserves Act but the Richtersveld was again overlooked. According to an inquiry into "Coloured Mission Stations, Reserves and Settlements" in 1945, the reason for this was that these communities were deemed to be "insufficiently advanced to be able to manage their own affairs as envisaged by the 1909 Act."[24]

With the discovery of alluvial diamonds at Port Nolloth and Alexander Bay in the 1920s, the situation of the Richtersveld community changed dramatically. The South African government's response to the discoveries of diamonds was to issue a series of proclamations (such as the Precious Stones Act 44 of 1927) which prohibited prospecting for diamonds on the Richtersveld and elsewhere. At the same time, the government moved swiftly to create reserves in Namaqualand. A commission recommended that 143,000 hectares of land traditionally occupied by the local community be cut off and given to white stock farmers and that the community be compensated for the loss of revenue previously generated through the lease of this land to white farmers.

The establishment of the Richtersveld reserve in 1930 was touted by the government as fair compensation for the lands taken over by the state. The Commission investigating the position of the Richtersveld stated in 1925:

> Although the inhabitants were not legally entitled to any compensation … the Commission recommends, bearing in mind the entire liberty which the Government has conceded to the people since the annexation of the country in 1847 to control and administer the reserve, that the sum of 2,000 pounds should be paid in compensation in respect of the area to be cut off.[25]

This was small consolation for the people of the Richtersveld. The loss of their land coincided with severe droughts in the region and the Great Depression. Residents of the Coloured Reserves were forced to find work on the diamond mines owned by De Beers diamond corporation. As anthropologist Peter Carstens points out in his book *In The Company of Diamonds*, preferential hiring for whites meant that Coloured workers were restricted to menial jobs at wages well below those paid to white workers. As in mines across the country, workers were required to live on the mine premises in residential compounds.[26] The socio-economic ramifications of the migrant labour system were as disastrous for the Richtersvelders as they were in other parts of South Africa, and indeed for indigenous labourers throughout sub-Saharan Africa.

The Coloured Rural Areas Act of 1963 was another watershed for the Richtersveld community. It provided for the privatization and subdivision of the reserves allocated to people classified as "Coloured" under apartheid laws. Even though colonial governments had stipulated that in most cases these areas were to be held in trust (by mission stations) for the indigenous inhabitants, the reserves were legally held by the Crown. The subdivision of the land carried out in the Richtersveld and other reserves (including Leliefontein and Steinkopf) caused widespread dissatisfaction and deprivation to the inhabitants. Because of the sparse annual rainfall in the area, which varies from place to place, having access to grazing lands in more than one area was essential to these pastoral communities. The majority of peasant farmers, who traditionally had grazing and sowing rights, were forced to live in the residential areas without access to land. The only people who benefitted from the scheme were those with other sources of income, such as the owners of shops or businesses. The residents of the reserves responded to the Act by taking their grievances to court to have the "economic units" scheme overturned. They won the case in 1988 on technical grounds – the department had not followed its own regulations in implementing the scheme – but the policy of privatization remained in place, and new enforcement regulations were introduced following the court case. A few years later, in 1993, the government transferred its alluvial diggings, including the land claimed by the Richtersveld people, to the Alexander Bay Development Corporation (Alexkor).[27]

The final straw for the Richtersveld people came in 1996 when the Minister of Public Enterprises announced the government's intention to privatize the state-owned diamond company Alexkor. The community's demands to be included in the discussions on the privatization bid were ignored. Anticipating that their situation would worsen if the changes went through, the community decided to launch court proceedings. The Richtersveld Community's claim for restitution of rights in land was submitted to both the Land Claims Court and South Africa's High Court in 1998.

THE RICHTERSVELD COMMUNITY V. ALEXKOR LIMITED & THE GOVERNMENT OF THE REPUBLIC OF SOUTH AFRICA (2000)

The plaintiffs in the Richtersveld case were the approximately 3,500 inhabitants of four villages in the Richtersveld reserve located in the Northern Cape Province. The entire reserve community was listed as the first plaintiff in the case, and the villages of Kuboes, Sanddrif, Lekkersing and Eksteenfontein were each listed separately as additional plaintiffs.[28] The territory they claimed is situated in the northwest corner of the province along the Atlantic coast from White Point (just south of Port Nolloth) to Alexander Bay at the mouth of the Orange River and east along the river valley contiguous to the Namibian border. (Map 2, *xvii*.) In addition to the restitution of their land, the community claimed rights to a new form of communal tenure of land within the reserve and to the mineral wealth in the area of their traditional lands or at least funds generated from the mineral wealth.[29] Their claims were based on both the provisions of the Restitution of Land Rights Act (Section 2 [1]) for dispossession after 1913 as a result of racial discrimination as well as ab-original title. The Richtersveld plaintiffs argued that the failure to recognize aboriginal interest in the land in South African law was a reflection of the racial discrimination which had characterized every aspect of its social and political structure for almost a century.

The Richtersveld case opened in September in the village of Kuboes and was later transferred to Cape Town in October of 2000. The case was heard by Judge Anthonie Gildenhuys and Wieshorn (Assessor) of the Land Claims Court. The community was represented by legal counsel with expert witnesses (anthropologists, sociologists and historians) as well as three lay witnesses, Willem Cloete, Elias Links and Paul Phillips. Along with the oral evidence and personal affidavits were "bundles" of documents, including maps, which were presented as evidence of the occupation and use of the territory in question by Richtersveld people for many generations. The claim was challenged by Alexkor, the state-owned diamond company, and the government, represented by the Department of Land Affairs and the Minister of Public Enterprises.

Like the hereditary Chiefs in the Delgamuukw case, who relied on oral traditions and history to prove their continuous occupation of claimed lands, members of the Richtersveld community brought their textual evidence to life with stories of their cultural and spiritual heritage. Although the Land Claims Court is specifically authorized under the Restitution of Land Rights Act (Section 30 [2]) to receive hearsay evidence, the Richtersveld plaintiffs had considerable difficulty establishing their eligibility for land restitution as a community. The requirement of the Restitution Act that claimant communities had to be the same as or part of the dispossessed community raised particular difficulties. For communities that had been forcibly removed (by colonial or subsequent white supremacist governments) to show that they were the same people that had been uprooted and resettled elsewhere was unrealistic at best. All that should be required of claimants, the Richtersvelders argued, was to prove that they possessed many elements of commonality with the dispossessed community.[30]

The diverse composition of the Richtersveld population was relevant to the case, because as the plaintiffs set out to prove, the community developed as a direct result of the apartheid system of racial segregation. For example, in 1949, a group of coloured people was moved from Calvinia, a few hundred kilometres south of the Richtersveld, and relocated to the Richtersveld village of Eksteenfontein. These people became known as the Bosluisbasters (Bush-tick Basters) – an unflattering title which reflected their neighbours' initial hostility towards them. The Eksteenfontein people were industrious and well organized, however, and they prospered in their new environment. While tensions remained between the newcomers and the Nama communities, they were united in their claim for land and had come to regard themselves as a single "community." Other more recent arrivals to the community were approximately 150 Xhosas who moved into the area in the early 1990s and settled in Sanddrif. They had all applied to become taxpayers and were included as plaintiffs in the land claim.

Expert witness S.M. Berzborn, a researcher from the University of Cologne, Germany, defined the term community as "a group of people who have a shared set of values and interact with one another, who define themselves as a community and refer to themselves as a group, and who are generally regarded by others as a community."[31] In her view, the Richtersveld community complied with all of these criteria. Based on eighteen months living in the region and on oral history interviews she had conducted with residents of the four villages, Berzborn cited the many social relationships between them, the extent of family ties and intermarriages, and social activities between the villages.[32]

Oral history, which in the Canadian Delgamuukw case had involved a visual display of crests and pageantry, also played an important part in the Richtersveld case. Paul Phillips, the grandson of Captain Paul Swartbooi Links, gave evidence to the court from his own experience and "on matters related to him by his elders." Phillips' paternal grandparents, who were of San descent, had settled in the Richtersveld with the permission of the Raad. His maternal great-grandfather was Petrus Cupido, a poor man without livestock who had had to live off fish and game in the vicinity of Dunvlei. He had died while hunting on the island in the Orange River mouth. When Phillips was born in 1941, his family lived in the small community of Brandbos, a grazing post for the Richtersveld community on the banks of the Orange River. His father was buried not far from Brandbos; but according to Phillips' testimony, his grave was no longer there because it was "cleared by the [diamond] mine in 1951 for the construction of irrigation works, chicken runs and pigsties."[33]

University of Toronto professor Peter Carstens, a social anthropologist who grew up in Namaqualand, confirmed that the Richtersveld today showed significant continuity with the past. As he told the court, when he had done fieldwork in the region in 1960, everyone in Kuboes and the surrounding hamlets lived in traditional mat houses, with the exception of the schoolteachers. The women of the community retained the high status they had enjoyed traditionally amongst the Nama and still controlled the milk supply. Most people still believed in traditional magic and sorcery and shared in the rich folklore traditions of the community. From an elderly local historian, Carstens learned the history of the struggles for power within the Richtersveld community through the nineteenth century. As Carstens stated, "If one examines the kinship system, the rules regarding marriage, the legends and mythology and also the perception of ownership of land (which strengthens the coherence of the community) the Richtersveld is still a predominantly Khoikhoi culture."[34]

The Richtersveld claim to aboriginal title followed similar lines to the Gitxsan and Wet'suwet'en claim with important variations. The Namaqualanders argued that they had "right in the land" by virtue of the fact that they "owned the land" and that they and their forebears had exclusive beneficial occupation and use of the land before it was annexed under colonial rule in 1847.[35] The ownership claim derived from the rule that a change in sovereignty does not affect the private property rights of its local inhabitants. Citing the Canadian cases of *Calder v. Attorney General of British Columbia* (1973) and *Guerin v. The Queen* (1984), the Richtersveld plaintiffs argued that their title to land was preserved and protected under this international convention.[36] The plaintiffs further argued that their right to the subject land was a special right which applied to them in the same way that it applied to the indigenous people of other nations. Here the plaintiffs drew clear parallels with Canada and other former British colonies:

It is a *sui generis* right recognized and protected in the United States, Canada, Australia and New Zealand by the development of their common law. They call the right by different names. In Canada they call it aboriginal title. We will also call it by that name. Our law has been or should be developed to recognize the same *sui generis* right.[37]

In anticipation that their case might be dismissed on the grounds that they could not prove "exclusive occupation of the land," since their communities were largely nomadic, the plaintiffs cited a Canadian case which addressed this specific problem, *Regina v. Adams (1996)*. In this case, the Canadian Supreme Court had stated:

> To understand why aboriginal rights cannot be inexorably linked to aboriginal title, it is only necessary to recall that some aboriginal peoples were nomadic varying the location of their settlements with the season and changing circumstances. That this was the case does not alter the fact that nomadic people survived through reliance on the land prior to contact with Europeans and, further, that many of the customs, practices and traditions of nomadic peoples that took place on the land were integral to their distinctive cultures.[38]

The Richtersveld case diverged from Canadian and other international cases in one important respect. The "right in land" on which the Richtersvelders based their case was not grounded in any existing recognition of aboriginal rights (as it was in Canada under the 1982 Constitution), but relied on the terms of South Africa's Restitution of Land Rights Act (1996), which supported the notion of aboriginal rights in spirit but not in words. As the plaintiffs stated in their submission, Section 25 (6) of the South African Constitution of 1996 placed an obligation on the government to address the issue of land dispossession despite the lack of specific legal or constitutional backing:

> It is clear that the definition of a "right in land" gives effect to a broader purpose underlying the Act as a whole and the constitutional provisions pursuant to which it was enacted. It is to afford redress to those people who were deprived of their rights and interests in land by the discriminatory laws and practices of the past, precisely because those rights and interests did not enjoy any or sufficient recognition and protection in law.[39]

Noting that aboriginal claimants have been refused recognition of aboriginal rights on grounds of being "insufficiently civilized" from a European perspective (as happened in a case in Southern Rhodesia in 1919 and in Justice McEachern's ruling in the *Delgamuukw* case), the plaintiffs argued that South Africa should instead follow more progressive precedents such as the *Mabo* case in Australia.[40] The new South Africa, the Richtersvelders claimed, stood at a legal crossroad similar to that of Australia (see Appendix).

But Judge Gildenhuys dismissed the case, explaining that even if the Richtersvelders had been able to prove that they had occupied the claimed territory for a continuous period before annexation, and that their dispossession had occurred after 1913, they had failed to establish their claim under the Restitution of Land Act on two counts. First of all, the claim did not fall under the Restitution Act since their dispossession did not occur under any law or practice designed to bring about spatial apartheid. Secondly, the plaintiffs had not convinced the court that their dispossession had resulted from racially discriminatory laws or practices. The court argued that the physical ouster experienced by the Richtersveld people in the early twentieth century was not racially motivated. When the state took over the alluvial diggings along the Atlantic coast and later erected fences to protect their property, the entire local population (including white farmers) was excluded from the area.

The Richtersveld community then took their case to the Supreme Court of Appeal. Although the Appeal court did not uphold their claim to aboriginal title in the claimed land, it found that their claim was permissible under the terms of the Constitution. Under Section 25 (7) of the South African Constitution (1996), "a person or community dispossessed of property after 19 June 1913 as a result of past racially discriminatory laws and practices are entitled, to the extent provided by an Act of Parliament, either to restitution of that property or to equitable redress." In the case of the Richtersvelders, the court found that dispossession by the state had occurred in the 1920s after diamonds were discovered, and that this dispossession was the result of racially discriminatory laws or practices.

The defendants, Alexkor and the Department of Land Affairs, were granted leave to appeal to the Constitutional Court, mandated by the Constitution to interpret legislation deemed to be a "constitutional matter." In their joint appeal, Alexkor and the government contended that the Supreme Court of Appeal had erred in three findings: that the Community's land rights had not survived annexation by the British Crown in 1847; that the Richtersveld Community did not have right in the land in 1913; and that the community was not dispossessed of land through racially discriminatory laws or practices.

However, on 14 October 2003, the Constitutional Court in Johannesburg rejected the appeal with costs and confirmed the Supreme Court of Appeal's decision on all three issues. In *Alexkor Ltd v. Richtersveld Community and Others*, the Constitutional Court ruled that the Richtersveld Community had indeed been cleared from the land under racist laws and therefore had a legitimate claim to ownership, including rights to the diamond mines at Alexander Bay.[41]

CONCLUSION

As these two case studies show, litigation has proved to be a hopeful avenue for the dispossessed peoples of both Canada and South Africa in reclaiming ancestral lands. But despite their significance as groundbreaking cases, neither case has produced the kind of sea change in jurisprudence that might have been expected – nor have the demands of the aboriginal plaintiffs been fully met.

The Court's ruling in the case of the Richtersveld community against Alexkor and the South African government is a good example of the Constitutional Court's critical role in the new democracy. Although South Africa's Constitutional Court has the capacity to provide leadership and direction to government departments and agencies, it does not have the mandate to oversee the implementation of its decisions. The powers of the Constitutional Court need to be strengthened to ensure that right-holders are indeed lifted from the bondage of poverty that propelled them into the legal arena in the first place. Although the Constitutional Court has ruled in its favour, the Richtersveld community must now find a way to translate the court's ruling into reality, either by filing a claim for the restoration of ownership and financial compensation with the Land Claims Court or negotiating a deal with the Department of Land Affairs and Alexkor Corporation.[42]

The *Delgamuukw* ruling produced similar mixed results. The question of aboriginal title remains contentious in Canadian courts. At the heart of the matter is the need to reconcile the rights of aboriginal people with those of the Crown or state. Justice Lamer's ruling, which held that the source of aboriginal title was grounded in both common law and the aboriginal perspective on land, leaves open the question of how aboriginal sovereignty can co-exist within the modern Canadian state. By placing the onus of proving title on First Nations, rather than on the Crown, Lamer has perpetuated what Brian Slatterly has called the "Myth of the Crown." Many First Nations have never assented to the proposition that the ultimate title to their lands resides in the Crown; the assertion has always been and remains the vestige of a purely "European" perspective of Canadian history.[43]

In his analysis of the significance of the Delgamuukw decision, Brent Olthuis challenges the "frozen rights" approach to aboriginal title imbedded in Justice Lamer's ruling and argues that Lamer should have been unequivocal in stating that these rights flowed directly from the traditional laws and customs of indigenous peoples and not from an estate held from the Crown. As Olthuis points out, "aboriginal laws are highly developed and quite capable of ensuring the appropriate respect for the land. Ignoring this fact in order to impose an 'outsider's' view of aboriginal law is a misguided initiative ... when it comes to reconstructing legal history, courts cannot take refuge in acts of state doctrine without forfeiting their moral authority and acting as passive agents of colonial rule."[44]

The ruling on the admissibility of oral testimony in Canada is also being questioned by the legal community. There needs to be a framework for assessing the weight of oral testimony, David W. Elliot argues in the *Manitoba Law Journal* in 2000. Claims derived from a hundred years ago, relating to very different societies, are not good material for our adversarial trial process. Elliot suggests that an alternative could be the establishment of an independent administrative tribunal with expert members, including aboriginal members. But this has been tried without much success. In the final analysis, no matter how progressive Canadian courts become with respect to aboriginal justice, unless government structures and attitudes change dramatically, the situation for many First Nations remains unchanged.[45]

However, many First Nations in British Columbia believe that Justice Lamer's ruling has greatly strengthened their political position. They believe that the new significance that the Court attributed to oral testimony will make it easier for them to prove their rights to specific areas. Moreover, the court's observation that aboriginal title includes minerals and other resources, and that infringements of this title requires compensation, suggests that their title has considerably higher value than they had previously expected.[46]

Given the controversial outcomes of both the Delgamuukw and Richersveld cases, two questions remain. To what extent have the First Nations of Canada benefited from the Supreme Court's qualified recognition of aboriginal rights? Secondly, would the inclusion of indigenous or "pre-existing" rights in the South African legal system enhance the restitution process in that country in any significant way?

In Canada, the constitutional rights of aboriginal peoples will probably remain in limbo until Canadian courts can find a way to "unfreeze" the current colonial notion of inalienability – that land held pursuant to aboriginal title cannot be transferred, sold or surrendered to anyone other than the Crown. In South Africa, the significance of aboriginal title is largely symbolic, since both the Constitution and the political agenda of the new democracy support land restitution. Although the sheer volume of claims and financial limitations make this a slow and unreliable process, mechanisms are in place to ensure that restitution in some form does take place.

Chapter Five
Negotiating Restitution

A restitution process that is simply aimed at getting claims "off the books" is likely to sow the seeds of poverty and conflict.

Surplus People Project Report, 2001.[1]

INTRODUCTION

The term "restitution" is defined in Webster's dictionary as the act of restoring to a person [or community] some thing or right of which they have been unjustly deprived. In post-apartheid South Africa, a special Restitution Commission was set up to ensure that as many people as possible who had been unjustly evicted from their ancestral lands were appropriately compensated. However, this has not proved to be easy. Africans have constitutional rights in the new democracy but have lost their previous leverage as an essential workforce to bring them into effect. Good farmland and the resources to make it productive are scarce. Finally, the current landholders, a predominantly conservative white community, have not yet bought into the concept that "South Africa belongs to all who live in it."

The Canadian government has established its own mechanisms to redress the injustices of the past towards aboriginal peoples. But as a minority population, North American Indians have always negotiated for their rights from a position of weakness. Special agencies within the Department of Indian Affairs dealing with land claims and residential schools, royal commissions and other "restitution" mechanisms have had a limited impact on the lives of most aboriginal communities. The most significant changes have been won through court rulings – notably those made by the Supreme Court of Canada. With their constitutional rights affirmed by the courts, aboriginal communities have gained confidence in negotiating the implementation of those rights with the federal and provincial governments. Since the 1990s, a number of indigenous communities have bypassed the difficult and costly process of litigation and have chosen to negotiate political acceptance of their demands for land rights and access to natural resources with provincial and federal governments. The final hurdle is convincing the Canadian public – particularly those with commercial interests in the claimed land – to participate in the restitution process.

RECLAIMING THE LAND IN SOUTH AFRICA

Of all the negotiated settlements between indigenous populations and the world's ruling powers that took place during the twentieth century, South Africa's was certainly the most dramatic and far-reaching. On the tenth anniversary of its first democratic elections on 27 April 2004, South Africans looked back on an incredible journey from the brink of civil war to a relatively peaceful, stable democracy.

The process began in the 1980s with negotiations between the ruling National Party under President F. W. de Klerk and the liberation movements, most notably the African National Congress led by Nelson Mandela. The meetings were fraught with conflict and uncertainty. When the negotiation process (known as Codesa) ended in March 1994 with the promise of a general election, white South Africans prepared themselves for massive retaliations by the previously disenfranchised majority. But the elections, declared "free and fair" by an international team of monitors, resulted in one of the most peaceful transfers of power in history. The final settlement revoked the iniquitous Native Land Act of 1913, which dispossessed the African peoples of South Africa of their land and dignity, and paved the way for a Constitution which would ensure the basic human rights of all South Africans.

When the land claims process was set up in the early 1990s, the apartheid government assumed there would be enormous resistance from current landholders. For this reason, it decided to set up a strong rights-based process with a special court established to resolve issues relating to the conflicting rights of claimants and current owners. At first the "willing buyer–willing seller" model chosen by the government seemed to work well. South African landholders (almost all white) were happy to divest themselves of their interests in farmland at a time when high interest rates and soaring debts made farming an expensive proposition.

In some respects, land restoration has turned out to be relatively simple. The major challenge facing the African National Congress government is to ensure that black farmers are able to prosper on their restored land. Writing in 1999, Andries du Toit, professor of agriculture at the University of the Western Cape, foresaw the problems that lay ahead. The restitution process, he declared, is "nothing more than a farce, paying lip service to land reform while granting minimal resources to the claimants.... The whole process constitutes merely symbolic restitution for public relations purposes."[2] The danger of restoring farmland to claimants without providing adequate resources to develop it continues to be a serious flaw of the restitution program.

THE RESTITUTION PROCESS IN SOUTH AFRICA

The Restitution of Land Rights Act provided five different ways to deal with land claims by people whose land had been taken from them after 1913: restoring the land from which they had been dispossessed; providing them with alternate land; compensating them with money; and giving them preferential access to government housing and the land development program. The Act has undergone several amendments. In 1999, the government did away with the need for a claim to be referred to the Court in cases where the interested parties had not reached an agreement as to how the claim should be finalized. The shift from judicial to administrative process meant that the Minister of Land Affairs was granted the power to settle claims through negotiation between the various parties. The result was a substantial increase in the number of claims resolved. Although the process was still painfully slow, 12,500 of the 67,000 claims registered were settled by June 2001. Two years later, on the ninetieth anniversary of the imposition of the 1913 Native Land Act, almost half of the registered claims were settled.

As in every area of administration in the new South Africa, apartheid has left a distinctive stamp on the land claim process. Because of the highly segregated nature of apartheid, there is no central office where land claims can be processed. The Commission on Restitution of Land Rights evaluates the claim and then passes it to specialists located in Commission offices throughout South Africa, who then do the work of validating claims. Regional offices are essential because of the segmented structure of apartheid administration (provincial and "homeland" departments kept separate records). Their task is to verify claims against government records to show which individuals and communities were moved, where they were resettled and what laws were in place at that time.

Moreover, the restitution process does not reach all South Africans who have suffered relocation and dispossession since 1913. Jacob Tshabangu, Project Officer in the Northern Province Land Claims Commission Office in Pietersberg, noted that the most prevalent class of landless people in his region are farmworkers and their families who were evicted from their land by white farmers. But because they continued to occupy the land under verbal agreements with the farm owners, and their eviction did not take place under any apartheid law, their claims are not eligible for consideration under the Restitution Act. As Tshabangu observed, the Constitutional recognition of property rights protects the rights of white landowners while failing to redress the injustice perpetrated on the African people as a whole.

CHALLENGES TO RESTITUTION IN SOUTH AFRICA

The scarcity of high quality farmland in South Africa is one of the major challenges to restitution. In Mpumalanga, one of South Africa's most fertile farming regions, more than 41 per cent of the commercial land is under claim. In February 2000, a group of white farmers under the leadership of the Transvaal Agricultural Union banded together to fight these land claims. Having appealed (unsuccessfully) to the Constitutional Court in 1996 to have the Land Restitution Act repealed, on the grounds that it infringed on their constitutional rights as landowners, the union has used every means at its disposal to maintain the status quo.[3] Claiming that the land reform program bars them from either improving their farms or conducting land transactions without the permission of a Land Claims Commissioner, the farmers established a defence fund and trained a team of lawyers and technical advisers to prepare legal responses to all potential claims.

In March 2001, the process of land redistribution was further challenged when a white farmer, Willem Pretorius, refused to sell his property, Boomplaats farm, for the price offered by the government and was subsequently served with an expropriation order. The land was to be returned to the original owners, the Dinkwanyane community, which had been forcibly removed between 1957 and 1961. But the controversy was finally resolved when Pretorius and the Land Claims Commission negotiated a settlement at a slightly higher figure. By that time, the case had become a *cause célèbre*. In response to the media attention, the Land Commission issued a press release announcing the successful resolution of the Dinkwanyane land claim. About three thousand people attended the "singing ceremony" to celebrate the return of the land to its original owners.[4]

However, for many white landowners, Boomplaats set an unwelcome precedent. The government was accused of using Zimbabwe-style tactics to obtain land, of being "anti-white," and of failing to protect the property rights of individuals in terms of the Constitution.[5] The conflict illustrated one of the major challenges in negotiating restitution: overcoming the racial prejudices of the past.

In addition to the competition for arable land, competition between indigenous communities also poses problems for the land claims process. Competition between urban and rural claims, between individual and communal claims, and between reforms that favour men and those that favour women represent fiercely contested areas and highlight the inherent danger of quick fixes. Another divisive factor within communities is the issue of women's right to the land and the problems of traditional social structures. Despite laws aimed at providing secure land tenure to farm workers, for example, women still rely on their husbands and fathers for access to housing and employment and have little security in their own right.[6] In their study on the relationship between women and land tenure, Catherine Cross and Michelle Friedman explain how women are disadvantaged by social assumptions and informal land practices not controlled by law. These become particularly important when land systems are under pressure from either overcrowding or economic change.[7]

At the root of these internal conflicts is the competition for limited resources. Urban claims have been dealt with more promptly than rural ones, mainly because rural claims tend to be advanced by a community and are therefore generally more complex (and more time-consuming to resolve) than claims by individuals. However, the downside of this bias towards individuals is that less money is available for rural communities to support development, and pay for education, housing, and health care for the most disadvantaged members of South African society.

In response to public pressure from black communities, the Minister of Land and Agriculture, Thoko Ndiza announced in February 2005 that the government had decided to extend the deadline for registering land claims to 2007. Although over two-thirds of the seventy-nine thousand registered claims had been settled, these were mainly in urban areas. The complexities of rural claims and the rising price of farmland in South Africa were the reasons given for the change in time line.[8]

CASE STUDY: MOGOPA COMMUNITY, NORTH WEST PROVINCE

The Mogopa land claim is an example of the complexity of the restitution program in rural South Africa. (Map 2, *xvii.*) It also illustrates how the return of land is only a partial solution to poverty. Situated in fertile farming country in South Africa's North West Province (formerly Transvaal), Mogopa was once a thriving agricultural community. The *Bakwena ba Mogopa* (the people of Mogopa) were a self-sufficient community that had purchased two farms in the Ventersdorp region in 1912 and 1934. Numbering about five thousand people, they not only lived off the land which they owned communally but also sold surplus crops through marketing cooperatives in town. Residents had well-built houses, churches and three schools, all built by the local people. But in 1983, the apartheid government moved in. Under Section 5 of the Native Administration Act of 1927, Mogopa was declared a "black spot" and slated for removal. The government's rationale for forcibly uprooting settled African communities which were surrounded by white farms was two-fold: their removal would swell the populations of the so-called African homelands and also create the illusion of a "white" South Africa.

When the Mogopa community was told that they were to be moved to Pachsdraai in the Bophuthatswana homeland, they refused to go. Assisted by local and international agencies, they launched a well-publicized resistance campaign. On 29 November 1983, church leaders, political groups, students, the Black Sash women's organization and journalists arrived at the village to witness the removal.[9] Because of the publicity, the removal date was postponed. Finally, on 14 February 1984, the farm was cordoned off and no outsiders were allowed into the area. The people of Mogopa were then ordered by the police to demolish their homes and pack their belongings. They were then loaded onto trucks and taken to Pachsdraai, near the Botswana border.[10] In 1987, while South Africa was still under apartheid rule, the Mogopa community took its land claim case to court. They won their case on a technicality. In an historic judgment, the Appeal Court ruled that the government should not have moved the residents without parliamentary approval. When one of their leaders, John More heard the court's decision, he was ecstatic: "This is the beginning of our struggle to get back our land."[11] But before the community could return to Mogopa, the government expropriated their land. The then-minister of Land Affairs, Hendrik Templar, defended the government's actions by declaring: "It is not government policy to allow black people to resettle or live in areas earmarked for white settlement.... Secondly, it would cause problems for the government in that other black communities would demand to be resettled on central government territory."[12]

In early 1988, some members of the community began to return to their land without government permission. They were charged with trespassing, and an eviction order was passed against them. But the Mogopa people were not to be deterred. They wrote to the Minister of Co-operation and Development stating that they wished to return to their original farms, and that they wanted reinstatement and damages for forced removal and for the expropriation of their land.[13] When they received no reply, they resorted once again to the courts. The Appeal Court ordered the government to negotiate with the current landowners for the sale of their land. Eventually the government was able to obtain an agreement that allowed the people who had returned to Mogopa to stay. In 1991, the government offered to return one of the farms to the Mogopa people, but only for residential purposes. The second farm, Hartebeeslaagte, which had previously been the breadbasket of the Mogopa community, remained leased out to white farmers as grazing land. The community then lodged a claim for the return of Hartebeeslaagte with the Advisory Commission on Land Allocation established by the apartheid regime. They received no response.

In 1994, Derek Hanekom, the new minister of Land Affairs under the Government of National Unity, received an urgent request from the people of Mogopa, reclaiming their second farm: "We urgently need Hartebeeslaagte back. We want to plough the land before the rain, so that it can be ready for the growing season. This is important, as we have no other means of support, and without its return stand in danger of being starved off our land." A member of the community, Daniel Molefe, later told the minister, "The government took my trousers, and now it has given back one leg. But how can I walk with just one leg?"[14] Hanekom managed to work out a deal with the tenant farmers of Hartebeeslaagte to allow the Mogopa community to return to their land. When the community heard the news they were overjoyed: "people shouted out loud, some began to ululate, other broke down and wept."[15]

However, after all this, the Mogopa community faces a massive task of rebuilding their village and making their land productive with minimal resources. Their homes, schools and churches were all destroyed the day the government bulldozers came to tear them down. Their cattle, cultural symbols of wealth and prosperity but also an essential source of food, were sold to neighbouring white farmers. Now the people have returned with small herds of goats, a few chickens and one or two horses to pull their hand-driven ploughs.

REBUILDING COMMUNITIES

There are hundreds of communities across South Africa in similar situations. However, some communities have fared better than others once their land was restored to them. Targeted for removal as a "black spot" in the early 1970s, African landowners in Cremin (near Ladysmith, KwaZulu-Natal) were expropriated in 1977; and a total of 2,856 people were removed to designated townships in the region. (Map 2, *xvii.*) The land was eventually sold to a white farmer. Although the people of Cremin were scattered across the province and lost touch with each other over the years, they never lost hope of returning to their own land one day. When the government announced its restitution policy following the 1994 elections, some of the Cremin people decided to submit a claim. Much to their delight, the claim was accepted four years later and settled under the Restitution of Land Claims Act. However, before the land could be returned to the community, the KwaZulu Natal Land Claims Commission had to negotiate the purchase of their claimed land from the current owner. A price, acceptable to both the Commission and the owner, was negotiated and the claim was settled. As the first land claim to be settled in KwaZulu Natal, the Cremin case was hailed as a landmark case. The official ceremony marking the handover of title deeds to the claimants was attended by both Prime Minister Nelson Mandela and Zulu King Goodwill Zwelethini.

In 2002, six years after this historic event, Cherryl Walker, former Land Claims Commissioner of KwaZulu Natal, visited the Cremin community farm. Cattle were grazing in the fields, small patches of mealies (corn, a staple of African diet) were growing, and a new brick school had been built on the site of the old one torn down by government bulldozers in 1978. Reconstruction of Cremin is taking place in a profoundly different era from the one in which it was founded. Building relationships with their white neighbours is a new experience for black communities, but one that is essential to the development and prosperity of the region. The greatest challenge of all is to rebuild a thriving, productive community with so few resources. The chairperson of the Cremin Trust told Walker:

> We are starting from scratch. What we are saying is that you
> cannot go back to your real cultures. Ja, because if you are old
> and want to bring back what you had, the time is too short.
> And if you are young, you might not get exactly what prevailed
> before.... It does not mean that we are back on our feet, but we
> are consoled.[16]

Many of the former members of the Cremin community have chosen not to return to their reclaimed land. The younger members, especially those who were born and have grown up in the relocation township of Ezakheni, stand in a different relationship to the land from their parents and grandparents who experienced the removal and fought for its return. Moreover, they are reluctant to exchange the relative comforts of township life for a rural one (without electricity or running water), where subsistence farming is the economic mainstay.

South African historian Rodney Davenport sees the restoration of land in rural areas as a production-based issue. In his view, the general condition of land in South Africa in terms of access to water and soil fertility demands that modern (as opposed to traditional) agricultural methods be used. The serious erosion of land in the former bantustans due to overcrowding demands particular attention. Davenport argues that government has an obligation to improve – or at least not to disturb – the potential of land to produce food and to do its utmost to prevent the intrusion of desert conditions. While conceding that rights should be respected, especially those deriving from ancient occupation where communities were moved because of apartheid government policy, dealing with rights without applying any form of restriction is a mistake.[17]

The Surplus People Project, an organization that strongly supports land claims, agrees that the resolution of claims could lead to either the development or deterioration of reclaimed land. However, other factors contribute to the continuing poverty of people when land is returned to them. If the land claimed is degraded through unsustainable use, then the future of successive generations will be in question. For claims to be successful, they argue, communities must drive the process. The successful completion of land claims depends largely on the involvement of all interest groups in the community to resolve conflicting claims and to propose participatory development for their areas.[18]

In her introduction to *Back to the Land*, a book about ten communities recently reconnected to their ancestral lands, Marlene Winberg writes: "Of course, inefficient farming methods will very quickly degrade land in a subcontinent where drought is endemic, and the ecology fragile. It would be tragic if those who returned to the land revert from landless poverty to landed poverty." But she goes on to remind us that massive state intervention was required to destroy efficient black farmers early in the century and then to subsidize the "efficient" farming empires that characterize white agriculture today. While it may not be feasible or even desirable to transfer the kind of "grand patronage" that underpinned apartheid land policies from white to black beneficiaries, it is vital for the government to provide meaningful support to those who are returning to the land, often after many decades. However, as so many returning communities clearly demonstrate, land represents much more than economic commodities to be managed and exploited. It is "a cultural anchor, a place of living, the core around which displaced people can begin to rebuild their interrupted sense of belonging."[19]

THE CONSERVATION FACTOR

A second factor in the provision of effective land restitution in South Africa is its constitutional obligation to protect and conserve the environment. Moreover, South Africa is a signatory to several international and regional environmental agreements, which compel it to prioritize bio-diversity conservation and sustainable resource use. This double commitment to land reform and bio-diversity represents a major challenge to the new government, especially in the overcrowded and environmentally sensitive rural areas. The following case study in northern KwaZulu-Natal illustrates this ongoing dilemma.

THE CASE OF KOSI BAY, MAPUTALAND (KWAZULU-NATAL)

Like aboriginal societies across North America, the people of Maputaland have always lived "off the land." For the past seven hundred years, the inhabitants of this beautiful coastal region close to South Africa's border with Mozambique have tried to conserve its natural resources as part of their way of life but this has not been easy. (Map 2, *xvii*.) Throughout its history, Maputaland's rich natural resources have attracted outsiders. As the result of a series of intertribal wars in the eighteenth century, the local Thonga people were incorporated into an expanding Zulu empire. Early European explorers were followed by elephant hunters. In 1917, an anti-nagana campaign (nagana was a cattle disease wrongfully believed to be carried by wild animals) led to the slaughter of thousands of head of game in this region. In the twentieth century, many acres of bush were destroyed to make way for sugar plantations and commercial forests. Then a dam was built on the nearby Pongola River, partially disrupting the finely tuned ecosystem.

Despite these intrusions, the fertile dunes that lie close to the coast, sustain a variety of exotic plants, and during the summer they become the nesting site for the rare leatherback and loggerhead turtles that migrate here from the east coast of Africa. The grasslands attract large herds of zebra and impala and the larger carnivores that followed them. The rich resources of the ocean yield a varied diet of fish and other seafood providing sustenance for the local people. The women weave mats and baskets from the reeds, and grasses provide thatching for their homes. They make wine from the palms and beer from the morula trees, a traditional African beverage.

In 1988, the entire area was declared a nature reserve, and the inhabitants were ordered to leave. About half the community did as they were instructed. But many stayed behind to fight for their ancestral lands. Today, three hundred thousand people are squeezed onto land surrounded by the scenic conservation areas of northern KwaZulu-Natal. Along the coastal region stretching south from Kosi Bay to Lake St. Lucia, eighty thousand people survive on a hundred square kilometres of land. Paradoxically, even though apartheid has been abolished, the community remains under threat of eviction from the provincial government's conservation officials – or "Nature" as the local people call them with some irony. Having initially formed part of the European colonial invasion and later of the apartheid dispensation, conservation officials are now agents of the democratically elected KwaZulu-Natal provincial government. Like their predecessors under the apartheid regime, who served eviction notices on the inhabitants of Kosi Bay in 1988, the conservation authorities continue to threaten the local people with removals, bans on hunting and snaring, and limits on the traditional use of game and fish stocks. The difference is that now the community is able to negotiate joint control over these resources through the Department of Land Affairs and the Land Claim Commission. It has the constitutional right to do so.

In the early years of democracy, the minister of Land Affairs became personally involved in hearing the claimants' case, assessing how restitution could best be achieved, and finally in making it happen. Derek Hanekom, South Africa's first ANC Minister of Land Affairs, criss-crossed the country meeting with dispossessed communities determined to regain control over their lands and lives. When Hanekom arrived at Kosi Bay in July 1994 in response to an appeal from the community, he was confronted by the stark contrast between the overcrowded and impoverished area allocated to the Kosi Bay community and the conservation area – a tourists' paradise. Journalist Marlene Winberg described what happened at the minister's first meeting with the community. The words of one of the local induna (headman) reveal the actual and psychological impact of its long struggle:

> We are grateful, minister, that you are relieving us of our sorrows. We are in fear of removal from our place. We need advice as to how to become real people, so that it will be even more beautiful than it is today. But we do not know how to achieve our goals.... We want to come up with a program to address our problems in partnership with the new government.[20]

A woman also spoke up, explaining the predicament experienced by women faced with the responsibility of feeding their families:

> We women are no longer working – we're just sitting. We eat wild pig. Mostly our children are hungry, and we have no one to support us. If I send a man to the forest to cut thatch or poles,

the conservation police will threaten him with guns or arrest him. We have no proper house. I need poles. The trees they found here were preserved by our forefathers. When we visit our graves, they point at us with firearms.[21]

After Hanekom had conducted further consultations, this time with the dreaded conservation people, a deal was struck which made the Kosi Bay community shared custodians of the nature reserve. With government support, the community opened up its own locally run ecotourism business. In 1995, the first group of tourists arrived at the small KwaDhapha camp.

The restoration of land and involvement of the Kosi Bay community in eco-tourism has only partially addressed the problem of poverty. Jobs inside the park have provided incomes for a limited number of people, but most local households (often headed by women) continue to rely on subsistence farming to feed their families. A study conducted in 2004 by Dr. Donovan Kotze of the Centre for Environment and Development at the University of KwaZulu-Natal, found that since most natural forest vegetation has very little direct value to local people, large sections of Kosi Bay swamp forests are being cleared for agriculture with detrimental ecological consequences. Although traditional methods of farming are generally protective of the environment, the study concluded that the cumulative effects of the cultivation of swamp forests by large and medium-scale farmers, as well as hundreds of individual plots for local consumption, is considerable. The solutions suggested by Dr. Kotze include the promotion of better management practices among farmers in the swamp forests and revisiting the issue of compensation in lieu of land restoration.[22]

Thembela Kepe of the University of the Western Cape argued in a paper written in 2004 that despite impressive land reform policies and legislation, conservation tends to receive preferential treatment over human rights and poverty alleviation. Her solutions approach the problem from a different perspective from those of Dr Kotze. First, the current "weak and fuzzy land tenure rights" of people who have succeeded in claiming conservation land need to be revisited and rectified, as they are hardly sustainable. Secondly, the overall approach to land restitution should be seriously reconsidered and strategies for alternative land use – other than eco-tourism – put in place to effectively address the high levels of poverty that exist in communities claiming conservation land.[23]

Legislation to establish an Indian Claims Commission in Canada came under serious consideration in 1961, after the Diefenbaker government introduced the Bill of Rights. Three years later, the National Indian Council of Canada organized a conference to study the question of land claims, funded by the Department of Indian Affairs. But nothing came of either initiative until the Liberal Party government issued its 1969 White Paper. Dr. Lloyd Barber (Vice President of the University of Saskatchewan) was appointed Indian Claims Commissioner, with the mandate to receive and study grievances and recommend a process for dealing with land claims. The mandate initially excluded the recognition of aboriginal rights (a matter that was deemed to be beyond its jurisdiction) but was later widened to include treaty rights. Although the Commission was short-lived (it lasted until 1977), it raised the profile of land claims and drew attention to the major difficulty in reconciling the interests of Indians and the provinces.

Then in 1973, a land claim process was established that is still in use today. It divides claims into two categories: "Comprehensive Claims" and "Specific Claims." The former applies to claimants who have never entered into treaties; the latter to treaty Indians who claim that their existing treaties have not been fully honoured, or that Indian reserves or moneys have been misappropriated, usually in violation of the Indian Act. The Department of Indian Affairs handles both Comprehensive and Specific Claims. After reviewing the documentation, the Claims Branch prepares a "statement of fact," which is then passed on to the Department of Justice to establish the legal merits of the claim. The court's main task is to interpret the extent of the government's lawful obligation in the case. The final decision on the validity of the claim is made by the Department of Indian Affairs, which also controls the amount of compensation to be paid (if any). Although Indian bands have gained more leverage in the bargaining process over the past decade (due at least in part to the wealth-producing resources in their territories), the process still requires the federal government to act as "judge and jury" in claims against itself, and is extremely slow.

Because land and resource management is a provincial rather than federal responsibility, each province has developed its own mechanisms for handling aboriginal land claims. The three prairie provinces have agreed to transfer unoccupied Crown land to the federal government in order to meet unfulfilled treaty promises. However, since the federal government has fiduciary responsibility for Indians and their lands, both Ottawa and the provincial governments are involved in final settlements.

Under Saskatchewan's Treaty Entitlement Agreement, the federal government provides compensation to Treaty Indians who were promised land under treaty, but for whom reserves were never set aside. In British Columbia, Quebec, the Northwest Territories and the Maritime provinces, where no colonial treaties were made involving land, provincial and territorial governments are required to negotiate the settlement of land claims.

The story of negotiated settlements in Canada varies across the country. The settlement of aboriginal land claims has been quicker and relatively simpler in the high Arctic and remote northern regions of Canada, where there was little outside interest in the land. Where competition for land and natural resources is part of the bargaining process, reaching agreements acceptable to all parties takes much longer. Satisfactory resolution depends on a number of factors, the margin of profit anticipated from the exploitation of resources being one of the most significant.

Between 1976 and 2005, a number of land claims across Canada have been settled, and native participation in the planning of major industrial projects is now considered part of the process. The people of the Mackenzie Valley are a good example. The Dene and Inuit peoples of the Northwest Territories and Yukon have found a way to reach a compromise with an industry that thirty years ago was believed to pose a serious threat to their people's cultural and economic survival. In 1976, the Canadian government placed a ten-year moratorium on a proposed pipeline along the Mackenzie Valley that was to carry oil and natural gas reserves from the Arctic Ocean to southern Canada. The decision not to proceed with the project was based on the report of a public inquiry led by Justice Thomas Berger. The report recommended that the government first settle outstanding land claims in the region before considering the pros and cons of the pipeline project. In 2003, having successfully negotiated most of their land claims, the people of the Mackenzie Valley were active participants in a new pipeline proposal involving a number of large Canadian oil companies, including Imperial Oil Resources, ConocoPhillips Canada, and Shell Canada Limited, as well as their own Aboriginal Pipeline Group.

By the end of the 1990s, the estimated value of High Arctic gas reserves exceeded $200 billion. Media reports indicate that dramatic increases in oil prices were instrumental in the renewed interest in the Mackenzie Valley, which helped to push forward both the resolution of land claims and the native peoples' willingness to participate in a new pipeline project. The Inuvialuit of the western Arctic, whose land claim was settled in 1984, also lost no time in taking advantage of this favourable turn in the market and negotiated four oil and gas concessions worth $75.5 million. (Map 4, *xix*.) Despite the market influences, these successful negotiations show that Indian groups gain bargaining power through each other's successes. Expectations, norms and precedents create an atmosphere favourable to Indian stewardship of the land they once lost.

THE LUBICON CREE, ALBERTA

There are also many examples of highly contentious cases where the outcome for aboriginal claimants has been far less encouraging. The case of the Lubicon Cree of Alberta falls into this category. This is a case that has attracted a lot of international attention but little government support. It illustrates the conflicts that can occur when no formal treaty rights apply. In these cases, native groups are forced to negotiate directly with provincial agencies (as the holders of Crown Land), rather than with the federal government with whom treaties were originally made.

The Lubicon Cree had been living between the Peace and Athabasca rivers and north of Lesser Slave Lake for thousands of years before the arrival of Europeans in North America. In 1899, when the Canadian government signed Treaty Eight with several other groups in the region, the Lubicon Cree were somehow missed out. For years, members of the Lubicon band made annual visits to Ottawa asking to be included in Treaty Eight. In 1933, when the Great Depression was driving hundreds of white immigrants into northern Alberta, the Lubicon Cree applied to the government for a land settlement. Finally, in 1939, the government responded and promised the band a reserve. The following year, a site was selected at the western end of Lubicon Lake and approved by both provincial and federal governments. The size of the site (25.4 square miles) was based on the band count of 127 members according to the terms of Treaty Eight from which the band had been excluded in 1899. However, the site was never surveyed. Disputes arose over the size of the band and their entitlements under the terms of Treaty Eight, and no settlement was made.

Then, in the 1950s, when mining and oil exploration companies entered the Lubicon territory, the prospect of securing a land base under treaty rights dwindled. The government allowed a village with close ties to the Lubicon band to be bulldozed and burned down to make way for exploration. In the 1970s, the Alberta government passed a retroactive law to stop the Lubicon people from declaring an aboriginal interest in the region. In 1979, oil development in the region reached its peak. Without an environmental study or investigation into the social impact on local communities (as had happened during the Mackenzie Valley oil pipeline dispute in 1976), resource companies had free rein to enter the claimed territory. Northern Alberta became the most active exploration and drilling field in the country. Over the next five years, more than four hundred wells were drilled within a fifteen-mile radius of the Lubicon band community.

The impact on the environment and on the Lubicon's traditional hunting economy was profound. Seismic crews set up "no trespassing" signs on their hunting grounds. Bulldozers ripped up trap lines and blocked animal trails. Fires, a perennial hazard in this wooded region, raged out of control. In 1980 alone, bush fires destroyed as much of Lubicon hunting territory as in the previous twenty years. Haying fields, berry patches and fishing streams were blocked off. Fur-bearing animals were driven from the area, as were moose and smaller game animals. The average income from trapping between 1979 and 1983 dropped from over $5,000 per trapper to less than $400.[24] While the oil companies produced revenues of billions (an estimated $1.2m per day), the Lubicon people were forced to live, in John Goddard's words, as "landless squatters dependent on welfare."[25] In response to the rapid social changes within their communities, the Lubicon Cree saw the settlement of their land claim as a gleam of light at the end of a tunnel. In their view, the restoration of control over their land and resources would enable the whole community to re-establish their connection to the land, even if it was on a different basis from the past. (Map 4, *xix*.)

In 1978, a new young chief, Bernard Ominayak, took over the band's leadership and a vigorous public relations campaign to force government action followed. The Lubicon erected barricades to stop construction when the provincial government proposed a road to provide easy access to the previously remote region. But the road was built anyway. However, by this time international human rights groups had started to take notice. The World Council of Churches meeting in Geneva in 1983 warned: "In the last couple of years, the Alberta government and dozens of multi-national oil companies have taken actions which could have genocidal consequences." In 1988, international attention was drawn to the plight of the Lubicon when the band campaigned for a boycott of the "Spirit Sings" exhibition at Calgary's Glenbow Museum in conjunction with the Fifteenth Winter Olympic Games. Partly in response to international pressure, the Alberta government under Premier Don Getty made some concessions relating to land and resources to the Lubicon in the "Grimshaw Agreement."

At this point, the federal government also began to take the Lubicon demands more seriously. Formal negotiations on Lubicon land rights began in 1988 with the Mulroney government. Derek Burney was appointed Chief of Staff to oversee negotiations between the band and Ottawa. The Lubicon agreed to a number of points, including the land area negotiated in the Grimshaw formula of ninety-five square miles to be set aside for a Lubicon reserve, seventy-nine square miles of which was to include full surface rights. The only concession the federal government made towards the economic development of the Lubicon was a trust fund of $5 million from which the band could draw "seed capital" to lever grants from existing federal programs. The main bone of contention for the Lubicon was their demand for compensation for what they claimed to be irreparable damage to their way of life. The band, once a self-sustaining hunting community, had become dependent on wage labour and transfer payments to supplement the limited hunting available. Although there was a marked increase in alcohol abuse and domestic violence in their communities, the Lubicon managed to maintain their cultural identity and retained Cree as their first language.

In 1989, the federal government offered the Lubicon a take-it-or-leave-it deal. Compensation was not included. The wording of the agreement obliged the Lubicon to "cede, release and surrender" all aboriginal rights to current and future legal actions related to aboriginal rights. The band also had to agree to withdraw its complaints from the United Nations Human Rights Committee and "to acknowledge the settlement of its grievances against Canada" before the compensation issue could be settled. But ultimately nothing in the offer was binding on the government. The Lubicon rejected the offer. When asked by a radio reporter what the Lubicon wanted, Ominayak replied: "Well, basically what we're looking at is to try and build a community that is going to be viable, both economically and as a community.... We've got people whose livelihood has been destroyed by the oil development. We don't want to just build a community where people are going to have nice houses but remain on welfare. We want to get out of that system. We don't want to get into it deeper."[26]

What happened after the Lubicon had rejected the proposed agreement underlines the competing interests of aboriginal societies in Canada and the government's willingness to play one group against the other. In order to secure its own interests and bring down the Lubicon, the federal government approached a dissident group with an offer it could not refuse. Henry Loubican, a resident of Grouard on Lesser Slave Lake, met with federal officials shortly after Ominayak turned down the deal in 1989. Soon afterwards, a separate band was formed of about 350 members – many believe it was created by the Department of Indian Affairs.

The "Woodland Cree," which was registered within weeks of its application for band status, accepted a settlement offer from Ottawa which Ominayak called "a formula to put welfare Indians in nicer houses."[27] The Loon Lake agreement followed, with a Woodland Cree–type land settlement.

Thus Lubicon society was slowly being torn apart. In some Lubicon communities families were divided, one family member joining the Woodland group, others crossing over to Loon Lake. Other factors were at work as well. Suicide, especially among the young people, as well as alcohol addiction and domestic violence were part of the destructive spiral endemic to many native communities. As Goddard noted, more and more people began channeling their frustration into drinking, fighting or joining evangelical congregations.[28] When the moderator of the United Church of Canada, Rt. Reverend Stan McKay visited the Lubicon community of Little Buffalo Lake in 1993, he described the conditions as "third world" and "totally unacceptable in Canada."[29]

During this period, a Japanese conglomerate, Daishowa Incorporated, completed a $5 million pulp mill north of Peace River and was preparing to move into Lubicon territory. A Toronto-based group called the Friends of the Lubicon took up the cause of the community. In 2000, as a result of the adverse publicity generated by a seven-year-long boycott of Daishowa products (organized by the Friends of the Lubicon), Daishowa finally agreed not to conduct logging operations on Lubicon territory until their land claim was settled. Shortly before this agreement was finalized, Ominayak reached an agreement with Petro-Canada that allowed oil exploration under certain conditions on lands claimed by the band. But still the federal government did nothing.

In January 2003, Amnesty International entreated Prime Minister Jean Chrétien to fulfill his election promise made over ten years before to bring a "swift resolution" to the Lubicon situation. But Chrétien retired from politics later that year, and the Lubicon continue to face pressure from ongoing resource extraction on their disputed land.[30]

THE B.C. TREATY COMMISSION

While most First Nations favour negotiation over court actions as a means to regain control over their lands and lives, the negotiation process with provincial and federal governments has been largely unsuccessful. The work of the British Columbia Treaty Commission is a case in point. Established under the B.C. Treaty Commission Act in 1995, the mandate of the Commission was to facilitate the negotiation of treaties in British Columbia among one or more First Nations. Its duties included the allocation of funds to enable First Nations to participate and to assist in conflict resolutions. After ten years (and an expenditure of $300 million), the Commission has failed to produce a single settlement. In the year 2000, all of the five settlements offered from a total of fifty claims were refused by the First Nation claimants.

Perhaps even more significantly, one quarter of aboriginal groups in British Columbia are entirely absent from the B.C. process. Government negotiators are perceived by aboriginal groups to be working hand in glove with the resource industries. The resource industries, in turn, regard the uncertainty engendered by aboriginal land claims as extremely damaging to their interests. For this reason, many of the large forest products companies are pushing the B.C. government to negotiate settlements that will convert existing reserve lands into treaty settlement lands. This is the format known as the "land selection model," which includes cash and resources as components of the package. Initially the proposed package offered cash in lieu of land – in other words the extinguishment of aboriginal title – which was fiercely rejected by aboriginal groups.

The revised formula of the B.C. government offers a percentage of land relating to the size of the aboriginal population in the claimed territory. This is unacceptable to the First Nation claimants on a number of grounds. First of all, it ignores their inherent aboriginal rights in the land and, secondly, with inadequate land bases the economic viability of their communities is at stake. The "co-management model," favoured (or, more accurately, insisted upon) by British Columbia's First Nations as the only sound basis on which to negotiate settlements, is rejected by governments and industries alike because (in their view) it perpetuates the "economic uncertainty" of undefined land rights. Hence the apparent impasse that currently exists.

CONCLUSION

In both Canada and South Africa, negotiating restitution involves reaching compromises with governments and industries. Some Canadian First Nations have been more successful than others in reaching agreements that are acceptable to all parties and that seem to offer long-term benefits for native communities. Almost all modern treaties or land claims – whether they are negotiated in the courts or through government – involve a conflict over natural resources. In some cases, aboriginal nations have taken advantage of development possibilities and established thriving business enterprises. But much more needs to be done to raise aboriginal employment and income levels.

Although agreements between federal, provincial and territorial governments and aboriginal groups may include benefits, the uneven negotiating power tends to tilt the balance in favour of government interests – and those of industries. This is especially true when the long-term release or extinguishment of aboriginal rights to land and resources is involved, rights which are affirmed in the Constitution. In recent years these issues have been brought before the Supreme Court for legal interpretation with some positive results. However, court decisions are only effective when governments comply with their rulings; having to resort repeatedly to litigation is a costly process. A possible alternative, suggested in a recent United Nations report, would be legislation on aboriginal treaty and constitutional issues. A step in this direction was taken in October 2004 with the introduction in the Senate of the First Nations Government Recognition Act (Bill S-16).[31]

The pattern of competition over scarce resources is repeated in South Africa, where the issue is further complicated by the legacies of apartheid. In reclaiming their land, indigenous South Africans confront the competing interests of white vs. black, rural vs. urban, and women vs. men. One of the major challenges facing the new government is balancing its constitutional commitments to reduce poverty, take care of the environment and make land available to all South Africans. Meanwhile, the vast majority of African people still live in poverty. Land is a central issue in the ongoing struggle for some measure of economic revival for the landless majority.

While the ANC government is committed to land reform and redistribution, without the active cooperation and participation of the current landholders, the prospects for meaningful restitution are disappointingly slight. What is needed is a realistic but uncompromising land policy that will encourage the generosity (and foresight) of the present landholders and provide mechanisms to enable the individuals and communities, that are reunited with their lands through the land claim process, to flourish.

Chapter Six
Self-Government

The road to political self-determination, the road to self-government, is directly linked to the role of economic development. If we are to have strong self-government, if we are to have a strong political direction, we have to have a strong economic base.

Blaine Favel, Chief of the Saskatchewan Federation, 1996[1]

RESTORING SOVEREIGNTY

The restoration of sovereignty to Canada's indigenous peoples lies at the heart of the land rights issue. As long as First Nations communities are denied the right to decide on their own form of government without coercion or interference, the recognition of their aboriginal land rights is a largely theoretical concept with little practical meaning. The reverse is also true: without a land base, self-determination is rendered almost meaningless. For this reason, Canada's first peoples have often linked the two rights together in land claims, whether these involved litigation or negotiations with the provincial and federal governments. In the view of First Nations, the right to self-government is an integral component of aboriginal entitlement deriving from the fact of first occupancy.

NEGOTIATING SELF-GOVERNMENT IN CANADA

In Canada today, many Status Indian, Métis and Inuit communities are seeking some form of self-government on their territories and reserves in order to regain control over their lives. This is a goal that underlies every land claim. However, there has been little consensus among First Nations on the shape self-government should take – or even if it should be sought at all. In most parts of Canada, Indian land claims involve conflict, both external and internal. The first conflict area is in defining self-government. Writing in 1971, during the furor over the Trudeau government's White Paper, William Wuttunee warned:

> Indians have a great love for their land which they regard as Mother Earth, but this love for the last remnant of their land has been their undoing. It has engendered a great devotion, to the point of heroic sacrifice, for a few acres of reserve land.[2]

In their socio-political critique of Indian self-government, Rick Ponting and Roger Gibbins warn of potential "thorns in the rose garden." Unrealistic expectations top the list. Other difficult issues are the rights of off-reserve Indians and the role of Indian representatives in the House of Commons. Would these representatives be integrated into existing parties, or would they form small factions with little influence?[3] Over the years, other concerns have gained prominence within native communities.

The growing awareness of the rights of Indian women added a new dimension to the controversies surrounding self-government within the aboriginal community. The issue of women's rights first surfaced in the 1950s when Mary Two-Axe Earley and others protested against the provision in the Indian Act linking a woman's status with that of her husband. In practice, what this meant was that by marrying a non-Status Indian, Indian women (and their children) lost their status while white women acquired Indian status by marrying a status Indian. Although the government eventually amended the Indian Act and repealed the discriminatory clause in 1985, the issue was not dealt with adequately in the legislation. Status Indian women who had "married out" before this date (and had thus lost their rights to land, housing and a range of other benefits on their home reserves) have found it very difficult to regain these rights and are often denied residence on reserves by the (often male) chiefs and elders. In 2005, problems still persist for many First Nations women across the country, despite several initiatives carried out by the Native Women's Association. For this reason, the protection of women's rights under the Charter of Rights and Freedoms remains an important issue for Indian women. Underlying the resolve of Indian women's groups to retain state-controlled protection is the increasing rate of domestic violence on reserves and the seeming inability of band leadership to address the situation.[4]

Most First Nation leaders insist that the self-government formula chosen must recognize the constitutionally entrenched rights of Canada's first peoples. The model of self-government presented by George Erasmus, former chief of the Assembly of First Nations, to a national conference on the subject in 1990 is one still shared by many aboriginal leaders today:

The kind of powers that would probably be acceptable to us are those that provinces already have in their areas of sovereignty.... This model would lend itself very nicely to what First Nations have always told the people in this country. You already have federal powers, and provincial powers. Let's look at First Nations powers. And we will have three major forms of government. Three different types of sovereignty. Two coming from the Crown, one coming from the indigenous people, all together creating one state.[5]

However, Erasmus's formula, which was reiterated in the 1996 Report of the Royal Commission on Aboriginal Peoples (on which Erasmus served as co-chair), has found little acceptance in government circles. Aboriginal sovereignty is a sensitive issue for Canada's non-aboriginal political leaders. In their view, recognizing aboriginal sovereignty (claimed by many Indian bands and nations across Canada) would dilute and undermine that of the nation as a whole. Sharing rights to the land is controversial enough, but sharing sovereignty with other nations within its borders is something few political leaders in Canada are willing to seriously consider.

Moreover, the notion of self-governing communities based on the protection of group rights (particularly on grounds of ethnicity) raises the spectre of South Africa's homeland policy in the minds of many Canadians. The very existence of reserves is frequently referred to in the media and elsewhere as "Canada's particular version of apartheid."[6] To establish a third order of government for First Nations living on reserves runs counter to the basic tenet of liberal ideology, wherein persons are incorporated into the polity as individuals, not as groups. Even those who do not espouse liberalism tend to see aboriginal self-government as a violation of Canada's status as a sovereign nation.

Historically, the Canadian government has always looked for a uniform way to deal with Indian issues. The search for an acceptable solution to the question of aboriginal sovereignty and self-government is no different. Given the complexity of the issue, it is not surprising that no one has been able to come up with a definition and one-size-fits-all model of Indian self-government. First of all, there is a lack of homogeneity among aboriginal communities themselves. Self-government is simply not applicable to a large proportion of the aboriginal population. Most non-status Indians and many Métis people live off reserves and have no land base on which to exercise their sovereign rights. As Douglas Sanders, an advocate of aboriginal rights, observed, "self-government can only be given content if special lands are set aside for these populations, the prospects of which are less than minimal."[7]

Nevertheless, various options and formulas for self-government have been put forward over the past few decades. In 1983, the Report of the Special Parliamentary Committee on Indian Self-Government (also known as the Penner Report) defined self-government as being very close to provincial status. In other words, virtually the entire range of law-making, policy development, program delivery, law enforcement and adjudication powers would be available to an Indian First Nation government within its territory.[8] Although many of the Penner Report's recommendations were reintroduced into the Royal Commission on Aboriginal Peoples Report thirteen years later, the issue of self-government remains unresolved.

Until 1999, when the Arctic Inuit negotiated for the creation of the territory of Nunavut, the federal government confined its definition of aboriginal self-government to limited control over local affairs. For example, the James Bay and Northern Quebec Agreement, signed in 1975 – Canada's first "Modern Treaty" – allowed limited autonomy for the Inuit and Cree inhabitants of the James Bay region. Stated in the simplest terms, this Agreement provided for local and regional administration in "Cree lands" and "Inuit lands" covering administration of justice, education, health, social services and economic and social development. In 1984, the federal government adopted a special local administrations scheme, wherein local band councils were granted increased authority over such areas as the management of band funds and the administration of bylaws. The Sechelt agreement in 1986 grew out of this new window of opportunity to negotiate for limited self-government.

THE SECHELT AGREEMENT

In 1976, the 650-member Sechelt band of British Columbia began to negotiate a new deal with the federal government. Their primary goal was to expand their land base and to gain maximum control of their lives through self-government. While the Sechelt band supported the efforts of the national aboriginal leadership to include the rights to self-government in the new constitution, they were determined to assert their claim to land as well. After a decade of negotiations, only some of these objectives had been achieved. Under the 1986 Sechelt Indian Band Self-Government Act, the Sechelt band was granted political and fee simple control over their reserve (of 26 square kilometres) north of Vancouver. The deal included $54 million in compensation but no general land claims settlement. The powers of the band council were to be similar in scope to those exercised by most municipal governments across Canada. This was far from the Sechelt objective of aboriginal self-government within the fabric of the larger Canadian society.

Although the Sechelt model represented some significant innovations for Indian self-government, including the replacement of authority of the Indian Act with a band constitution, it fell short of the objectives of Indian leadership across the country, which were to entrench the right to self-government and aboriginal title in the 1982 Constitution. This was an important issue for First Nations communities. As J.R. Miller noted in 1989, "Native organizations are understandably suspicious that the acceptance of municipal-style self-governments might be only the prelude to their being abandoned constitutionally by Ottawa and con-signed to the provinces."[9]

The view taken by historians John Taylor and Gary Paget was that the Sechelt agreement represented "a coincidence of interests." Each of the players – the Sechelt band, the provincial and the federal governments – had something to gain from its conclusion. As Chief Stanley Dixon had stated at the outset, the objective was "to work with our neighbour communities to improve the quality of life for all citizens."[10] However, the Sechelt gained very little in terms of quality of life for their people, and their struggle for a viable land base continued. For the federal govern-ment, the Sechelt agreement represented at least partial evidence of its willingness to follow through on the promise to assist any community that wanted to move towards self-government. However, as the Minister of Indian Affairs, David Crombie, was careful to point out, Sechelt was not a model for others to follow.[11]

As for the government of British Columbia, the Sechelt formula fit-ted perfectly with its overall policy towards native people. The province's objective was to demonstrate that self-government could be achieved without constitutional entrenchment. Moreover, the agreement would set a precedent for resolving native grievances through self-government rather than through the framework of comprehensive claims settlements. In contrast to the federal government, the province saw the Sechelt deal as a model for self-government for other bands across the province. Indeed, through this agreement, the province was providing a clear sig-nal to other Indian groups that it was willing to discuss municipal-level self-government rather than land claims.[12]

THE INUIT PEOPLES OF THE NORTHWEST TERRITORIES

Like many other aboriginal communities, the people of the eastern Arctic took advantage of the federal government's offer to negotiate comprehensive land claims with native people who had never signed treaties. In 1976, the Inuit Tapirisat of Canada (renamed Inuit Tapirisat Kanatami in 2001) presented its first claim to the federal government. From the outset, the Inuit dreamed of dividing up the Northwest Territories to establish their own territory where they would have control over their lives and destinies.

For more than four thousand years, Inuit people had occupied the land, marine waters and islands of a vast area stretching from the Mackenzie River Delta in the west to the Labrador coast in the east, and from the southern reaches of Hudson Bay to the High Arctic islands in the north. The Inuit belong to a wider community of Arctic people (Greenland, Alaska and the western tip of Siberia are all part of the circumpolar Arctic region) and have an identity as a separate people or nation distinct from other indigenous peoples of North America. In living "off the land," they have developed and sustained a unique way of life. Although the people have adapted to the changes introduced by European peoples, Inuit culture has not been submerged by those changes.

In the early twentieth century, as the economic returns from whaling and the fur trade decreased, government intrusion in the Arctic region increased. In the 1940s, Canada built air bases in the Arctic for refueling European warplanes. The postwar period was a time of enormous change and hardship for the Arctic communities: forced relocations of Inuit people, high rates of disease, the removal of children to residential schools, and the movement of people from the land into more centralized settlements all had a profound effect on the traditional patterns of everyday life and land use in particular.

As the Inuit themselves acknowledge, not all the changes brought about by European intrusion were negative. The federal government provided new health, educational and social services. Later, a major housing scheme was introduced to provide modern, prefabricated dwellings for Inuit families. As settlements grew to include a growing non-Inuit population, new types of jobs were created, and new ideas about economic development were introduced into the region. For example, soapstone carving and printmaking, traditional crafts practiced by many Inuit artists, gained international markets.[13] Marketing cooperatives were established to help sell local products and earn foreign currency to obtain imported goods.[14]

The dream of creating an Inuit territory from the Northwest Territories began to take shape in the 1970s. Although the idea of combining the land claim settlement with a self-government agreement met strong resistance from the government, the persistence and determination of the Inuit paid off. One of the toughest obstacles to a final agreement was the issue of boundaries between the new territory, its neighbours, and overlapping claims of Indian communities. Once again, a compromise was reached by establishing three regions: Qiqitaaluk (Baffin), Kivallik (Keewatin) and Kitikmoet (Central).[15] In 1990, the Federal government and the Inuit of Northwest Territories signed an initial Agreement in Principle, which included a clause pledging a new territory and a political accord to deal with the self-government issue. It took a further nine years for the settlement to be completed.

THE NUNAVUT LAND CLAIM

On 1 April 1999, the Canadian government officially proclaimed Nunavut (meaning "our land" in Inuktitut) Canada's third territory, after more than a decade of negotiations with the Inuit people of Northwest Territories. (Map 4, *xix*.) The atmosphere of euphoria that day, as the Nunavut flag was raised for the first time, was likened by Inuit journalist, Zebedee Nungaq to Inauguration Day in South Africa in 1994. On that day, television images of the new president Nelson Mandela and Archbishop Desmond Tutu dancing on the podium had renewed hope for millions of subjugated peoples worldwide. No wonder the sense of joy in this northern Canadian community brought South Africa to mind: "What a satisfying delight then to observe Nunavut's birth.... I can just see Desmond Tutu dancing the 'toya-toya' [*sic*] over this event," wrote Nungaq. "The dream is now reality and we have crossed the threshold of history on a forward roll.... What an honour to be part of Nunavut's Freedom Day!"[16]

Despite the superficial similarities, the people of Nunavut stood at a different kind of threshold to South Africans celebrating their newly won democracy in 1994. Freedom represented different things to the Inuit of Nunavut and South Africa's black majority. For the people of Nunavut, the objective of their negotiations was initially to have their own territory with the same powers and status as a province. Notions of self-government were beyond the government's land claims policy; thus, it was difficult to persuade the government negotiators to accept any formula that linked the conclusion of the land claims agreement to the establishment of a Nunavut territory and government. But in 1990, a compromise was reached. In the summer of 1993, two pieces of legislation were presented to Parliament for scrutiny and approval: the Nunavut Land Claims Agreement Act, which ratified the Nunavut Agreement, and the Nunavut Act, which created the Nunavut territory and government.

As the 1995 report by the Nunavut Implementation Commission explained, the Inuit representatives brought a range of political and proprietary demands to the land claims table. As a result, the final agreement included many new rights: fee simple ownership of surface and mineral rights; hunting, fishing and trapping rights; and joint Inuit/government management boards to plan and regulate the use of Nunavut waters, lands and resources.[17] While each of these rights had to be carefully negotiated with government representatives, the issue that required the most skill and patience was the creation of a new territory with its own territorial government. The Inuit negotiators emphasized that this would be a "public" government answerable to a legislative assembly elected by all citizens meeting residence and age qualifications. But it was still a hard sell. Even when agreement was reached on the issue of Nunavut being subject to Canada's Bill of Rights and Freedoms, government resistance continued.

Before the Nunavut agreement was signed, two other northern land claims reached settlement. In 1975, the federal government had signed a final agreement with the Inuit of Northern Quebec, which included surface rights to 3,147 square kilometres; exclusive hunting, fishing and trapping rights on the remaining 33,631 square kilometres; and compensation of $90 million. In 1984, a similar agreement was signed with the Inuvialuit of the Western Arctic. The Western Arctic Claim Agreement (also known as the Inuvialuit Final Agreement) extinguished Inuit title to the western Arctic in return for ownership of ninety-six thousand square kilometres along with benefit payments of $45 million plus $10 million for economic development. A third claim, by the Inuit of Northern Labrador is still being negotiated.

While the land covered under the Nunavut Land Claim agreement (352,191 square kilometres) is larger than either of the previous settlements, the conditions followed much the same pattern as the previous Arctic agreements. Like the Yukon Act and Northwest Territories Acts, the Nunavut Act includes provisions for such things as the office of the federally appointed commissioner, law-making powers of legislatures, and the role of the federal government. Like the other two territories (and unlike the ten provinces of Canada), Nunavut is not constituted as a "Crown in right of the territory": in other words, its Crown lands are controlled by the federal government, not the territorial governments.

Unlike the federal arrangements with the Northwest Territories and Yukon governments established in 1908, which were unilaterally imposed on the local populations, Nunavut resulted from the effort of the aboriginal people themselves. As a result, the Nunavummiut (the Inuit and non-Inuit people of Nunavut, a total of 18,000 people) have considerable say in the control and management of their land. While previous Arctic agreements were exclusively about land and land use, the Nunavut settlement is also about joint sovereignty, albeit a qualified form of sovereignty. Although the concept of "sovereignty" in the Canadian context does not imply absolute autonomy or the creation of a separate, independent state, the Nunavut agreement shifted the goal posts in significant ways. The wording of the commitment to create the Nunavut Territory is open to interpretation, but it would appear that Nunavut has a constitutional dimension not shared with the other territories.

Another distinctive feature of the Nunavut agreement is its inclusiveness. Although Inuit people make up 85 per cent of the population of Nunavut, the government includes both Inuit and non-Inuit residents. Inuktitut and English are the official languages. Nunavut Tunngavik Inc (NTI), established in 1993 as the Inuit corporation responsible for implementing the Land Claim agreement, was responsible for setting up the new Territory of Nunavut. As a non-profit organization controlled by and accountable to the Inuit of Nunavut as defined in Section 39.1.6 of the Nunavut Land Claim agreement, NTI's mandate is to "constitute an open and accountable forum organized to represent Inuit of all regions and communities of Nunavut in a fair and democratic way, that will safeguard, administer and advance the rights and benefits that belong to the Inuit of Nunavut as an aboriginal people, so as to promote their economic, social and cultural well-being through succeeding generations."[18]

The very scale of the Nunavut undertaking means that it cannot be overlooked. The new territory comprises 20 per cent of the landmass of Canada, and its boundaries extend over a larger marine area than the boundaries of any other Canadian province or territory. Moreover, Nunavut's international significance is not confined to the circumpolar area. Clearly, the agreement is an extremely important feather in Canada's cap. As one internal report declared, at a time when the global community is increasingly conscious of the legal rights and moral claims of aboriginal peoples around the world, Canada's commitment to the Inuit people stands out as a "concrete expression of its willingness to share a genuine degree of legislative and administrative power with aboriginal citizens."[19] It also encourages other aboriginal communities to claim sovereign rights over their territories. Furthermore, with the Nunavut agreement in place, it will be more difficult for the Canadian government to argue that the recognition of aboriginal sovereignty negates the fundamental rights and freedoms of individual aboriginal and non-aboriginal citizens.

Like black South Africans, who belong to the wider community of African people across the continent, the Inuit identify with the indigenous peoples who inhabit the circumpolar world; but they also see themselves as citizens of Canada. Instead of seeking separation or secession from Canada, the Inuit's goal (as it is for many First Nations leaders) was to be included as equal partners in Confederation. In words reminiscent of South Africa's century-long struggle for political equality, the Inuit delegation to the Canadian Senate in 1983 stated: "We believe we have the right to participate fully and equally in Canadian political life and in the electoral process."[20]

Demographically, the situation in Nunavut is more like that of South Africa than that of the Sechelt reserve, whose residents comprise a tiny fraction of the total population of British Columbia. The Inuit, on the other hand, make up 85 per cent of the population of Nunavut, close to the black majority of 87 per cent in South Africa. Because of their numerical strength, the Inuit negotiators focused on political equality and basic human rights as the central point of their land claim. Rather than claiming special status based on inherent aboriginal rights, the driving force behind their fourteen-year battle for self-government was their belief in their inherent right to self-determination as members of the human family. The Inuit position was founded on the principle of the interdependence and equality of all individuals and peoples and on the irreversible connection between Inuit and their lands. This was different from the Sechelt agreement, where no land base was involved.

The Sechelt and Nunavut cases illustrate how different situations have produced different results with respect to the content and form of self-government attained. In the case of Nunavut, the government was prepared to grant both a land base and sovereignty (albeit limited) over the newly formed territory. The Sechelt, on the other hand, having negotiated a form of self-government with the provincial and federal governments, had to make a separate claim for their land base. In 1995, the Sechelt tabled a comprehensive treaty proposal with the British Columbia Treaty Commission for land and a share in resource revenues. But in 1997, they withdrew from the process, declaring they had reached a stalemate with the Commission over revenue sharing. In 2005, the Sechelt held an internal referendum on whether to pursue the land claim through the courts. The results were in favour of going to court, but the costs (an estimated $10 million) are more than the band leadership is prepared to pay.

However, it would also be naïve to conclude that Nunavut's future is without problems. Nunavut is different to other parts of Canada in that it was never "homesteaded" (for obvious reasons); but it did not escape colonization. The burden of poverty inherited by the new government stems from destruction of the traditional economy due to the anti-fur lobby campaign, the debilitating levels of suicide and family violence, and heavy dependence on interim financial transfers from Ottawa. Its unemployment, poor educational levels, low income levels, and over-crowded housing conditions are the familiar legacies of a mismanaged past. For all its optimism and hopes for a brighter future, Nunavut has many challenges ahead in bringing social health and healing to its youthful society.

REVERSING "SELF-GOVERNMENT" IN THE FORMER BANTUSTANS

In South Africa, where the majority population reclaimed its sovereignty in 1994, the objective of creating viable and harmonious communities is especially challenging. The African National Congress government, which took over from the Government of National Unity after the second national elections in 1999, is faced with one of the most skewed land distribution structures in the world. One third of the entire population of South Africa (about 2.1 million households) continues to live on 13 per cent of the land in the former bantustans. The fact that the former bantustans were regarded by the apartheid government as "self-govern-ing" autonomous states has added to the complicated process of land restitution. (Map 1, *xvi.*)

The issues are complex and easily misunderstood. The areas that comprised the ten former bantustans are by no means homogeneous. They display diverse settlement patterns, population distributions, land tenure rules and relationships, structures of government, land uses and ecological conditions. In some provinces (KwaZulu Natal, Limpopo and parts of the Eastern Cape, for example), communal tenure areas are wholly or partly subject to institutional arrangements of the chiefs or Traditional Authorities, as they chose to call themselves in the 1980s. Others are linked to old and new institutional arrangements within municipal authorities or government departments.[21]

The dual system of land rights introduced under colonial and apartheid governments continues in post-apartheid South Africa because of the difficulties of undoing history. Laws involving arbitrary racial distinctions have been repealed, but remnants of the old Bantu Areas Land Regulations of 1969 are still in place. The problem is compounded because of ambiguities in the 1996 Constitution. On the one hand, the Constitution promises in Section 25 (6) that

A person or community whose tenure of land is legally insecure as a result of past racially discriminatory laws or practices is entitled, to the extent provided by an Act of Parliament, either to tenure which is legally secure or to corporate redress.

However, on the other hand, the Constitution also recognizes the authority of Traditional Authorities, the former "puppet" chiefs of the apartheid regime, who controlled the allocation and use of land in the former bantustans. The issue of constitutional recognition of Traditional Leaders is complex but deserves some attention as an important political backdrop to land restitution.

The role of the traditional chiefs in African communities changed over the centuries, mainly due to European influences. The apartheid system and previous colonial systems had used government-appointed "chiefs" or traditional leaders in positions of almost complete control over the allocation of land and management of resources on so-called Native reserves, which later were renamed African homelands or bantustans. While these appointments were often made from members of a chiefly family, the rule of lineage was rarely followed. Moreover, the colonial powers maintained control over the traditional authorities by defining land as a customary communal holding. In other words, the land was to be used by the community rather than by individuals. As Professor Mamdani explains,

The genius of British rule in Africa … was in seeking to civilize Africans as communities, not as individuals. More than anywhere else, there was in African colonial experience a one-sided opposition between the individual and the group, civil society and community, rights and tradition.[22]

The practice of co-opting traditional leaders (always male) to serve the European agenda reached its peak in the apartheid period. In 1951, the Bantu Authorities Act expanded and cemented the powers of chiefs to serve the interests of the apartheid state. Mamdani uses the analogy of a "clenched fist" to describe the chiefs' wide-ranging powers held in place by state coercion and intimidation:

Not only did the chief have the right to pass rules (bylaws) governing persons under his domain, he also executed all laws and was the administrator in "his" area, in which he settled all disputes. The authority of the chief thus fused in a single person all elements of power, judicial, legislative, executive and administrative. This authority was like a clenched fist, necessary because the chief stood at the intersection of the market economy and the non-market one. The administrative justice and the administrative coercion that were the sum and substance of his authority lay behind a regime of extra-economic coercion, a regime that breathed life into a whole range of compulsions: forced labour, forced crops, forced sales, forced contributions and forced removals.[23]

However, the power held by chiefs in the apartheid era was far from absolute, since they owed total allegiance to the white government that appointed them and paid their salaries.

One of the primary powers the chiefs had at their disposal was control of land allocations. No application for land could be considered without the signature of the tribal authorities. This power was often abused by charging unauthorized fees to applicants. These fees could be paid in money or in goods – chiefly, alcohol or livestock. In 1999, in the Tshezi communal area on the Wild Coast of the Eastern Cape, tribal authorities used fee extraction to illegally allocate cottage sites to white entrepreneurs. These were dubbed "brandy sites" by the local people because of the alcohol payments that had been demanded. Abuse also occurred in the delivery of state pensions, the judgments of tribal courts, and applications for migrant labour permits.[24]

Given their controversial position, it is difficult to understand how the traditional authorities have won recognition in the post-apartheid dispensation. But the African National Congress (ANC) has always had a close relationship with tribal chiefs. When the ANC was formed in 1912, chiefs were among the founding members. Chiefs were also present at the Congress of the People in 1955. However, the position of chiefs became increasingly ambiguous during the apartheid era, when they were perceived to be stooges of the government. In the 1980s, when the ANC was attempting to broaden its support as widely as possible, many members of the newly formed Congress of Traditional Leaders in South Africa (Contralesa) became ANC supporters. The exceptions were Zulu tribal leaders belonging to the Inkatha Freedom Party (IFP), who were strongly opposed to the ANC. By this time, the bantustans had been completely discredited, and apartheid itself was in decline. The ANC was a government in waiting. Although some members of Contralesa played both sides of the field during the chaotic final months of apartheid rule, their participation in the negotiations between the National Party and the

ANC was essential for a peaceful transition to democracy to take place. From beginning to end, the negotiations were built on compromises. The recognition of Traditional Authorities in the draft Constitution was one such compromise.

When the tenure reform mandated by the 1996 Constitution was initially implemented, the land rights of farm dwellers were given precedence over those of former bantustan residents. Proposed policies that applied to the former bantustans lagged behind, largely because of the complexities involved. As Dr. Sipho Sibanda, Director of Tenure Reform Policy in the Department of Land Affairs observed, any proposed legislation in the area of land tenure "does not have the luxury of starting with a clean sheet." Some of the present occupants have "Permission to Occupy" (PTO) status, some occupy the land under customary law, and some are beneficiaries of a state-administered trust. Whatever rights the new government might confer on landholders within the former bantustans, they would inevitably conflict with the "old" apartheid institutions of management: "The task of the new government is therefore to ensure that mechanisms are in place to minimize the potential for abuse of power and ensure that the broad principles of democracy, equity and transparency are applied."[25] Moreover, because some bantustan residents were forced off land to accommodate "refugees" from other areas, there are problem of overlapping land claims. To add to the confusion, systems of administration and record keeping have broken down, if they ever existed. The loss of records, uncertainties about which laws apply, and the unauthorized issue of permits have created an urgent need for clarity and reform.

When Derek Hanekom took over the portfolio of Minister of Agriculture and Land Affairs after the 1994 elections, he proposed a Land Reform Bill to create statutory rights for existing land users on the former bantustans to decide for themselves what administrative role the traditional chiefs would play. The Bill was held back before the 1999 elections because it threatened to stir up the hornet's nest – as one commentator called it – of traditional leadership. Two years later, Hanekom's successor, Thoko Didiza, proposed a Bill that was equally controversial. The draft Communal Land Rights Bill was intended to open the way to transfer state land to communities still controlled by former bantustan leaders. However, critics of the proposed legislation accuse Didiza of introducing a policy with echoes of apartheid by effectively consolidating the power of chiefs over the land. At issue was the role of unelected traditional leadership in the allocation of land in the new democracy and the status of rural woman.[26]

Under pre-existing laws, the only tenure rights available to communities in the former bantustans (referred to in the Communal Land Rights Bill as "old order rights") were informal, with title vesting paternalistically in the state or (in KwaZulu-Natal) in the Ingonyama Trust. Under customary law and practices, the land was reserved for men who were issued Permission to Occupy (PTO) certificates. African women were treated as perpetual minors, accessing land and inheritance rights only through the male members of their family (husbands, fathers, sons). Widows were likely to be taken by their deceased husband's brother as an additional wife and thereby lose rights to their husband's land and property. By maintaining the system of PTOs in the proposed Bill, the discrimination against women would continue. In 1997, 63 per cent of households in the former bantustans were holders of PTO certificates, 26.6 per cent were not and 9.6 per cent were uncertain whether they had permission to occupy or not.[27] The issue of gender is therefore taken very seriously in debates over land tenure reform. Although women have full protection under the Constitution and are entitled to own and farm land on an equal footing with men, the old order institutions have cast a long shadow on their present rights.

One of the ways the government is trying to address the problem of land tenure in the former bantustans is to strengthen municipal institutions and thus build local capacity. Prior to 1994, municipal governments existed only in urban areas, and traditional authorities administered whatever municipal functions were available in the bantustans. But the new Constitution requires that municipal governments be established across the country. Although many traditional leaders oppose the appointment of elected councillors, regarding them as a threat to their own powers, local government is largely considered an essential building block in the democratic process.

CONCLUSION

The restoration of sovereignty to subjugated communities (even if it is only partial restoration, as in the case of Nunavut) does not begin with a clean slate. The majority of communities reclaiming their land in South Africa and Canada have all the social indicators of underdevelopment. To be effective in the long-term, land claims in these countries must be settled in such a way that they represent a major step in overcoming the existing social, political and economic inequality experienced by indigenous peoples. This means enough land to meet their needs, a fair share in the development of resources on these lands, and jobs and economic opportunities to end the poverty and unemployment that afflict so many aboriginal communities. Upgrading of educational, housing, and health standards, maintenance of language and cultures, and meaningful control over local affairs are the essential ingredients for the development of healthy, viable communities.

The loss of land and land rights of the African population of South Africa and its association with the loss of citizenship under the laws of apartheid represent one of the most enduring legacies of the colonial and apartheid periods. The objective of the South African government is to extend the full set of rights and duties embraced by the notion of sovereignty (citizenship) as enshrined in the Constitution to all its citizens, including those who were deprived of any citizenship or human rights in the country of their birth. The dilemma it faces is how to acknowledge the cultural identity and traditions of African peoples, as represented by the institution of Traditional Leadership, on the one hand, while honouring the constitutional demands of democratic governance and individual and equal human rights on the other.

Part Three

Dealing with Legacies

Chapter Seven
Restoring Dignity

When the divide between rich and poor is not as glaringly defined
in terms of the settler and the indigenous, only then will an inclusive
new nation emerge.

Mathatha Tsedu, 1998.[1]

THE HUNGER FOR DIGNITY

On 30 April 2004, when Thabo Mbeki was inaugurated as President
of South Africa for a second term of office, he promised to restore the
human dignity of all South Africans. For a millennium, he said, there
were some in the world who were convinced that to be African was to
be less than human. This conviction made it easy to trade in human beings as slaves, to colonize countries, and, today, to consign Africans to
the periphery of the global economy. The journey South Africans have
undertaken as a new democracy is about redressing the harms that were
caused by land dispossession and to restore dignity to those whose humanity has not been fully recognized. This is Canada's journey as well.

Speaking to the Northeastern Alberta Aboriginal First Nations
Association in October 2000, Matthew Coon Come, then National Chief
of the Assembly of First Nations, described the devastating impact of
dispossession on the living conditions in many First Nations communities across Canada:

> More than half of our people are still dependent on welfare
> and our nation as a whole has no source of its own revenue, no
> tax base, no direct benefit from natural resources of our land.
> Our nations are totally dependent on the Crown for housing,
> sanitation, education, health care, fire protection, social facilities.
> We are still considered the white man's burden.... The land
> and resources of our people have been alienated. We have been

dispossessed of our lands and resources. They have been taken away through all kinds of procedures under the pretense of legality. This dispossession is still going on.... We have gone from being the owners of everything, the natural equity of thousands of years of conservation and care, to become the dependents of a state that is reluctant to provide even the bare necessities of life.[2]

As Coon Come rightly points out, the relationship between the poverty and despair experienced by reserve communities and the loss of land and independence is unmistakable. Responsibility for the residents of Canada's 2,787 Indian reserves rests with the Department of Indian and Northern Affairs. Today more than half the status-Indian population live in cities. A federal interlocutor and some of the provinces are responsible for providing social services to Métis and non-status Indians. Thus the human rights situation of Canada's aboriginal peoples results not only from different geographical settings but from a variety of social and cultural factors as well. Added to this are the different approaches to public policy by the various agencies and complex sets of laws and jurisdictions governing relations between the state and various categories of aboriginal peoples. Many Canadians, unaware of these complexities, blame the federal government for spending large sums of taxpayers' money with very few visible results. Aboriginal people see the solution in reclaiming their territorial bases and taking responsibility for the administration of their own lives. Land alienation and loss of human dignity lie at the root of many of the problems that plague indigenous communities.

The purpose of this chapter is to acknowledge the legacies of colonial and post-colonial dispossession in Canada and South Africa and then to examine some recent initiatives designed to restore dignity and wholeness to indigenous communities. The task that confronts Canadians and South Africans today is to reverse the trends of history which have produced societies that are deeply divided along cultural, ethnic and economic lines and to build new societies that are inclusive and respectful of each other's needs.

LEGACIES OF DISPOSSESSION IN CANADA

In 2003, the United Nations ranked Canada the best country in the world to live in. Two years later, based on a special investigation into the economic conditions of Canada's aboriginal population, Canada had dropped to eighth place in the world. In March 2005, the United Nations' Commission on Human Rights published a report on "the situation of human rights and fundamental freedoms of indigenous people" in Canada that reflected the ongoing impact of dispossession on reserve communities across Canada. According to UN special investigator Rodolfo Stavenhagen, the areas of greatest disparity between aboriginal and non-aboriginal reserve communities were health, housing, education, employment, and social welfare. In every case, these disparities can be linked directly or indirectly to land loss and to the absence of cultural and political self-determination.

The United Nations report confirmed that illness of almost every kind occurs more often among aboriginal peoples than among other Canadians. In some cases, diseases such as tuberculosis, that have been virtually extinguished in the rest of Canada (as in other developed countries of the world), persist in the third-world conditions often found on Indian reserves. Infectious diseases occur at a higher rate among aboriginal people than other Canadians, as do chronic and degenerative diseases. Other diseases that have reached critical proportions in aboriginal communities are diabetes and HIV/AIDS (Acquired Immune Deficiency Syndrome and the virus associated with it).[3]

The linkages between land loss and health conditions are well known. The extremely high rates of diabetes among aboriginal populations in Canada can be traced to the fact that indigenous people no longer have access to their high-protein traditional diets. Like their ancestors who had no resistance to influenza and measles, today's aboriginal populations do not have digestive systems adapted to European food. Thus, Indians living on reserves can expect to die seven to eight years younger than other Canadians. Moreover, infant mortality rates on reserves remain twice the national average, largely due to maternal malnutrition and distances from major healthcare centres.[4]

Although the disparities are not as pronounced as they are in South Africa, the health sector in Canada is under particular stress to address the glaring health problems in aboriginal communities. John Williams, former Director of Ethics at the Canadian Medical Association (CMA) has done sabbatical work in South Africa. In his paper "Ethics and Human Rights in South Africa," Williams draws some important lessons for Canada from the South African experience: "The current South African commitment to reduce these inequalities between white and non-white citizens might inspire a similar commitment to address aboriginal health issues in Canada.... Although the breaches of medical ethics observed in Canada are not on the level of those documented in South Africa, they still jeopardize the profession's ability to advocate on behalf of physicians and patients." Ethics is still a marginal and poorly resourced subject in many Canadian medical schools, Williams points out. Most importantly, vigilance is required to ensure that the medical profession in Canada avoids both the direct violations of human rights such as those performed under apartheid by some South African physicians, and complicity in an unjust system that violates the basic principles of human rights and ethics.[5]

To close the human development gaps between aboriginal and non-aboriginal Canadians, the government must address a wide range of related issues. Housing, education, welfare and social services are among the most urgent. Closely related to health levels among First Nations is the problem of poor housing. In 1996, more than ten thousand homes on reserves had no indoor plumbing. One reserve in four had a substandard water or sewage system. Poor sanitation and lack of running water are among the major causes of gastroenteritis epidemics. As Chief Ignace Gull of the Attawapiskat First Nations community testified to the Royal Commission in 1994: "We are forced to dump our sewage in open pits and use outdoor privies at 30 or 40 below, winter temperatures. This practice causes people of all ages to get sick."[6]

Land loss and the consequent segregation of Indian communities on reserves has made unemployment – one of the most obvious indicators of poverty – high on the list of priorities for band leaders and political decision-makers alike. Geographic isolation on reserves that are often located far from major centres deprive residents of employment opportunities readily available to other Canadians. The lack of public transportation, poorly maintained roads, and extensive distances from airports add to the isolation of native communities from access to job markets. Indian Act provisions concerning income tax exemptions on salaries earned on-reserve is a further disincentive to reserve residents to live and work off the reserve. The connection between loss of land and the economic conditions on reserves is obvious to reserve residents, who watch billions of dollars in logs, minerals, fossil fuel and hydro electricity being exported from their territories with little or no benefit flowing to them.

This is particularly evident in the province of British Columbia, although non-native residents are reluctant to admit it. In April 2005, west coast writer Will Horter pointed out the double standards that many white residents of British Columbia apply to the exploitation of natural resources on native lands:

What non-native community facing severe unemployment, health and suicide issues would sit idly by when resources (natural capital) are shipped off in vast quantities, while governments dither about process and companies and shareholders get rich? Not many![7]

The facts speak for themselves. British Columbia's billion-dollar timber industry relies on the forests in unceded aboriginal lands with minimal payback to the First Nations affected. The mining industry in that province claims to generate $4 billion a year – and barely a token of this amount is shared with the native landholders. The fossil fuel industry also makes billions of dollars a year ($77 billion according to one report) in gas revenues. The environmental and social impact of these industries is an additional financial burden on First Nations communities. Moreover, the damage caused by abandoned mines, acid mine drainage, and leaking tailing ponds contaminates the soil and destroys the habitats of wildlife on which many native communities depend to supplement their diets.

Over the past two decades, Canada has made major efforts to improve the standard of healthcare on reserves. Unlike South Africa, where remote rural areas have very few health services, there are nursing stations in virtually all the isolated northern reserves and helicopters available to airlift patients to hospitals. In some regions, hospitalization of Indians is higher than it is for non-native communities.[8] How then to explain the ongoing disparities between the standard of health on reserves and the rest of Canada? One possible reason is that health services are provided largely by white doctors and nurses who usually do not speak the local languages and whose services are hampered by the cultural gap. In recent years, federal and provincial educational programs have produced a growing number of native health professionals; but there is still frustration because the federal government continues to control native health services through the Department of Indian and Northern Affairs. In spite of administrative and financial difficulties, a number of bands are taking control of their own health services with some positive results.

A host of social problems affecting aboriginal youth, women and men in reserve communities stem directly from loss of land and culture. Among the most destructive is the high rate of substance abuse, often starting in childhood. Local band councils, community groups and government agencies are trying to address the problems of endemic drug addiction and alcoholism among reserve communities. However, there is still a long way to go. Aboriginal self-government and the opportunity to regain control of their lives is seen as a critical step in bringing healing and dignity to aboriginal communities. George Erasmus, National Chief of the Assembly of First Nations in 1989, wrote:

> As people of the First Nations of Canada we have a vision of the
> sort of country we want to live in and to build in collaboration
> with other Canadians.... We should have tribal courts run by
> our own people. We should administer our own child-care and
> social services. We should take control over our own education,
> as we have already begun to do. In this visionary Canada we
> would be free to express in our actions our tremendous concern
> for the environment.... Once our jurisdiction was recognized we
> would ... establish sustainable economies that would consider
> the long-term future of our children and grandchildren.[9]

The issue of autonomy over health services is now being addressed by
some aboriginal communities through land claim agreements. Other
native communities are asserting their sovereign rights directly through
reserve-based institutions and programs. For example, the Mohawk of
Kahnawake (the *Kanjen'Keha ka*) near Oka, Quebec, have established the
Kahnawake Schools' Diabetic Prevention Project (KSDPP) to conduct
research on the prevalence and prevention of diabetes among aboriginal
people. For generations, studies like this were conducted by non-aboriginal researchers and institutions. The Kahnawake project is an indication
of the determination of First Nations to take control over their own lives
and communities.

Education is another key area where autonomy of aboriginal communities is essential. First Nations children learn from an early age that
their ancestral traditions and cultures are less important than those of
non-native peoples. Canadian school curricula has historically ignored
aboriginal history and culture or has dealt with these topics in inappropriate or disrespectful ways. But this is changing. Many reserve communities have established their own schools and curriculum. The establishment of the First Nations University of Canada, formerly Saskatchewan
Federated College (open to both First Nations and non-First Nations
students), has special programs to create awareness of the diversity and
richness of First Nations and Métis cultures, histories and current issues
affecting First Nations communities.

LEGACIES OF DISPOSSESSION IN SOUTH AFRICA

In post-apartheid South Africa, legacies of colonial and apartheid policies are reflected in the huge disparities in economic and social conditions between those who have been dispossessed of their land and the
current landholders. For all the talk about a "rainbow nation," the divide
between rich and poor is still glaringly defined in terms of the indigenous

Rural African home near Nylstroom, Northern Province.

and European populations. President Mbeki's characterization of South Africa as "two nations" – a rich nation (mostly white) and a poor nation (almost entirely black) – is totally appropriate.

Three of the most obvious indicators of this widening gap between black and white South Africans are housing, health and economic development. But there are, of course, many others, including access to quality education, meaningful employment, and an enhanced standard and quality of life. All of these have been available to white South Africans for the past fifty years under the same laws that deprived the black population of both their land and civil rights.

South Africa's teaming squatter camps around large cities like Johannesburg, Cape Town and Durban, where anywhere from forty thousand to two million people live in makeshift dwellings constructed from cardboard boxes, plastic bags and corrugated iron, stand in stark contrast to the comfortable white suburbs where many Africans are employed as domestic workers or gardeners. In the rural areas, particularly in the former bantustans, unemployment and poverty levels for thousands of African households (consisting mainly of women, children and the elderly) are even higher.

Under the Reconstruction and Development Program (RDP), introduced by the new government in 1994, housing was high on the list of priorities to "uplift" those most adversely affected by apartheid. Joe Slovo, the first ANC housing minister, estimated that half the black population lacked a secure roof over their heads and called for half a million homes

African homes in Khayelitsha township near Cape Town.

to be built in the first five years. Not only was this target not met, but the RDP houses (labeled "kennels" by the residents) were also often even tinier than the "matchbox" houses built for urban Africans in the apartheid era. Financial restraints have seriously affected almost every sector. The government's answer was the GEAR program (Growth, Employment and Redistribution), which replaced the RDP in the late 1990s. This new policy, which focused on markets as the key instruments of development, was welcomed by the investment and business sectors, but did little to relieve the misery of the poor.

The economic system of a market-driven economy, which has served the white minority well, seemed on the surface to be the logical choice for black South Africans seeking the same goal of economic growth. Sick of sharing a few crumbs from the table, the black majority are now in a position to actually have a share in the wealth of the country. In its 1999 election poster, the ANC promised to deliver "a better life for all." The only drawback is that only a few can find a place at the table. The vast majority are excluded and in many cases are rendered even more impoverished by the transition to democracy.

John Pilger, a British journalist and filmmaker, has identified some of the root causes of the continued poverty. In order to avert civil war, the African National Congress negotiators had been forced to compromise their left-leaning ideals articulated in the 1955 Freedom Charter, which had assured all South Africans of a share in the country's wealth. The

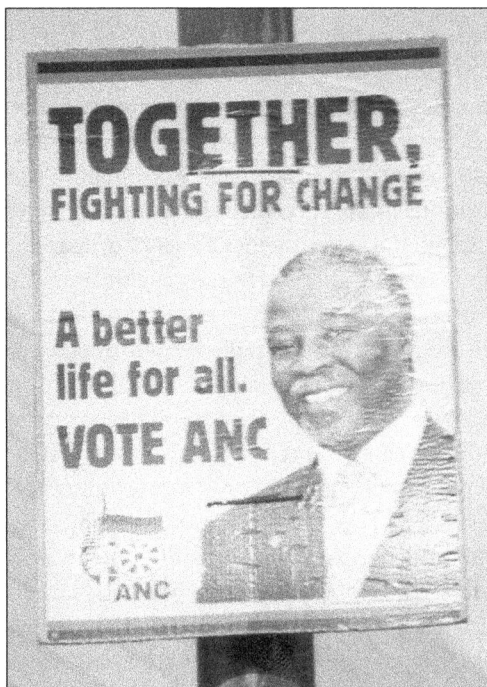

African National Congress election poster, 1999.

land would belong to all who worked it, and all the major monopolies, the mines and financial institutions, would be nationalized. However, Mandela and his colleagues were forced to abandon these communistic ideals and to support the continuation of a market economy. As Pilger observes, this was nothing new. Under white rule, there had been a long and bloody history of a market economy in South Africa. Cecil John Rhodes paved the way in the late nineteenth century, advocating the dispossession of Africans and their "removal" to cheap labour reserves for white-owned gold and diamond mines and industries. The Oppenheimers followed in Rhodes' footsteps and grew rich on the brutal migrant labour system.[10] In post-apartheid South Africa, Harry Oppenheimer's theory of "trickle down" wealth has been adopted by President Thabo Mbeki and his Minister of Finance, Trevor Manuel. While this policy favours the development of a small black elite, it has not addressed the enormous legacy of poverty the ANC government has inherited.[11]

Inequities based on racial groupings that vastly favoured white South Africans were an integral part of the apartheid system. This was especially apparent in the provision of health services. A survey conducted in 1983 reported that in urban South Africa the doctor-patient ratio was 1: 330 for whites and 1: 12,000 for Africans. In the bantustans, there was one doctor for every 14,000 people in the Transkei, 17,000 in Bophuthatswana and 19,000 in Gazankulu.[12] Government figures estimated infant mortality in these areas to be between 20 and 25 per cent of live births. Malnutrition was (and remains) one of the main causes of infant mortality.[13]

Health conditions in the rural areas have not dramatically improved since 1994, although the government's target of primary health care (for children and nursing mothers) and the systematic immunization of children against infectious diseases has made a significant difference in the areas where the program has been implemented. But the economy-driven hospital closures, layoffs, and privatization of health care have raised serious ethical and human rights dilemmas for health care delivery.[14]

The provision of clean water (communal taps) to previously neglected rural black communities was a major achievement of the new government in the first years of democracy. However, in 1998 the ANC government decided to privatize water throughout the country. Water became a commodity to be sold for profit on the open market and the benefits of clean running water are now available only to those who can pay for it. In the rural areas, multinational water companies installed prepaid meters on communal taps or stand pipes. Not only were the meters unreliable, but the scheme inhibited local people from obtaining sufficient water for their daily needs. As a result, health levels plummeted. In 2003, a major cholera epidemic swept through the community of Ngwelezane in KwaZulu-Natal. David Hemson, a researcher with the Human Science Research Council of South Africa reported that three hundred people died from cholera and 350,000 were affected. The cost of setting up emergency hospitals and tents for re-hydration were enormous. Many blamed the privatization of water for the outbreak because local people had reverted to the old way of fetching water from rivers and streams, most of which are polluted. Although the government denied that lack of access to clean water caused the epidemic, the publicity was effective: Ngwelezane received a new standpipe and a low, flat rate for their water.[15] However, in other areas, the risk of communities contracting diseases from contaminated water continues.

The spread of AIDS (Acquired Immune Deficiency Syndrome), and the virus associated with it, HIV, is a growing problem in South Africa affecting thousands of men, women and children. Children who have lost both their parents to the disease, have become double victims. With about 1,600 South Africans infected daily, HIV/AIDS has taken centre stage in the massive health problems that face the new government. The direct impact of poverty on the prevention and treatment of HIV/AIDS

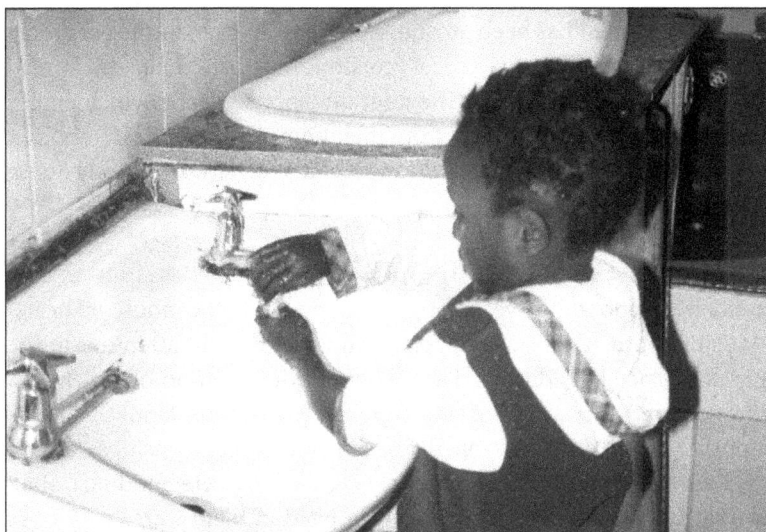

Child in Aids Orphanage near Durban, KwaZulu-Natal.

has become increasingly apparent over the past several years. Poor people are less likely to have access to educational program relating to the spread of HIV/AIDS or to be able to pay for medical treatment. Moreover, malnutrition contributes both to the effectiveness of medications and to the recovery rate of HIV/AIDS patients.

The ANC government (and President Mbeki in particular) has been heavily criticized for delaying the provision of free treatment to AIDS sufferers. Finally, in 2003, the health minister Manto Tshabalala-Msimang announced a plan to provide free anti-retroviral drugs in public hospitals. The plan, which AIDS activists and health professionals have been urging for years envisages that at least one service point (clinic) would be provided to every municipality across the country by 2005. Although the government has committed over R12.1 billion to the plan, and the international community is also providing funding, the program is barely making a dent in the rampant spread of the disease across the country. Apart from the logistics of setting up clinics and the sheer number of patients involved, there is also an acute shortage of health professionals to ensure that the drugs are properly administered.[16]

Women, who remain on the lowest rung of the economic scale, are particularly vulnerable to AIDS. In 1994, the women's organization Black Sash reported that in rural KwaZulu Natal, the prevalence of HIV in women was more than four times that of men.[17] More recent reports show a similar trend developing across the country. The rise in HIV infection in women has been attributed, at least in part, to the escalating rate of rape cases in South Africa. Prostitution has also helped to spread the disease in South Africa. The migrant labour system, which entails long absences of male workers from their homes and families, is another important contributing factor to the spread of HIV/AIDS among South African men and women.

THE PROBLEM OF "INVISIBILITY"

In her book about the lives of migrant labourers in the industrial heartlands of South Africa, Mamphela Ramphela brought attention to the appalling social conditions that lay behind the eruption of violence in parts of South Africa in the late 1980s and early 1990s. Until the media reports of so-called Black-on-Black violence in the townships, neither the migrant labour hostels (huge barrack-like concrete buildings, often several rows deep) nor the people who lived in them were "visible" to the white public in racially segregated South Africa.

The conflict began when migrant workers, armed with traditional Zulu weapons of assegais and spears, as well as firearms, began to savagely attack the African residential community surrounding their hostels. The unprovoked attacks can be partly explained by the state-orchestrated conflict between the ANC and the Inkatha Freedom Party. However, the psychological and sociological climate engendered by the inhuman and degrading conditions endured by thousands of hostel dwellers provided the ideal conditions for this "orchestration" of violence to take place.

The hostels were originally built to accommodate male workers who had labour permits for ten months of the year in the cities and then had to return to their homes in the bantustans. Women and children were forbidden by law to live in the hostels. Even as temporary "homes," the hostels were, and still are an affront to human dignity. They exist because of the country-wide housing crisis deliberately created by the apartheid government in order to discourage "surplus" Africans from settling in urban areas.[18]

As Ramphele writes in *A Bed Called Home*, the physical space constraints in the hostels of the Western Cape (where most of her research was conducted) is overwhelming. The common denominator of space allocation in the hostels is a bed and nothing more. The "beds" in question are wooden bunks or concrete slabs the size of a narrow single bed, without mattress or spring – occupants have to provide their own. Since the demise of apartheid and the removal of the Group Areas Act, whole families including children now "live" in an allocated area of 1.8 square metres, and share living, cooking and ablution facilities with hundreds of other families. Privacy of a sort is created by a flimsy curtain and practicing the art of "imagining space where there is none."[19] These "bed homes" are distributed in different types of hostels, with varying degrees of intensity and configuration across the country; but all bear the mark of a system designed to rob the inhabitants of their human dignity and self-esteem.

South Africans have to acknowledge the legacy of apartheid, particularly the space constraints imposed on black people. In Ramphele's words, it is not going to be easy for people who have had to "shrink" to now stand up and walk tall. Habits developed over the years of oppression will die hard.[20] The hostel experience suggests that many Africans still face real barriers to participation in normal life. These barriers reinforce the notion of being a "victim of circumstance" rather than an active agent in the unfolding historical process. As Ramphele concludes, the "victim image" is a valuable asset in the personal struggle for survival, despite pulling a person down, because it releases one from responsibility in social relations: "Many of our informants repeatedly indicated that they saw themselves as victims of both the wider political system and the power games played in community politics.... In a sense this becomes a self-fulfilling prophecy and leads to low levels of effective participation."[21]

Some of the deprivations of hostel life in South Africa find echoes in the situation of Canada's aboriginal peoples, especially those who live in squalid conditions on reserves or in urban ghettos. In these situations, the support structures of traditional social life have been whittled away by generations of residential school experience. The compulsory separation of Indian children from their parents and communities paved the way for the current syndrome of unemployment, alcoholism, substance abuse and domestic violence. Even those who manage to escape the cycle of dysfunctional home life and move to the cities find the experience of non-acceptance by the wider society equally destructive. A disproportional number of urban native people end up in prison compared to the general population. The 2005 United Nations study found that 17 per cent of prison populations across the country were comprised of aboriginal men, women and children, who make up only 4.4 per cent of the total population.

Peter Carstens has compared the psychological impact of reserve life on Canada's Okanagan people and in "Coloured" communities in South Africa. His work documents the conflicting situations people face when they try to come to terms with their marginal positions in their respective societies. Frustration induces a complex chain of reactions involving both avoidance and acceptance, often marked by aggression. Indians sometimes give the impression of their acceptance of their situation. However, often their concealed anger finds expression in joking relationships with each other and with whites. Overt aggression against whites rarely occurs, perhaps because the hidden taboos produced by the system tend to internalize and displace aggression. Therefore, many kinds of personal violence are resolved locally on a personal level. Among the Okanagan, there are many kinds of feuds that are resolved by shouted insults or fist fights. Often drinking is involved. Vandalism is another form of displaced aggression, often directed at public property as a rejection of white institutions. In Carstens view, there is an urgent need to study the social and psychological effects of the Indian Act and the concomitant reserves. Too often Canadian policy-makers and the public at large erroneously attribute self-destructive behaviour to "traditional Indianess," when really they are indicators of a reserve culture.[22] Métis writer Maria Campbell uses a powerful metaphor for this destructive legacy:

> My Cheechum (grandmother) used to tell me that when the government gives you something, they take all that you have in return – your pride, your dignity, all the things that make you a living soul. When they are sure they have everything, they give you a blanket to cover your shame.[23]

The higher-than-average suicide rates among aboriginal Canadians, frequently involving young people, must also be located within the historical context of the reserve system. As Carstens points out in a recent article, the syndrome of suicidal risk behaviour, many of which are themselves pathological, are "flags of sinister distress" in reserve communities. These warning signs have been recognized for a long time. In 1992, Justice Murray Sinclair, an aboriginal judge, told a conference on suicide prevention that the extremes of violence (including suicide) among aboriginal people is essentially a function of their history. When people have been oppressed for generations, their reaction to the restraints imposed on them can quickly become violent – a violence that is often directed towards self, family, friends and others in the local community.[24]

Aboriginal Canadians are not alone in experiencing this debilitating cycle of self-abuse and violence towards others. Writing about the impact of the "victim image" on Afro-Americans, S. Steele explains the powerful impact of victimization on the psyches of oppressed people. "Oppression conditions people away from all the values and attitudes one needs in freedom – individual initiative, self-interested hard work, individual responsibility, delayed gratification, and so on. It is not that these values have never had a presence in black life, only that they were muted and destabilized by the negative conditioning of oppression."[25]

This kind of insight is helpful in understanding the processes that give rise to a culture of victimization, although it is not intended to defend or camouflage the ugly destructiveness of behaviour that leads to the fetal infection of infants, the serious neglect and often abuse of children, domestic violence, rape and murder. The failure of band leaders to take responsibility for the breakdown of social order in their communities and the financial mismanagement and corruption in the administration of reserves is unacceptable under any circumstances. Situations where unattended children die in house fires, young people burn to death from sniffing gas, and the suicide rate is among the highest in the world are indicative of the extreme conditions under which many native communities are now living. They are also the direct result of dispossession – of land and human dignity.

LAND MATTERS: RESTORING DIGNITY

The vast majority of South Africa's rural population is either fully or partially dependent on land and land-based resources in order to survive. The only external sources of income are wages (usually earned in towns through domestic work or in shops and industries); remittances from family members who work as migrant workers on mines or in factories; and income from informal economic activities and state welfare grants. Land-based sources include crop and livestock production and the harvesting and processing of natural resources. The production of food crops has played a vital role in sustaining African households in the former bantustans, particularly in the eastern half of the country, where the climate is conducive to rain-fed cultivation. In these mixed farming areas, a high proportion of households are involved in crop production along with a number of other livelihood activities. Maize inter-cropped with other food crops and vegetables are produced on small plots of land mostly for home consumption. But depending on the size of arable holdings, levels of production are often not sufficient to meet the subsistence needs of households, necessitating the purchase of maize and other staple foods. In areas where population density is high, there are significant numbers of households without access to arable land apart from a small home garden.

In their 2003 report on rural land use and livelihoods, Maura Andrew, Charlie Shackleton and Andrew Ainslie discuss the ways in which rural households make full use of the land they have.[26] Until the 1990s, most

African women carrying firewood, Gauteng.

surveys of rural households found that the sale of crops amounted to less than 10 per cent of household incomes. However, more recent studies show that the contribution of agriculture to rural households has been underestimated. In some areas, crop sales may represent as much as 20 per cent of a family's income. Livestock farming is another important source of livelihood for rural families. The ownership of cattle and other livestock was a key element in the pre-colonial economies of African people in southern Africa and has remained so. The range of livestock farmed today includes cattle, sheep, goats, horses, donkeys, pigs, chickens, geese, turkeys, pigeons, rabbits and ducks. By keeping this type of livestock, rural families are able to obtain: meat, milk and eggs for home consumption; equity as an investment; income from the sale of animals or by-products such as hides and skins; the means to pay *lobolo* or bride-wealth, and cow dung (used to line the walls and floors of their huts). The horses and donkeys are also useful for draught or transport purposes.

In addition to farming, communal land is harvested for a whole range of resources used by rural communities, from wild spinaches and edible fruits to fuel wood and grass hand-brushes. Many rural households make use of edible insects, wood for fences or kraals (animal pens), medicinal plants, wild honey, and reeds for weaving. These resources are extracted from home gardens as well as neighbouring fields. More specialized resources, such as some medicinal plants, weaving fibres, and durable household poles, are only found in certain parts of the countryside around villages. Knowledge of these resource areas and their availability is often of vital importance to economically vulnerable households. Moreover, there are often marked disparities between wealthy and poor households in the use and dependency on natural resources. Poorer households are more likely to sell natural resources to generate cash income than more affluent households. For many families, the harvesting of natural resources is their only means of livelihood. For others, it represents supplementary income for specific items, such as school fees, books or uniforms. Thus, overall, access to land and natural resources is pivotal to rural life.

The South African government is beginning to address the problem of land-related poverty in a number of different ways. In 1997, the White Paper on South African Land Policy introduced several programs designed to benefit disadvantaged people. Some programs provide grants to buy or improve land under the direction of the Department of Land Affairs. Others distribute subsidies for housing construction administered by the Department of Housing. The amount of the housing subsidy depends on the income of the household. Only households earning under R1,500 ($400 CAN) per month qualify for the full subsidy amount of R23,000. A requirement for accessing the housing subsidy is that tenure must be secure. Beneficiaries must have a secure right to the land on which the house is to be built. Generally, subsidies are made available only to beneficiaries who possess registered title to a property in the form of ownership, a lease or a deed of grant. The rural housing subsidy used in the former bantustans is more flexible. Beneficiaries must have at least informal rights to the land on which they will live, but these rights must be uncontested – something that can be difficult and time-consuming to prove. Granting such a subsidy also requires the written consent of either the tribal authority or the provincial Department of Land Affairs office. A large section of the former bantustan population does not have secure land tenure, and so the housing subsidy has not been of significant benefit to rural communities. In 2003, over eighty-seven thousand urban households had received housing grants, as opposed to 501 rural households.

Thus town-dwellers benefit more from certain government programs than people living in rural areas. However, there are programs designed specifically for rural communities. Among these are ventures that involve the sharing of land-based resources between landholders and landless people. In his paper published by the Programme for Land and Agrarian Studies (PLAAS) in February 2004, David Mayson describes the various types of joint ventures that have been initiated with government support. Although the Department of Land Affairs gave specific support to the joint ventures program in its 1997 White Paper, the most significant players are corporations and businesses which have direct interests in developing mutually beneficial partnerships with previously disadvantaged people. The fact that the "private sector" is the primary initiator and driver of most joint ventures (including those funded by the government) means that there is a certain amount of risk involved for the African partner.

One type of joint venture that has provided small-scale black farmers with improved livelihood opportunities is contract or out-grower farming. This is an agreement between the farmer and processing markets or firms, in which the farmer agrees to supply an agreed quantity of goods of a specified quality. In return, the farmer is paid for the produce, but also receives support, such as bank credit, training and assistance with the purchase of machinery and other resources. Contract farming has been most common in the former bantustan areas, where women are involved in the production of cash crops such as cotton and sugar (albeit on communal land accessed through a male family member). The downside of these schemes is that they do not give African farmers secure and independent access to land and capital. Moreover, access to land is only granted for the production of a specified crop, leaving less arable land available for food production.

A more favourable type of joint venture for disadvantaged people is a sharecropping or share-produce arrangement. These are agreements in which instead of paying a predetermined amount of rent for farmland, the tenant agrees to give the landlord a share of the harvested crops. In the past, sharecropping agreements were inherently unequal. Sharecropping was a mechanism used by Africans to retain some hold on land which had been taken over by white farmers. In post-apartheid South Africa, the balance of power is not quite as unequal. For example, workers on a grape farm agreed to work the land of a neighbouring farmer in exchange for half the crop, which is then bottled and sold under their own wine label. Another example is where a community dispossessed in the 1970s has received their land back through the restitution process but lacks the resources to farm the land productively. The community has entered into a reciprocal agreement with a neighbouring white farmer which satisfies the needs of both parties. Each party receives 50 per cent of the profits from the venture: the community provides the land (and grant money for capital equipment) and the white farmer contributes cattle, machinery and management expertise.

In his assessment of joint ventures as a mechanism to assist small-scale black farmers to make a better living, David Mayson points out that the main beneficiaries of these schemes are white commercial farmers and corporations. While these schemes mobilize private sector resources and help poor people to overcome the many barriers to enter the market economy, they do not address the long-term problem of economic redistribution. In Mayson's words, "[j]oint ventures are generally unequal arrangements, and the dominant partners will seek to ensure their own interests are promoted. It is important for farm workers, small-scale farmers and their facilitators to understand this and to seek ways to increase their resources (including land) and benefits from the scheme."[27]

Bridging the power gap between white landholders, who have been the beneficiaries of farm subsidies and government schemes for almost a century, and newly recovered black farmers is not going to be easy. But the emergence of joint ventures is an encouraging sign that there is a willingness on both sides to join hands and make the land work for their mutual benefit.

In Canada, access to land and natural resource is also a critical issue for Canada's aboriginal peoples. According to the Canadian Human Rights Commission, the social and economic situation of the aboriginal population is among the most pressing human rights issues in Canada. While the Commission is not mandated to monitor the human rights of First Nations under the Indian Act (as stated in section 67 of the Canadian Human Rights Act) it has called for special measures to be implemented to reduce the economic and social gaps that exist between aboriginal and non-aboriginal Canadians. One of its recommendations is to establish an Aboriginal Employment Preference Policy. It has also called upon the Canadian government to ratify the International Labour Organization Convention concerning Indigenous and Tribal Peoples in Independent Countries.[28]

As in South Africa, Canadian governments, both federal and provincial have also introduced programs designed to bridge the human development gaps between aboriginal and non-aboriginal Canadians. In 2002, the Quebec government and the Cree and Inuit of Northern Quebec struck a follow-up agreement to the 1975 James Bay and Northern Quebec Agreement. This agreement, known as "La Paix de Braves," provided for the transfer of Quebec's socio-economic responsibilities to the Cree through the establishment of several joint councils that deal with economic development, forests, mines and hydroelectric management.

In an effort to deal more effectively with land claims based on aboriginal and treaty rights as recognized in the Constitution, the federal government passed legislation designed to affirm the existence of aboriginal rights in certain areas without the contenders having to bring the matter to the Supreme Court for legal interpretation. The First Nations Recognition Act (Bill S-16) was introduced in the Senate in October 2004 but has yet to be ratified by parliament.

CONCLUSION

Among the problems that face both Canadian and South Africans societies is how to reverse the social attitudes and political systems that have been in place for at least a century. In his book, *Citizens Plus*, political scientist Alan Cairns offers what he considers a middle ground solution to the impasse in negotiations between aboriginal peoples and the Canadian state. Former policies were based on the premise that Canada's first peoples would eventually be absorbed into the mainstream society, Cairns argues, but "history changed direction on us." Even though aboriginal peoples were written out of Canadian history, they refused to die out as social Darwinism had foretold. "We are like the new élite of Central and Eastern Europe whose book shelves were groaning with tomes dealing with the transition from capitalism to communism. The reversal baffled and confounded them. In much the same way, the material on our shelves assumed the goal of assimilation. Although we are now moving towards a different goal, the specifics are unclear. Moreover, the problems that confronted us in the past have not gone away, and the solutions are more elusive than ever."[28]

What is lacking in both countries is a fundamental concern for the common good. This is what George Soros, the Hungarian-born billionaire and philanthropist has to say about social justice and the market economy (*laissez-faire*) ideology:

> By taking the conditions of supply and demand as given and declaring the intervention of government as the ultimate evil, *laissez-faire* ideology has effectively banished income redistribution. I can agree that all attempts at wealth redistribution have failed, but it does not follow that no attempt should be made. Wealth does accumulate in the hands of the owners, and, if there is no mechanism for redistribution, the inequities can become intolerable. The claim that the accumulation of wealth is in accordance with the survival of the fittest is negated by the fact that wealth is passed on by inheritance.[30]

The truth is that no society can afford to ignore the common good. *Laissez-faire* or the trickle-down theory will benefit the wealthy at the expense of the poor. But there will be no stability or social justice until the legitimate demands of the dispossessed have been met. Soros sees the solution in "open societies," where institutions dedicated to the common good are allowed to flourish and where people with conflicting views and interests live together in peace. The key to fostering such societies is to recognize our interdependence as human communities.

Chapter Eight
Reconciliation

But true reconciliation cannot be imposed; neither can it occur
between cultures and societies that are enormously uneven in power.
The kind of reconciliation that can bring real peace can only occur
between partners whose independence, strength of purpose and inner
cohesion allows them fully to understand and share with the other.

Edward W. Said (1996)[1]

THE PURPOSE OF PUBLIC INQUIRIES

As public inquiries aimed at establishing a new relationship between
aboriginal and non-aboriginal peoples, Canada's Royal Commission on
Aboriginal Peoples (RCAP) and South Africa's Truth and Reconciliation
Commission (TRC) have certain features in common. Both commissions
were focused on reconciliation (the healing of wounds inflicted on indigenous peoples by governments and institutions) and gave indigenous
peoples the opportunity to tell their stories in their own words. The
commissions were held in the 1990s: Canada's RCAP was established in
1991 and South Africa's TRC in 1994. However, the circumstances that
gave rise to South Africa's truth commission and the part it played in
that country's transition to democracy place it in a completely different
category from Canada's Royal Commission on Aboriginal Peoples. The
Canadian commission was almost routine by comparison. Over the past
century, the Canadian government has held a series of similar inquiries
into the grievances of Canada's first peoples, none of which has radically
changed the situation of aboriginal peoples or their relationships with
government and the country as a whole.[2]

CANADA'S ROYAL COMMISSION ON ABORIGINAL PEOPLES

The Oka crisis in the summer of 1990 alerted the Canadian public to the
smoldering anger within the aboriginal community.[3] Television coverage
of the seventy-eight-day standoff on the Kanesatake reserve, which ended
with the arrest of thirty-nine Mohawk leaders, shocked and shamed

many Canadians. Two of the Mohawks charged were found guilty: Ronald Cross (known as "Lasagna") and Gordon ("Noriega") Lazore. They each served sentences of two to four years. The cost of the standoff to Canadian taxpayers came to well over $200 million. The fact that the incident made headline news around the world was further inducement for the government to take the matter seriously.

In 1991, the Conservative Party government of Brian Mulroney established the Royal Commission on Aboriginal Peoples to recommend ways to "restore justice to the relationship between Aboriginal and non-Aboriginal people in Canada." Four aboriginal and three non-aboriginal commissioners were appointed to investigate the issues and advise the government on its findings. Former Grand Chief of the Assembly of First Nations, George Erasmus, and Justice René Dussault co-chaired the commission. After almost five years and thousands of hearings held across the country, the Commission published its report in 1996. As a starting point to establishing a new relationship between aboriginal and non-aboriginal Canadians, the Commission affirmed that Canada's first people are "nations within Canada – collectivities with their own character and traditions [and] have a right to their own autonomous governments, and a special place in the flexible federalism that defines Canada." This status of nationhood was based on "their original occupancy of the country, the treaties that recognized their rights, the constitution that affirms those rights, and their continued cohesion as peoples."[4]

One of the primary objectives of the Commission was to give aboriginal people across the country the opportunity to express their grievances and talk about the difficulties they face. George Erasmus made this point very clearly:

> Rest assured, at the very least, the Commission will provide the
> opportunity for disclosure. A big part in traveling the country
> is for people to tell us their experience. We want to hear it. We
> want Canadians to hear it also. We will also be asking people
> to think about what they would like to occur in future – to find
> solutions and make recommendations for healing and so forth.[5]

The Commission saw its mandate as primarily forward-looking and solution-oriented. As co-chair Dussault expressed it, in order to build a new relationship between aboriginal and non-aboriginal peoples, it is not productive to dwell on the sins of the past. "You don't build a new country out of a feeling of guilt ... but because it's pleasant and fruitful to work together towards the future."[6] However, in its final Report, the

Commission admitted that "it would be false and unjust to attempt to wipe the slate clean," ignoring both the wrongs of the past and the treaty rights flowing from previous relationships.

Reflecting the evidence presented to the Commission, the final report dwelt extensively on the nation-to-nation relationship between aboriginal and non-aboriginal societies. The image of the two-row wampum, representing peaceful co-existence, was strongly advocated. While it acknowledged that the relationship between aboriginal and non-aboriginal peoples in Canada had "long been troubled and recently has shown signs of slipping into more serious trouble," the Commissioners concluded optimistically that "the relationship can almost certainly be mended, indeed turned from a problem into an asset and one of the country's greatest strengths."[7]

The report also made special mention of the relationship of the government with the Métis community. Although the Métis were recognized in the Constitution as an aboriginal people, they have not been able to negotiate modern treaties or agreements with the federal and provincial governments. The Commission urged the government of Canada to deal with Métis people on a nation-to-nation basis so that they can negotiate agreements on the same basis as other aboriginal peoples.

One of the major revelations made to the Commission was the treatment of aboriginal children in church-run residential schools owned and funded by the government. The impact of residential schools on generations of aboriginal people across the country was a common theme in much of the testimony. The traumatic effects of being separated from their homes and communities at a very young age, then being punished for speaking their languages and sometimes abused, was seen as the direct cause of the serious social problems facing many aboriginal communities.

Even when healing centres were established, the hurt continued. Dominic Eshkakaogan of the Ojibwe Cultural Foundation in Sudbury, Ontario told the Commission:

> In spite of [the healing process] the hurt is still there whenever residential schools are brought up. It brings back memories, it brings back tears. Even as an old man we cry. We cry when we remember those years.[8]

Eric Morris, an educational worker and president of the Teslin Tlingit Council in the Yukon, was one of a number of witnesses who called for a special inquiry into the residential school system:

I don't want to rub salt in the wounds by talking about residential schools.... But, the schools broke family ties, cultural traditions. The government system destroyed our oral traditions and our stories and legends were sort of "laid dormant" and did not move anywhere. Violence came afterwards. As villages became "alcohol and drug free" many hurts and pains of the past began surfacing and that is why we are calling for an inquiry into the residential schools.[9]

In response, the Commission recommended that the government institute a National Public Inquiry into Indian Residential Schools in order to enable aboriginal people to "stand in dignity, to voice their sorrow and anger, and be listened to with respect." It also called for further research into the social effects of residential schools, to identify the abuse that occurred, and to recommend remedial actions by governments and churches, including apologies, compensation and funding for treatment. In its Report, the Commission made clear that it did not believe funding was the only solution to the overwhelming social problems afflicting so many native communities. "To make the plan (its recommendations) work at all, first wounded spirits must be healed and real hope restored to young native people."

CRITIQUING THE RCAP PROCESS

Of all the government-appointed commissions relating to aboriginal Canadians, the Royal Commission of 1991–96 was by far the most important and far-reaching. The 2005 report of the United Nations Human Rights Committee refers to the Commission as "the most thorough study ever carried out; its numerous recommendations have opened the way to solutions of long-standing problems afflicting the relations between these peoples and various orders of Government in Canada."[10] The government's response in 1998, an action plan named "Gathering Strength" presented a broad-based approach designed to increase the quality of life and to promote the self-sufficiency of aboriginal Canadians. Thus the Royal Commission held out possibilities of addressing the legacies of dispossession including new legislation to compensate First Nations for the injustices of the past.

However, the Commission hearings have been criticized as intrinsically flawed because they failed to provide an acceptable forum for aboriginal people to voice their pain and anger. Although many aboriginal people who testified to the Royal Commission in Canada remarked on the sense of release they felt in coming before the Commission, there were some who expressed a profound sense of frustration. Among these was a woman elder from the Cariboo Tribal Council who said: "I'm angry that nothing has ever been done about [the legacy of residential schools]. I've been angry for fifty years, and all anybody ever does is to try to talk me out of it! And that makes me angry too!"[11]

Roland Chrisjohn and Sherri Young, the authors of a published report on residential schools presented to the Commission in October 1994, take the Commission to task for what they consider to be its one-sided perception of the residential school issue. In their view, by focusing attention on the need for "healing" and "reconciliation" within aboriginal communities, the Commission drew attention away from the individuals who committed such acts of abuse against children in their care – and the institutions responsible for their appointment and supervision. Chrisjohn and Young are skeptical about the efficacy of this one-sided approach to the healing process. Moreover, they blame the churches for using "therapy" as a way of avoiding responsibility for the treatment of aboriginal students in residential schools:

> We cannot see into the hearts and minds of those who have
> called so strongly for therapeutic or conciliatory responses
> to the Residential Schools, whether ecclesiastics, judges, or
> therapists of any stripe. Instead, we point out that unanimity has
> come about in the absence of any evidence to favor it. We ask if
> such unanimity really benefits Aboriginal Peoples. And we call
> attention to manifest economic, political and legal reasons such
> a smoke-screen would be created in the first place.[12]

The deep-seated distrust of aboriginal peoples towards the Canadian government and churches is indicative of the wide gap that exists between the two worlds of aboriginal and non-aboriginal Canadians. Although the notion of a deliberately set "smoke-screen" may represent an extreme view, and bear little relation to reality, there is enough "smoke" to warrant raising the important question of accountability on the part of the perpetrators of aboriginal abuse. The rank and office of those who victimized aboriginal children, whether they were school administrators or clergy, should not be allowed to shield or immunize them from being held accountable.

Another area of concern for some First Nations people is that by giving prominence to the issue of residential schools, the Royal Commission may have diverted attention away from the systemic violation of human rights in Canada and the wider issues of land and treaty rights and self-government. As inexcusable as the schools were as instruments of oppression and subjugation, they do not represent the total picture, any more than Australia's "stolen generation" represents the whole of that country's history (see Appendix) – or South Africa's victims of gross human rights abuses heard by the TRC represent the history of apartheid. The hardships and deprivations endured by aboriginal peoples run much deeper and cover a far wider range of concerns than the residential schools alone represent. Thus the Commission has created fresh divisions within the aboriginal community by favouring one group over others. A case in point is the administration of the government's "Healing Fund" which is earmarked specifically for survivors of sexual and physical abuse in residential schools. Survivors of residential schools who experienced cultural or psychological abuse are not eligible to apply for compensation. The result has been that growing numbers of former students are claiming compensation through the courts.

SOUTH AFRICA'S TRUTH AND RECONCILIATION COMMISSION

The Truth and Reconciliation Commission was established as part of the compromise between the apartheid government and the liberation movements to ensure a peaceful transition to democracy.[13] While apartheid South Africa was not formally a military state, the generals who operated the National Security Management wielded almost unrestrained power. Their demand for automatic amnesty during the negotiations of 1993 forced the African National Congress (South Africa's largest liberation movement) to find a middle path to satisfy both parties. While it rejected a Nuremburg-style inquiry on philosophical grounds, the African National Congress was prepared to consider an alternate process which would provide a forum for full disclosure of the crimes committed, while denying the right of automatic amnesty to any perpetrator.

Appointed under the Promotion of National Unity and Reconciliation Act in December 1995, the Truth and Reconciliation Commission (TRC) was assigned the task of establishing as complete a picture as possible of the causes, nature and extent of the gross violations of human rights committed from 1 March 1960 to 5 December 1993. Archbishop Desmond Tutu was appointed chairperson, and Dr. Alex Boraine, his deputy. The Commission consisted of three committees: the Human Rights Violations Committee, which was to conduct investigations and hearings into petitions relating to human rights violations submitted to the Commission; the Reparations and Rehabilitation Committee, which was to investigate the issue of compensation; and the Amnesty Committee, which had to grant or withhold amnesty to the thousands of applicants who admitted their role in the deaths and torture of their countrymen and women. There was also an Investigative and a Research Unit.

The TRC submitted its report to President Nelson Mandela in October 1998 after two and a half grueling years of hearings held across the country. Since the hearings received extensive media coverage, South Africans were exposed almost daily to revelations about their traumatic past on national radio and television. In improvised courtrooms fashioned out of town halls, community centres and churches, people came forward to tell their stories of terror, mutilation and death. The Commission received 21,300 statements from victims and nearly eight thousand applications for amnesty. As the TRC process got underway, it became obvious that the Commission's optimistic objectives to "put the past behind us and move into a peaceful future" were probably both unrealistic and unattainable.

For many who watched the proceedings on television, the most memorable part of the proceedings was the extraordinary role played by TRC Chairperson, Archbishop Desmond Tutu. Certainly no one could have provided an atmosphere more conducive to reconciliation and healing than this dynamic Anglican clergyman. That he wept openly with the emotionally distraught and anguished survivors who testified to the Commission, pleaded with Winnie Madikazela-Mandela to admit her part in the crimes she was accused of committing, and treated everyone from the intransigent former President P.W. Botha to the most remorseful abuser with equal respect and dignity was apparent in the broadcasts. However, some faith communities who did not share Tutu's theological interpretations of the TRC's mission felt alienated and excluded by the "powerful presence" of the Archbishop and the visual display of Christian symbols (Tutu wore his purple cassock and cross to the hearings). As Muslim activist Faried Esack pointed out, the result of this sense of exclusion was that few Muslims were able to "own" the TRC process.[14]

CRITIQUING THE TRC

For all the careful thought and discussion that preceded South Africa's TRC process, opinions about the usefulness and success of the commission vary widely, as did public expectations for what it might accomplish. For those who were looking for what Professor Mahmood Mamdani calls a "grand concluding narrative" to accompany South Africa's entry into a global economy after decades of isolation and international censure, the TRC played its part admirably. Widely covered in the foreign media, the TRC was generally reviewed much more favourably abroad than inside the country. For many, the Commission's most valuable contribution was to hold up a mirror to South Africans showing them a deeply troubled society, a society torn apart and distorted by the obsessive policies of white supremacy. One of its greatest achievements, according to some commentators, was to make it impossible for the white community to deny all knowledge of what had happened; but other commentators criticized the process for failing to address some of the key concerns of the majority (black) population.

The international community has been rightly impressed by the role of the TRC in restoring dignity and recognition to thousands of its citizens. However, there are other aspects of the TRC process which send a more cautionary message. Writing in 1998, journalist Antjie Krog observed, "the jury is still out as to whether the Truth Commission has been successful as an agent of reconciliation and reparation. And South Africans are discovering that the relationship between truth and reconciliation is far more complex than they ever imagined."[15]

One of the most compelling criticisms of the TRC process for many black South Africans was made by Professor Mamdani, head of the African Studies Department at the University of Cape Town. By focusing on human rights abuses as "the narrative" of the past, Mamdani argued, the TRC confronted apartheid through a narrow lens that excluded the experiences of the vast majority of the population. The consequence of paying special attention to a small minority who had been victimized by agents of the state (or agents of the opposition forces in some cases) was that the impact of the apartheid system on millions of South Africans remained unexamined and unaddressed.

A second criticism of the TRC – and one of the most controversial – was that it was only empowered to provide restorative justice not retributive justice: to punish offenders for their actions. As Elizabeth Kiss wrote in *The Economist*, "We've heard the truth. There is even talk about reconciliation, but where's the justice?"[16] This was one of the compromises made with the ruling apartheid government before the truth commission was established. But many families of victims were angry that the people who had harmed their loved ones were going to escape punishment by requesting and receiving amnesty.[17] Among those who campaigned vigorously to have amnesty declared unconstitutional before the TRC began its work was the Biko family. Steve Biko, the leader of the Black Consciousness Movement, had been brutally murdered in police custody in 1977. The Biko family eventually accepted the *bona fides* of the TRC process once the announcement was made but were nevertheless openly jubilant when his killers were refused amnesty.[18] While restorative justice is needed to rebuild community spirit, for many people there was also a need for retribution.

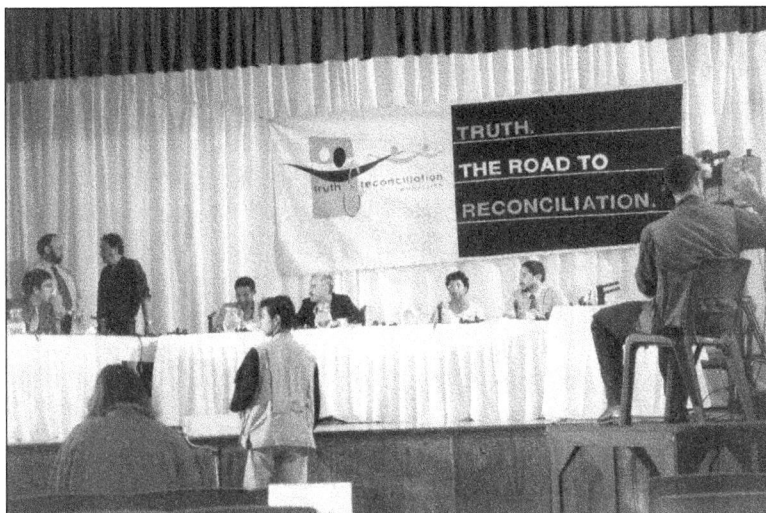

TRC hearing relating to General Magnus Malan, former Minister of Defence.

Some of the perpetrators who testified to the TRC and applied for amnesty were subsequently charged in the criminal courts. Eugene de Kock, a former commander of the security police's C-10 counter-insurgency unit at Vlakplaas farm outside Pretoria was sentenced to 212 years in jail after a twenty-one-month trial. Because of the non-political nature of some of de Kock's crimes, he will serve time in jail even if his amnesty application had been granted. But in another key trial, former defence minister Magnus Malan and his fifteen co-accused were acquitted of all charges related to the 1987 KwaMakutha massacre, due to insufficient evidence.[19]

Finally, the TRC has been faulted for setting up a dichotomy between the perpetrators of abuse and those they abused. This dualism of "perpetrator" and "victim" evaded the issue of systemic repair, and most significantly of all, it failed to recognize and address the other critical player in the South African tragedy: the beneficiaries. This was a critical failing because it meant that the influential but silent "accomplices" of apartheid – the white minority who had benefitted in every respect from the apartheid system – did not have to face the country. The distinctive characteristic of the apartheid system, Mamdani argues, is the link between the perpetrators and the beneficiaries. "It is the link between power and privilege, between racialized power and racialized privilege."[20]

The merging perception of the dominant culture as beneficiary, perpetrator and victim has had important consequences. Sometimes the merging was seen as part of the "South African miracle." No longer were there sharp and clear distinctions between "white" (beneficiaries) and "black" (victims); people became changed by the TRC process and the exposure it provided to the excesses of apartheid. One of those deeply affected by the TRC process was Afrikaner poet and journalist, Antjie Krog. In the closing paragraph of her book, *Country of my Skull*, she describes the strange confusion of emotions she is left with after her two-year assignment as special radio reporter on the TRC hearings:

> I am filled with an indescribable tenderness towards this Commission. With all its mistakes, its arrogance, its racism, its sanctimony, its incompetence, the lying, the failure to get an interim reparation policy off the ground after two years ... it has been so brave, so naively brave in the winds of deceit and rancour and hate.... For all its failures, it carries a flame of hope that makes me proud to be from here, of here. But I want to put it more simply. I want this hand of mine to write it. For us all; all voices, all victims.

> Because of you
> this country no longer lies
> between us but within
> it breathes becalmed
> after being wounded
> in its wondrous throat
> In the cradle of my skull
> it sings, it ignites ...
> I am changed for ever. I want to say
> forgive me
> forgive me
> forgive me
> You whom I have so wronged, please
> take me
> with you.[21]

Krog's imagery exquisitely sums up the dilemma of being both beneficiary, as a member of the privileged white "race," and perpetrator by association as a member of the ruling Afrikaner nation. In addition, she also feels victimized by the shocking and shaming revelations of the TRC that turned her world upside down.

But the opposite effect can also occur. Mamdani observes that the more South Africa's beneficiaries are outraged by the violations of human rights under apartheid, the less they feel responsible. Not only do they see no need to be forgiven, but they also experience forgiveness as a humiliation. Consequently, those victimized by apartheid become outraged by the complacency, callousness, and indifference they perceive, and so they feel that forgiveness is undeserved. As a result, they demand justice. So the TRC has in some ways ended up fueling the very demand for justice it set out to displace. What South Africans must do now, Mamdani insists, is search for a form of justice which can heal without compromising or diminishing the truth.[22]

REPARATIONS

One of the major disappointments that came out of the TRC process was the ANC government's refusal to honour its commitment to compensate the victims of gross human rights abuses who testified to the Commission. In 1996, the Commission's Reparations Committee recommended that twenty-two thousand people should receive compensation of up to R150,000 each to buy homes, educate their children, and pay for medical care. In 1998, the Government of National Unity (headed by President Nelson Mandela) agreed with the Commission's recommendations and promised greater equality of resources to all South Africans: "Unless there are meaningful reparations, the process of ensuring justice and reconciliation will be flawed." But as of January 2000, only eight thousand people had received interim payments of R2,000 each. As one newspaper editorial put it, the TRC's forty pages of recommendations were met with "deafening silence" by the ANC government.[23]

When Thabo Mbeki succeeded Mandela as president, he defended his government's decision not to honour its pledge of reparations by questioning the justness of paying individuals for the suffering they had endured. Finance Minister, Trevor Manuel, went so far as to discredit some of the claimants saying that "there were many Oscar contenders among those who appeared before the TRC," and argued that individual reparations were not necessary because the government was trying to uplift all the country's poor through its policies.[24] By asserting that the socio-economic implications of apartheid were being dealt with by other structures, notably the Land Claims Commission, the Gender Commission, and the Youth Commission the government side-stepped its commitment to the TRC process.

UNCOVERING THE TRUTH

Both Canada's Royal Commission on Aboriginal Peoples and South Africa's Truth and Reconciliation Commission raised a number of critical issues relating to the restitution of land rights and the restoration of dignity to aboriginal peoples. The most important lesson to be learned from both commissions is that "reconciliation" cannot be seen as an end in itself, merely the healing of a relationship that has turned sour. If this is how it is perceived, then the process of reconciliation holds out little hope for the disadvantaged partner. The act of reconciliation must change the relationship in fundamental ways in order to redress the injustices of the past.

As South Africa's experience clearly showed, the only kind of truth commission that can produce meaningful reconciliation between aboriginal and non-aboriginal communities must uncover the "truth." Mary Burton, who later became a TRC Commissioner, outlined the essential nature of the truth-telling process in the South African context at a conference in 1994. Her words are equally valid for Canada:

> We need to have a commission of truth that can establish the
> facts and we need to give it teeth. It must gather in the stories to
> reach that truth which is, in a way, already known and accepted.
> But we need to make it legitimate through that process. We
> need to tell and record and validate that truth. We need to
> acknowledge wrongs, not only in terms of injustice and hurt, but
> also the terrible loss.[25]

In his usual evocative language, poet Breyten Breytenbach described the purpose of truth-telling as "the obligation to live together in full knowledge of the past with at least a semblance of decency and tolerance and order, when the foulness of the crimes committed by some of us against others is still propagating its stench."[26]

As post-apartheid South Africans learned very quickly, one of the ways of evading "the truth" is to offer an apology. In 1996, the leader of the National Party, F. W. de Klerk, expressed his "deep regret" about apartheid in a speech to Parliament but has yet to admit his party's role as a deliberate, willful agency of human suffering. In his 1999 autobiography, de Klerk revealed his perceptions of the truths brought to light by the Commission. Describing the confrontational relationship that had developed between himself and the TRC Chairman, Archbishop Tutu, de Klerk wrote:

> The pity is that Archbishop Tutu and I – and the essentially
> decent communities that we respectively represent – are still
> so deeply divided by our different perceptions of the truth of

our country's troubled past. At the time of writing, the TRC has not yet produced its report. My fear is that, judging by its performance thus far, it will attempt to impose its own one-sided version of the truth on all South Africans, based on those aspects of the truth that fit its preconceived notions of our history.... My fear is that if the commission fails to produce a report which takes into account the perspectives and good faith of all the parties to our conflict, their efforts will lead neither to truth nor to reconciliation.[27]

By persisting in depicting the Afrikaner National Party government as an "essentially decent community" that acted in "good faith," de Klerk failed to acknowledge responsibility for the heinous crimes committed under his party's fifty-year administration. In fact, by denying all knowledge of the reprehensible actions of anti-insurgency police units, such as the Civilian Cooperation Bureau and the notorious Vlakplaas Unit, de Klerk passed the blame onto the foot soldiers who carried out their orders to such brutal effect: "I am convinced that the great majority of the members [of cabinet and the State Security Council] remained unaware of such operations until they were finally exposed by the Goldstone Commission or by the media."[28]

The truth about what was actually known to political leaders may never be revealed. There were reports that politically sensitive records relating to the activities of government departments had been destroyed in the weeks prior to the 1994 elections. For this reason, the Commission conducted a special investigation into the alleged destruction of records. Verne Harris, an archivist at the National Archives of South Africa and a member of the investigative team, has reported that "swathes of official documentary memory, particularly around the inner workings of the apartheid state's security system, have been obliterated." While a surprising amount of documentation survived the purge, Harris notes, the work of the Commission was gravely impeded by the loss of many critical "pieces of the past's puzzle."[29] As the TRC report indicated, "the destruction of state documentation probably did more to undermine the investigative work of the Commission than any other single factor."[30]

Anglican priest Father Michael Lapsley and lawyer Albie Sachs, survivors of separate assassination attempts by the apartheid regime, point out the enormous barrier to reconciliation presented by the non-repentance of government officials. In his Christian tradition, Lapsley says, repentance involves amendment of life, not glibly speaking about a new South Africa "as if it was like putting on a clean shirt."[31] This failure to recognize the enormity of the past places serious roadblocks in the path of reconciliation. Albie Sachs summarizes the problem:

> It is enormously frustrating to me to know there are millions of people who want to share this country, to share their humanity and open up their hearts – not just Mandela who is noted for this. But they cannot do it because the other side will not acknowledge that apartheid was more than a mistake.[32]

In Canada, official apologies to aboriginal peoples have become the centrepiece of the move towards "reconciliation" and the establishment of a new relationship with First Nations. In fact the only response elicited by the Royal Commission to date has been an apology from the Department of Indian and Northern Affairs (DIAND) plus the establishment of a Healing Fund for the survivors of physical and sexual abuse in church-run residential schools. In 1998, at the launch of "Gathering Strength," the government's official response to the RCAP Report, Jane Stewart, then minister of Indian Affairs, included a Statement of Reconciliation. Expressing regret for the many past policies and actions that have eroded the political, economic and social systems of Aboriginal peoples and nations, she told First Nations people that the government was "deeply sorry" and offered an apology to the victims of residential schools who suffered physical and sexual abuse. On 4 May 1998, at the launch of the $350-million fund to develop a community-based healing strategy for victims of the legacy of abuse, the Department stated: "Reconciliation has been our first priority because we cannot look forward without first looking back and coming to terms with the impact of our past actions and attitudes."[33]

The United States issued a similar statement of apology in September 2000. The Federal Bureau of Indian Affairs apologized to indigenous Americans for "the legacy of racism and inhumanity" including massacres, forced relocations and attempts to quash languages and cultures. "Never again will we attack your religions, your languages, your rituals or any of your tribal ways. Never again will we seize your children, nor teach them to be ashamed of who they are. Never again." In presenting this apology, the head of the Bureau, Kevin Gover, a Pawnee Indian, said that by acknowledging this legacy, the Bureau accepted the moral responsibility of putting things right. One hundred and seventy-five years after the creation of the agency as Indian Office of the War Department, the Bureau recognized its role in the "ethnic cleansing" of western tribes, the deliberate spread of disease, the decimation of the mighty bison herds, the use of the poison of alcohol to destroy both body and mind, and the killing of women and children – a tragedy so ghastly that it cannot be dismissed as merely the inevitable consequences of the clash of competing ways of life. In the United States, some native leaders welcomed the apology, while others called for an apology from the entire federal government, not just the department responsible for Indian Affairs.[34]

Chief Stewart Phillips of the Penticton Indian Band and president of the Union of B.C. Indian Chiefs gave short shrift to verbal apologies on both sides of the border. "Those kinds of statements from government represent a bunch of cleverly staged hand-wringing to make governments look good, while they continue to promote policies that lead to our marginalization." However, when Jane Stewart presented her apology on behalf of the DIAND, expressing "profound regret" for past actions, Phil Fontaine, Grand Chief of the Assembly of First Nations, accepted the apology on behalf of the AFN.[35] Not all First Nations leaders approved of his acceptance.

Canada's mainline Christian churches have also apologized. An explicit acknowledgment of the churches' culpability regarding residential schools came from the Oblates, a Roman Catholic order which ran many residential schools for indigenous children across Canada. In a statement read by Reverend Douglas Crosby, O.M.I., to the annual religious pilgrimage at Lac Ste-Anne, Alberta on 24 July 1991, the Oblate Order issued a full apology to the native people of Canada:

> We wish to apologize for the existence of the schools themselves, recognizing that the biggest abuse was … that the schools happened … that the primal bond inherent within families was violated as a matter of policy, that children were usurped from their natural communities, and that, implicitly and explicitly, these schools operated out of the premise that European languages, traditions, and religious practices were superior to native languages, traditions and religious practices.[36]

The United Church of Canada as well as the Anglican and Presbyterian churches have since offered their own apologies. The United Church of Canada offered two apologies, first in 1986 and again in 1997. The latter, a statement of Repentance and Apology to the First Nations of Canada for the harm caused by residential schools, was accompanied by the establishment of a Healing Fund. Despite these expressions of remorse and promises of a new relationship, the survivors of the residential school system have taken matters into their own hands. By November 1999, former residential school students had filed over six thousand claims against the four churches (Roman Catholic, Anglican, United and Presbyterian) and federal government. The number has increased each year since. Many claims allege physical and sexual abuse; but the main thrust of the litigation is for compensation for the loss of language and culture as a result of the residential school experience.

The notion of apologies without meaningful actions to go along with them is not readily understood by aboriginal peoples: even the words "I'm sorry" have no equivalent in many Canadian First Nations languages. Elijah Harper, Commissioner of the Indian Claims Commission and a former residential school student, has explained that in his tradition when a wrong has been committed, "the onus was placed on the perpetrator to make it right or to do something to make it okay. Reconciliation to me means making things right. How do you restore dignity, self-confidence and worthiness by saying 'Here's a million dollars?' I think there needs to be a human element, an emotional attachment to that – much more than money is being transacted."[37]

The skepticism of aboriginal peoples is not difficult to comprehend. The gulf between words and action remain a barrier to true reconciliation between aboriginal and non-aboriginal communities. Numerous commissions and government reports have urged changes in the legal relationship between aboriginal peoples and Canada, including self-determination. The Penner Report, published in 1983, gave strong endorsement to the principle of self-government within Canadian confederation.[38] But to date, the Canadian government has not chosen to implement any of them, including the Royal Commission's 1996 recommendations advocating aboriginal governments as a "third order of government." Similarly, there has been no action to implement an aboriginal lands-and-treaties tribunal to replace the Indian Claims Commission, as recommended by the Commission. During his term as prime minister of Canada, Jean Chrétien proposed major amendments to the Indian Act (last revised in 1951), but the Act and the Department of Indian and Northern Affairs remain in place.

Apologies and talk about "reconciliation" are ways of dealing with problems without any real changes taking place. Speaking of the reconciliation process in Latin American countries, Tina Rosenberg warns that short-term solutions can have great long-term costs. Beware of the words "amnesty" and "reconciliation," she cautions, because amnesty can be confused with amnesia and reconciliation with recurrence. False reconciliation risks allowing a century-old cycle of crime and impunity to continue.

> If the state still believes it did the right thing and behaves in a manner in which crimes could be repeated, it is not ready for reconciliation. The kind of reconciliation that lets bygones be bygones is not true reconciliation ... If, conversely, the victims in a society do not feel their suffering has been acknowledged, then they too are not ready to put the past behind them.... This is an important problem related to reconciliation: if people do not believe that justice will ever be done the door is left open to private acts of vengeance and retribution, and that can be dangerous for a society.[39]

The essential purpose of truth-telling is to confront the dark side of the past and to ensure that such things never happen again. The onus is on the whole society to make the radical changes necessary to establish a new kind of relationship with those who were formerly oppressed. In the words of Albie Sachs:

> We have to acknowledge that we, as a country and as South Africans, assume an historic responsibility for what happened. Many of us fought against it, all of us are going to give the guarantee that it will not happen again. Our future relationship will be based on the principle of dignity, equality and respect.[40]

The chilling testimonies in the TRC hearings brought light to bear on the darkest side of South Africa's psyche. They laid bare the signs of a deeply wounded and sick society.

For meaningful reconciliation to take place in Canada, there would need to be a thorough investigation into its treatment of indigenous peoples in order to create a society and a culture that values human rights over everything else. The need for transparency is still urgent. In September 1995, First Nations activist Dudley George was killed at Ipperwash Provincial Park during a confrontation with the Ontario Provincial Police over the land rights of the Stoney Point People. The public inquiry into the incident, held nine years after George's death in response to pressure from a number of organizations, was carefully monitored by aboriginal and non-aboriginal groups alike. In calling for the inquiry, the ecumenical Aboriginal Rights Coalition drew attention to the need for stricter controls over police deployment in matters involving aboriginal communities.[41] Neither the federal nor provincial governments nor the justice system have been transparent in all their dealings with aboriginal peoples, even though there are laws which provide public access to information.

Finally, as Chilean law professor Jose Zalaquett told South Africans in 1996, the purpose of dealing systematically with the legacy of atrocities is moral reconstruction, rather then crime and punishment. To put back in place the moral order that has broken down or has been severely undermined, or to build up a just political order where none has existed in historical memory, are the primary objectives of a truth commission. This entails the building of a political culture and setting in place values and institutions and policies that will guard against recurrence.[42]

CONCLUSION

By persisting in seeing reconciliation as primarily a question of people-to-people relations – the establishment of a "renewed relationship," as the RCAP Report phrases it – meaningful changes are unlikely to take place. Government-driven attempts to fashion a new relationship out of the old one have failed to acknowledge that the existing system is founded on the alienation of aboriginal peoples from their land and resources. As South African theologian, Itumeleng Mosala observed, reconciliation can never be achieved on the terms of the dominant society. It is indigenous peoples, who have been alienated from their source of identity and survival, who must dictate and determine the terms of reconciliation.

> Reconciliation must have something to do with the reversal of our alienation; and our alienation is not alienation from white people first and foremost. Our alienation is from our land, our cattle, our labour which is objectified in industrial machines and technological instrumentation. Our reconciliation with white people will follow from our reconciliation with our fundamental means of livelihood.[43]

A crucial point is being made here. Once indigenous people have been reconnected with their land and resources, which represent their "fundamental means of livelihood," only then will their reconciliation with the dominant society be possible.

Chief John Joe Sark of the Mi'kmaq Grand Council came to a similar conclusion. As he told the Royal Commission in 1994, Canada's aboriginal peoples are not looking for "sympathy, good intentions, or charity from non-aboriginal Canadians: they are demanding justice and recognition of their aboriginal rights and treaties including the right to self-government. Only when these rights have been recognized and land claims have been equitably settled will there be a level playing field and the fair chance for aboriginal peoples to coexist in peace, harmony and prosperity with other Canadians."[44]

Conclusion

WHY LAND RIGHTS MATTER

A common hunger for land and human dignity has compelled many indigenous communities worldwide to reclaim their territories, farms and hunting grounds and to demand an equitable share in the wealth-producing resources they contain. For the indigenous peoples of Canada and South Africa, the recognition of land rights represents the first step in their recovery from an abusive past which has stripped them of their basic means of livelihood and of their dignity as human beings. As the case studies in this book clearly demonstrate, land represents much more than economic commodities to be managed and exploited. As Joe Seremane, South Africa's first land claims commissioner expressed it, "Land is a birthright. The umbilical cord between us and mother earth that tells us where we belong. Like the womb, earth is the source of life. When we die, we return to the earth. This is why land is important."[1] When the issue of land rights are viewed from this perspective, it becomes clear that indigenous peoples are not asking for charity. Nor, as the Gitxsan and Wet'suwet'en chiefs in the *Delgamuukw* case argued, are they asking for some frozen rights from an historic icebox. They are asking for what they believe is rightly theirs – they are asking for justice.

There are many reasons why countries like Canada and South Africa should feel compelled to respond to their demands. Apart from Constitutional obligations to protect the human rights of all their citizens, there are practical reasons for providing mechanisms for land restitution. In Canada, there are recognized treaties between the state (or Colonial powers) and First Nations, that must be honoured. This is required by the justice system and rule of law under which Canada is governed. Secondly, although the aboriginal population is not very large, it is capable of arousing strong public opinion. Confrontations over land, such as those that occurred at Oka in 1990 and at Ipperwash Provincial

Commemoration of the Oka Crisis, Kanesatake, Quebec, August 1991.

Park five years later, are costly both in dollars and in public image. The federal government has a vested interest in preventing such outbursts of Indian anger from happening again.

The South African government has different reasons for addressing the issue of land rights. A century of white supremacist rule has created a situation of widespread poverty and hunger for land, affecting the vast majority of South Africa's indigenous population. In February 1994, before the elections were even scheduled, 353 rural communities held a Land Conference to set out its demands for the new South Africa. The Preamble to the Land Charter that emerged from this conference begins with these words:

> We, the marginalised people of South Africa, who are landless and land hungry declare our needs for all the world to know.
>
> We are the people who have borne the brunt of apartheid, of forced removals from our homes, of poverty in the rural areas, of oppression on the farms and of starvation in the bantustans. We have suffered from migrant labour which has caused our family life to collapse. We have starved because of unemployment and low wages. We have seen our children stunted because of little food, no water, no sanitation. We have seen our land dry up and blow away in the wind, because we have been forced into smaller and smaller places.

Aboriginal land rights demonstration, Ottawa, Ontario, June 2001.

> We look forward to the birth of a new South Africa. But for
> us there will be nothing new until there is land and services and
> growth. These are the biggest difficulties facing our country in
> the future.
> We will not sit back and watch the wealth build up in the
> cities, while on the edge of the cities, in the small towns and in
> the countryside, we continue to suffer and starve. These are our
> demands.[2]

This, then, is the driving force behind South Africa's land policy: the
overwhelming urgency to address the demands of thousands of landless
people and to build a new country on the foundations of racial equality
and human rights for all South Africans.

THE TASK OF NATION-BUILDING IN SOUTH AFRICA

In South Africa, the task of knitting together a society torn apart by
decades of racial discrimination and conflict is being addressed on a
number of fronts. Since his release from prison on 11 February 1990,
Nelson Mandela has shown South Africans a new image of itself; the
image of a non-racial, inclusive society. The foundation stone of the
new South African democracy is racial inclusiveness. In one of his first
public addresses at a rally in Durban, Mandela declared: "We are com-

mitted to building a single nation in our country. Our new nation will include blacks and whites, Zulus and Afrikaners, and speakers of every other language."[3]

One of Mandela's most important gifts to South Africa – and indeed to the world – is his wonderful knack of walking through the invisible barriers that continue to divide South African society. At a 2002 centennial celebration of the Anglo-Boer War (1899–1902) in South Africa, Mandela astonished the entire country by attending a wreath-laying ceremony commemorating Danie Theron, a Boer scout who had been killed in the war, at the Voortrekker Monument in Pretoria. Instead of seeing Theron as a member of the "other side," as an Afrikaner and therefore one of his oppressors, Mandela chose to see him as a freedom fighter, someone who, like himself, had fought for the liberation of his people. Mandela's words that day chartered a new course for South Africans to follow: "That we have had grave and deep differences with some of the political leaders from this [Afrikaner] community, and with the racial policies emanating from them, in no way detracts from our sense of appreciation for the role of Afrikaners in building our common land."[4]

Thabo Mbeki, who took over from Mandela as president in 1998, has expressed his vision of a new South Africa through the spoken word. This was no reformulation of an often-told story, but a narrative of inclusiveness that holds out the possibility of wholeness and healing. Here is a brief extract from Mbeki's statement as Deputy President on the occasion of the adoption of the Republic of South Africa's Constitutional Bill on 8 May 1996:

I am an African. I owe my being to the hills and the valleys, the mountains and the glades, the rivers, the deserts, the trees, the flowers, the seas and the ever-changing seasons that define the face of our native land....

I owe my being to the Khoi and the San whose desolate souls haunt the great expanses of the Beautiful Cape....

I am formed of the migrants who left Europe to find a new home on our native land. Whatever their actions, they remain still part of me ...

In my veins courses the blood of the Malay slaves who came from the East. Their proud dignity informs my bearing, their culture a part of my essence.

I am the grandchild of the warrior men and women that Hintsa and Sekhukhune led, the patriots that Cetshwayo and Mphephu took to battle, the soldiers Moshoeshoe and Ngungunyane taught me never to dishonour the cause of freedom …

I am the grandchild who lays fresh flowers on the Boer graves…

I know what it signifies when race and colour are used to determine who is human and who is not.…

All this I know and know to be true because I am an African![5]

Implicit in this statement is Mbeki's vision of an African Renaissance – a revitalization of African languages, African traditions, African domination in all spheres of life in order to restore the dignity and prosperity of all his people.

In post-apartheid South Africa, the task of retelling the past from a more inclusive perspective has been taken up by a broad range of people, from community leaders and museum directors to playwrights and politicians. In 1999, for example, the Griqua descendants of Saartje Baartman, a Khoikhoi woman who was taken to Europe in the nineteenth century and displayed as a "Hottentot Venus," demanded the return of her remains to South Africa from the Musée de l'homme in Paris. Another Khoikhoi woman, Krotoä (Eva), who was banished to Robben Island in the 1600s as an unfortunate misfit, has been reclaimed by an Afrikaner writer as *onse ma* (our mother).[6] Most significantly of all, Khoikhoi and San communities are demanding the restoration of their stolen land and restitution in the form of compensation and a share in the wealth produced on their ancestral lands.

The history of black South Africans is also being retold. The Voortrekker Monument in Pretoria, with its larger-than-life engraved murals of white women and children being massacred by the Zulus, and vivid tapestries celebrating the heroism of the Voortrekkers, no longer dominates the depiction of South Africa's past. Ordinary people, like Muriel Ncwana in Guguleto (Cape Town) are celebrating their cultural heritage – in this case, by opening a restaurant serving traditional Xhosa cuisine. Over the past decade, memorials to heroes like Stephen Biko, the Black Consciousness leader, and Hector Peterson, the first victim of the 1976 Soweto Student Uprising, have been erected, streets and towns renamed, and museums constructed to recall the bravery and sacrifices of the men and women who faced the onslaught of a terrible regime. The Robben Island Museum, housed in the former prison where Nelson Mandela and many others were incarcerated, is a vivid reminder of the irrepressible power of the human spirit. In December 2001, the Apartheid Museum opened in Johannesburg. Like the Holocaust Museum in New York, to

Xhosa restaurant in Guguletu township, Cape Town.

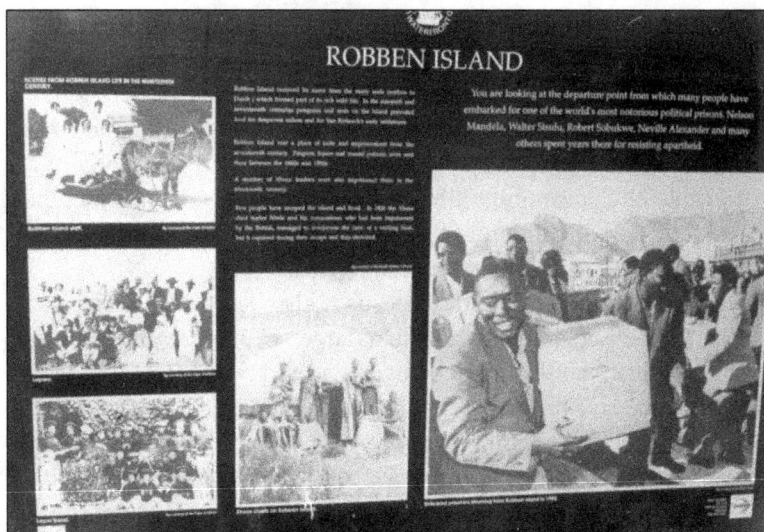

Robben Island Museum poster at Cape Town's Waterfront complex.

which it has been compared, the Apartheid Museum ensures that South Africa's chilling history will never be forgotten.[7]

South Africa's Truth and Reconciliation Commission was also an attempt to recognize and validate the hidden past. The hundreds of stories that were told at the TRC hearings, as vital as they were to the people concerned (whether victim or perpetrator), represent only a fraction of

Statue of Steve Biko, East London, Eastern Cape.

the stories of pain and injustice that could have been told. Even if a wider time frame had been provided by the Commission to include stories of gross human rights violations from colonial times, the Commission could not have uncovered all the stories there are to tell. The stories of dispossession experienced by African children who watched their mothers nurse and care for the white children of their employers; the stories of farmers who were forced off their land to work as sharecroppers or labourers on the lands that once were theirs; the stories of African men who left their homes and families for months at a time to work as poorly paid migrant workers in white-owned mines and industries – these represent a small part of the South African experience. Some of these stories are emerging in the land claim process, but many will never be publicly made known.

THE POWER OF STORIES (CANADA)

For too long Canada's story has focused only on the needs and interests of its dominant society. The founding narrative – the image Canadians have of themselves – tells of a mosaic of many cultures melded into one and dominated by two "founding nations," British and French. According to this founding myth, aboriginal peoples are expected to eventually adopt the languages and cultures of the dominant society and become assimilated as minority populations within Canadian society.

Political scientist Alan Cairns would like to see First Nations incorporated into the Canadian nation and given some special recognition as the first occupants of this country that would make them "Citizens Plus." He laments the fact that aboriginal and non-aboriginal communities in Canada "do not meet as common members of a single society, sharing citizenship, common memories and mutual pride in past achievements." History divides us, he argues, and it is overcoming these divisions, "at least to the extent that we can take pride in each other's presence in our common country," that is the goal towards which Canada must steadily work.[8]

The problem with this image of a blended society is that it ignores some major facts of history. The fact that Indian lands are protected under the Royal Proclamation of 1763, that treaties and agreements were negotiated with aboriginal nations by representatives of the Crown and federal and provincial governments, and that the 1982 Constitution recognizes the existing aboriginal rights of the indigenous peoples are inconvenient truths that have been largely ignored by the dominant society over the past hundred years. The onus has fallen on aboriginal people to assert their rights and to force legislators to recognize the special place of aboriginal people in Canada.

The oral histories of aboriginal people tell their own versions of Canada's history. The stories and myths of "empty lands" and "disappearing races" that supported four hundred years of dispossession are now being challenged by the proud history of aboriginal nations whose strong traditions continue to adapt to changing times. Aboriginal people are telling their stories through the various royal commissions, through their organizations, through the court cases of residential school survivors, through land claims and negotiations for territorial rights and self-government. Each of the aboriginal groupings defined by the federal government and recognized in the Canadian Constitution, tell their own story of dispossession and broken promises. In recent years, the demands of aboriginal peoples for self-determination and economically viable territories are receiving attention from governments and from the courts.

As the Royal Commission on Aboriginal Peoples report pointed out, aboriginal Canadians are not an "inconsequential minority group with problems that need fixing and outmoded attitudes that need modernizing." They are the original occupants of the nation, many with treaties that recognized their rights; a constitution that affirms those rights and their continued cohesion as nations within Canada. They have a right to a special place in the flexible federalism that defines Canada.[9] The constitutional and legal framework now exists for the Canadian government to implement the appropriate public policy that would give aboriginal people the opportunity to be self-governing entities in Canada.

Canada's aboriginal peoples have entered the twenty-first century with new assertiveness and determination. Speaking as Grand Chief of the Assembly of First Nations at an Indigenous Peoples' Conference in 1991, Ovide Mercredi articulated the spirit of confidence that other native leaders are affirming:

> If we believe in sovereignty, then we must practice that belief
> and put mechanisms in place to assist others. We must develop
> an indigenous agency for development and not wait for others
> to take on what is our responsibility. The time for grieving
> over past injustices is over. It is time to pay attention to hurts
> collectively and to move forward.[10]

Establishing international connections is a vital part of a worldwide movement in aboriginal solidarity. One of the ways in which aboriginal peoples are supporting each other in reclaiming their lands and resources is through the courts.

The British case system, which is adopted by most former British colonies, has proved to be a helpful tool for indigenous peoples claiming land based on aboriginal rights. One example is the case of the Richtersveld community in South Africa which claimed rights to ancestral land (including rights to the diamond mines) based on precedents established in similar cases in Canada and Australia. The *Mabo* case in Australia was fought on similar grounds (see Appendix). Although the courts do not always decide in the aboriginal party's favour, aboriginal plaintiffs are becoming more skilled at using the court system to their own advantage. Learning the language of the dominant society has become a necessary part of their survival strategy. For Canada's First Nations, the Constitutional recognition of existing aboriginal rights is vital to the land restitution process. It is the responsibility of the courts – in particular, the Supreme Court of Canada – to interpret what these rights entail. It is the task of governments to implement the courts' decisions and to ensure that justice is done.

Appendix
Australia and New Zealand

The pattern of British colonial dispossession and political domination in North America and southern Africa was duplicated with some variations in Australia and New Zealand. Today, a common hunger for justice and human dignity is forcing Australian Aborigines and the Māori of New Zealand onto the political arena. Without the constitutional protection enjoyed by Canada's First Nations and South Africa's black majority, the first peoples of Australia and New Zealand are relying on the justice system in their respective countries to support their demands for land and treaty rights.

Unlike Canada, South Africa and New Zealand – where prior occupancy of the local inhabitants was initially acknowledged – the colony of Australia was established on the doctrine of *terra nullius*, the belief that the land was devoid of human habitation. British settlers – so the argument went – were legally entitled to claim sovereignty and ownership over the entire continent on grounds of "first possession." When the British flag was hoisted over the penal settlement at Sydney Cove on 17 February 1788, as many as half a million Aboriginal people, living in hundreds of tribal groups across the continent, were instantly dispossessed of their ancestral lands. In the words of Australian historian, Henry Reynolds: "From that apocalyptic moment forward they were technically trespassers on Crown land even though many of them would not see a white man for another thirty, another fifty years.... English legal witchcraft was so powerful that it had wiped out all tenure, all rights to land which had been occupied for 40,000 years, for 1,600 generations and more."[1]

As the settlers moved further into the interior, it became obvious that the land was far from empty. Against fierce resistance, local populations were forced off their land to make way for European settlement. Many died from diseases like smallpox and syphilis, hundreds were murdered outright. As Australian historian Clive Turnbull observes, "from early in the story of European contact with Aborigines, we came upon the two factors which most contributed to their hostility and ultimately to their destruction: the gratification of the lusts of the invaders and the greed for land."[2] The crimes committed against indigenous Tasmanians are among the ugliest in Australian history. Although the notorious "Black Line" expedition – a human chain consisting largely of soldiers, settlers and convicts – failed in its objective to rid the island of every living aboriginal man, woman and child, very few Aborigines survived the invasion of Europeans on their shores.

While clearly fallacious, the myth that the country had been settled legitimately by right of first possession remained rooted in white Australian psyche and law until well into the twentieth century. As recently as 1971, the notion of *terra nullius* was upheld by the Supreme Court of Northern Territories in its first land claim case, *Milirrpum v. Nabalco Pty Ltd*. As in Justice McEachern's 1987 ruling in Canada's *Delgamuukw* case, the Australian court deemed that the Aborigines' relationship to land did not constitute legal interest in property recognizable in Australian law. Some concessions were made, however, in 1976 when the commonwealth (federal) parliament enacted a law that allowed Aborigines in the Northern Territory to apply for grants to own land provided it was not required for mining for the "national interest." Some of the southern states subsequently followed suit.

In 1988 the aboriginal peoples of Australia presented the prime minister Bob Hawke with a Statement calling for aboriginal self-management, a national system of land rights, compensation for loss of land, respect for aboriginal identity, an end to racial discrimination and the granting of full civil, economic, social and cultural rights. The Barunga Statement, which was written on bark, was eventually hung in Parliament but the government has never responded to its demands.

It was not until 1992 that indigenous Australians made any real headway towards reclaiming the land taken from them in 1788. Ed Mabo, on behalf of the people of Murray Island, made Australian legal history when he claimed ownership of ancestral territory by virtue of native title In *Mabo v. Queensland*, the Australian High Court ruled, by a majority of six to one, that the theory of *terra nullius* was inappropriate in a country which had so clearly been occupied. It also ruled that indigenous rights to land had not been extinguished by European occupation. In Justice Brennan's words: "whether the Islanders had been colonized by settlement, cession, conquest or declaration, their title in the land had not been surrendered."[3]

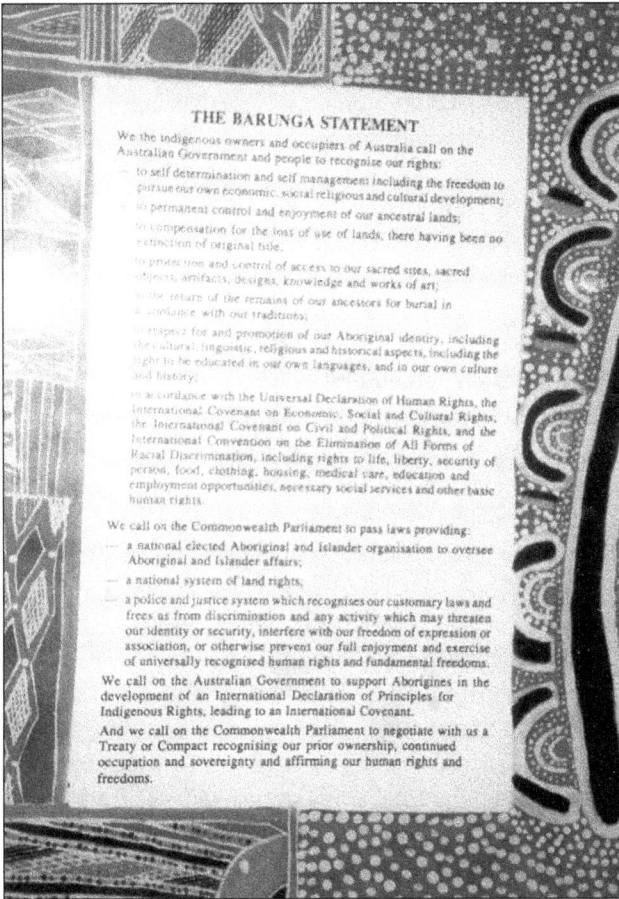

THE BARUNGA STATEMENT

We the indigenous owners and occupiers of Australia call on the Australian Government and people to recognise our rights:

to self determination and self management including the freedom to pursue our own economic, social religious and cultural development;

to permanent control and enjoyment of our ancestral lands;

to compensation for the loss of use of lands, there having been no extinction of original title.

to protection and control of access to our sacred sites, sacred objects, artifacts, designs, knowledge and works of art;

to the return of the remains of our ancestors for burial in accordance with our traditions;

to respect for and promotion of our Aboriginal identity, including the cultural, linguistic, religious and historical aspects, including the right to be educated in our own languages, and in our own culture and history;

in accordance with the Universal Declaration of Human Rights, the International Covenant on Economic, Social and Cultural Rights, the International Covenant on Civil and Political Rights, and the International Convention on the Elimination of All Forms of Racial Discrimination, including rights to life, liberty, security of person, food, clothing, housing, medical care, education and employment opportunities, necessary social services and other basic human rights.

We call on the Commonwealth Parliament to pass laws providing:

— a national elected Aboriginal and Islander organisation to oversee Aboriginal and Islander affairs;

— a national system of land rights;

— a police and justice system which recognises our customary laws and frees us from discrimination and any activity which may threaten our identity or security, interfere with our freedom of expression or association, or otherwise prevent our full enjoyment and exercise of universally recognised human rights and fundamental freedoms.

We call on the Australian Government to support Aborigines in the development of an International Declaration of Principles for Indigenous Rights, leading to an International Covenant.

And we call on the Commonwealth Parliament to negotiate with us a Treaty or Compact recognising our prior ownership, continued occupation and sovereignty and affirming our human rights and freedoms.

Barunga Statement display at the Tiagarra Aboriginal Culture Centre & Museum, Victoria, Australia.

The *Mabo* decision, quickly followed by the *Wik* case, substantially changed the law of the land in Australia and brought Australian common law into line with the contemporary situation in other western nations, including Canada and New Zealand. In 1993, the Keating Government introduced the Native Title Act to deal with the implications of the *Mabo* decision. The Act set forward procedures for dealing with Native Title claims – but also retrospectively validated the interests of non-indigenous landholders. In an historic compromise, indigenous groups accepted this validation process in exchange for guaranteed rights to negotiate. In theory, these mechanisms should have made the hearing of claims more efficient. In practice, the massive level of opposition to claims by state governments and other parties, resulted in lengthy and expensive court cases. A case in point was the claim of the Yorta Yorta nation that went into appeal in 1999. The Yorta Yorta lost their claim to their ancestral territory because they did not have written proof of their aboriginal rights. As Jacqui Katona, an Australian aboriginal writer and human rights activist, points out,

> By inventing the concept of native title to suit its own purposes, the Dominant Nation has us tied up in knots. On the one hand it acknowledges a past wrong, while at the same time it prevents Aboriginal people from reclaiming their land because they have been excluded from it in the first place. And because the court will not listen to their oral evidence, the legal system now decides that their rights over the country are "extinguished."[4]

Over the past decade, the Australian government has been looking for ways to diffuse the anger of its historically disadvantaged aboriginal communities. In 1994, the commonwealth government announced "reconciliation" as a national goal, and established a Council for Aboriginal Reconciliation to suggest strategies to address the issue of indigenous rights. Attention has been focused on the forced removal of children of Aboriginal descent from their homes between 1910 and 1960. In 1997, Australia's Human Rights and Equal Opportunities Commission held a public inquiry into what became known as the "Stolen Generations." The Inquiry considered public and confidential evidence from hundreds of Aborigines; detailed many stories of childhood abuse and its devastating effects; and made fifty-four recommendations calling for reparation to all victims. The Commission's Report heightened public sympathy for aboriginal rights in Australia and caused acute embarrassment to the Australian government prior to the Olympic Games in Sydney in 2000.[5] However, the call for compensation for the damaging effects of the policy on aboriginal communities, produced minimal response from the Howard government.[6] While Sydney's "Sorry Day" parade in May 2000 drew an estimated crowd of two hundred thousand people, the Prime Minister, John Howard, was conspicuously absent. His refusal to deliver a formal apology to the indigenous population for their treatment at the hands of white immigrants has further alienated the aboriginal community and their supporters.[7]

In New Zealand, where British navigator James Cook established relatively cordial relations with the local inhabitants on his 1769 and 1777 visits, indigenous land rights were never in question.[8] The New Zealand Polynesians, who had inhabited these islands for at least a thousand years before the arrival of Europeans in the 1790s, were formidable warriors

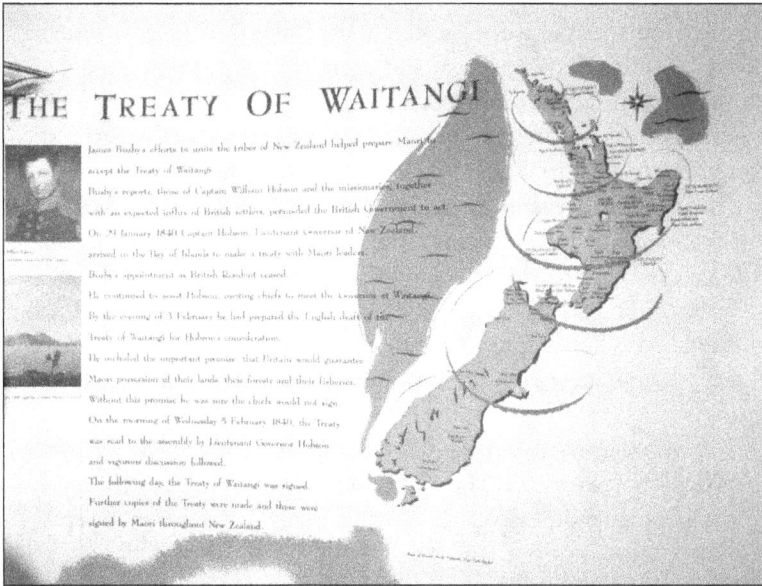

Treaty of Waitangi (1840) display at the Te Kapa Museum, Wellington, New Zealand.

but also highly skilled traders. The European sealers and whalers who established settlements along the coast – and later in the interior – were in no doubt that the country belonged to the Māori (as the local people now named themselves).[9] Organized colonization of New Zealand began in earnest in the late 1830s when the New Zealand Company (owned by a British family) established settlements in Wellington, Nelson and New Plymouth. When the British government decided to annex New Zealand (ostensibly to protect the local people from negative European influences, especially the introduction of the musket) it hoped to do this with Māori consent. Captain William Hobson was dispatched to the Bay of Islands in 1840 and, with the help of British Resident, James Busby and Church Missionary Society missionary Henry William, drew up a treaty by which the New Zealanders themselves would cede sovereignty of their country to the British Crown.

This single treaty, the Treaty of Waitangi (1840), has dominated Māori-state relations ever since. The fact that there were two official versions of the Treaty – one in English and one in Māori – has played a critical role in the country's history. According to the English version, both the chiefs of the United Tribes of New Zealand (established by the British Resident James Busby in 1835) and the chiefs of the independent tribes outside the Confederation "ceded their Sovereignty to Her Majesty the Queen of England." The Māori version, when translated back into

English, replaces the word "sovereignty" (*mana*) with "governorship" (*kāwanatanga*). Thus, the legal and moral validity of the Treaty hangs on the translation of the word "sovereignty."

In his paper on the centrality of the Waitangi treaty to Māori justice, New Zealand historian R.J. Walker argues that the missionaries, who had held preliminary discussions with some of the chiefs, knew that any loss of *mana* was an anathema to the chiefs. As it was, there were many who refused to sign the treaty. When the northern chiefs assembled at Waitangi on 5 February 1840, at the invitation of Governor William Hobson, many spoke against it, recognizing intuitively that their sovereignty was at stake. Chief Tareha was emphatic on this point:

> We, we are only the chiefs, the rulers. We will not be ruled over.
> What! Thou a foreigner up and I down. Thou high and I, Tarehu
> the great chief of the Nga Puhi tribes low! No, no, never, never.[10]

When Hobson arrived the following day, forty-three chiefs signed because they saw no other alternative. As each chief signed, Hobson shook their hand saying '*He iwi tahi tātou*' (We are now one people). The missionary W. Colenso had the task of giving out blankets and a parcel of tobacco to each chief.[11]

After the Treaty was signed, and the pace of systematic settlement increased, the real meaning of the Treaty revealed itself in the competition for land that ensued. In June 1843 a posse of fifty armed settlers was sent out to enforce the New Zealand Company's claim to Māori land at Warau. A new spirit of nationalism developed within the Māori community, inspired by the separatist Kotahitanga movement. In 1858 the first Māori king, Te Wherowhero was elected. The king came to symbolize *mana whenua* (sovereignty over the land) but the intention was to establish two parallel sovereignties, similar to the North American notion of the two-row wampum. However, Governor Gore Browne set out to crush the King movement on the grounds of "disloyalty to the Queen." A series of land wars ensued. To pay for the wars, three million acres of land was confiscated under the New Zealand Settlement Act of 1863. In order to gain possession of the remaining sixteen million acres still in Māori hands, the Native Land Court was established in 1867. The Court functioned to transform tribal lands from communal to individual title. Those named on the title to a block of tribal land were regarded as trustees by their people, but they had the power to sell it if they wished. Beset by "land sharks and shyster lawyers," the title holders were induced to part with their property for paltry sums. By 1960 only four million of the original sixty-six million acres of Māori land was left in their hands. As Walker puts it, the guarantees entered into by the Crown at Waitangi were "as insubstantial as mist in the noonday sun."[12]

For all its veneer of humanitarian idealism, the colonization of New Zealand was substantially no different from any other example of nineteenth century imperialism (with the possible exception of South Africa). Hobson's "one people" objective to amalgamate the settler and indigenous population under the same political and judicial system, failed to produce more than nominal equality in economic and social life. Although Māori people had full civil rights, the government essentially represented a white settler electorate (four Māori members of parliament represented the interests of the Māori population) who were determined to maintain their dominion over the Māori and to acquire their land on terms the Europeans considered satisfactory.[13]

To some extent, the "amalgamation" policy in New Zealand meshed with Māori aspirations. Historian Alan Ward records that, in the 1960s, many Māori leaders embraced the notion of "ambiculturalism" as well as "inclusion." By "ambiculturalism" they meant not only the tolerance of cultural differences, as in "pluralism," but the recognition of the validity of the two cultures and the ability of each to make creative use of the other.[14] Unfortunately, self-interest on the part of the white community – the knowledge that giving Māori greater control over their land would hinder land purchasing – frustrated that approach. In Ward's view, had some accommodation of Māori demands been made, genuine "ambiculturalism" may have been possible.[15]

Unlike South Africa, where the African peoples were united against a common oppressor, tribal identity prevented the Maori from acting as a pressure group commensurate with their numbers. However, by focusing on the Waitangi Treaty, some measure of unity was attained. Having appealed unsuccessfully to the British government for decades, their petition to have the Treaty ratified was finally tabled in the New Zealand Parliament in 1934. Years went by and nothing happened. The decision of the Māori Affairs Committee thirteen years later to have the Treaty reprinted and copies hung in the schools, was seen by the Māori as a hollow gesture. In 1971, the annual "celebration" of the Treaty (Waitangi Day) became the focus of radical Māori protest action. In terms very like those of Canada's constitutional debate in the late 1970s, Ngā Tamatosa (The Young Warriors) proclaimed that unless the Treaty was ratified, Waitangi Day would be declared a day of mourning. The Tamatosa protest was supported by a submission to government by the Māori Council citing fourteen statutes which contravened the Treaty.

The journey to dignity and the restoration of Māori land rights has been long and painful. After more than a century of political, statutory, and judicial denial of the Waitangi Treaty, the chiefs still assert that they have never relinquished sovereignty over their land. To date the Treaty confers a moral and political (but not legal) obligation on the part of government – but it has never been ratified by Parliament and is therefore not enforceable in a court of law.

As in Australia and South Africa, "reconciliation" has become the operative word in dealing with the legacies of the past. In keeping with its previous cosmetic responses to Maori demands, the government established the Waitangi Tribunal in 1976 to hear Māori grievances. However, the measure was not retroactive to 1840. It was only authorized to deal with infractions dating from 1975, when the Treaty of Waitangi Act came into force. Despite these obstacles, Māori confidence in their own future has manifested itself in a new political assertiveness over the past two decades. The objective is to renegotiate their rights in a nation-state through the articles of the 1840 Treaty.

Notes

PREFACE

1 The Republic of South Africa will be referred to hereafter as South Africa.
2 International Defence and Aid Fund for Southern Africa (IDAF) was an anti-apartheid organization that raised funds for the legal defense of political prisoners in South Africa and humanitarian aid for their families. It was based in London, England, having been banned in South Africa by the apartheid government in 1966. IDAF, as it was known around the world, was disbanded in 1991 after the release of Nelson Mandela from prison and the unbanning of the African National Congress and other liberation movements.

INTRODUCTION

1 South Africa's total land mass is 1.23 million square kilometres and the province of Ontario covers an area of 1.08 square kilometres.
2 Rodney Davenport and Christopher Saunders, *South Africa: A Modern History*, 5th ed. (London: Macmillan, 2000), 428.
3 Before Confederation, Ontario and Quebec were known collectively as the Province of Canada. Under the terms of the British North America Act (1867) the parts of the Province of Canada formerly known as Upper Canada became Ontario and the parts formerly known as Lower Canada became Quebec.
4 In 2004, the number of Canadians reporting aboriginal ancestry was just over one million, a figure that includes 720,740 Métis (people of Euro-Aboriginal descent) and 41,800 Inuit.
5 The Afrikaans language evolved from the Dutch spoken by the first white settlers at the Cape consisting of immigrants from Holland, Germany and France. The process of creolization was also influenced by the languages spoken by slaves from Indonesia and Asia, Khoikhoi as well as people of mixed descent. While the language of officialdom remained Dutch, the new creolized form (known as "Cape Dutch") developed into a separate language by the nineteenth century. See Christopher Saunders and Nicholas Southey, *A Dictionary of South African History* (Cape Town & Johannesburg: David Philip, 1998), 4.
6 The eleven official languages of South Africa are: English, Afrikaans, Zulu, Xhosa, Swati, Ndebele, Southern Sotho, Sipedi, Tswana, Tsonga, and Venda. However, English is the lingua franca of most South Africans and is the official language most frequently used in the spheres of politics and business.
7 Zebedee Nungaq, "Kicking the Tires of History," in *Nunavut News*, Special Edition, 85 (1999): 20–21.
8 Cited in Frederika Hackshaw, "Nineteenth Century Notions of Aboriginal Title and their Influence on the Interpretation of the Waitangi Treaty," in I.H. Kawharu, ed., *Waitangi: Māori and Pākehā Perspectives of the Treaty of Waitangi* (Aukland, New Zealand: Oxford University Press, 1989), 97.
9 *Johnson v. McIntosh* (1823), cited in Richard H. Bartlett, "Parallels in Aboriginal Land Policy in Canada and South Africa." *Canadian Native Law Review* 4 (1988): 28.
10 T. J. Lawrence, *The Principles of International Law*, 4th ed. (London: MacMillan, 1919), 151, quoted in Henry Reynolds, *The Law of the Land* (Ringwood, Victoria: Penguin Australia, 1987), 12.

11 *Johnson v. McIntosh* (1823), cited in Hackshaw, "Nineteenth Century Notions of International Law" in Kawharu, ed., *Waitangi*, 98.

12 Quoted in *Victims or Victors? The Story of the Victorian Aborigines Advancement League* (South Yarra, Victoria: Hyland House Publishing, 1985), 10.

13 S. Bannister, *Humane Policy: or Justice to the Aborigines of New Settlements...* (London: 1830; reprint, 1968), vi.

14 Noël Mostert, *Frontiers: The Epic of South Africa's Creation and the Tragedy of the Xhosa People* (London: Pimlico, 1992), 35.

15 Ibid., 107.

16 There are about 850,000 San people living today in remote regions of the Kalahari Desert in South Africa, Botswana, Namibia, Angola, Zimbabwe and Zambia. See Peter Godwin, "Bushmen: Last Stand for Southern Africa's First People," *National Geographic* (February 2001): 94.

17 Paul Olivier, "TRC to Probe San 'Executions': SADF under Spotlight." *Cape Argus*, Cape Town, 13 September, 1997.

18 Godwin, "Bushmen," 112–16.

19 Charles Van Onselen, *The Seed is Mine: The Life of Kas Maine, A South African Sharecropper 1894–1985* (New York: Hill and Wang, 1996), 96.

20 Hugh Brody, *The Other Side of Eden: Hunters, Farmers and the Shaping of the World* (Vancouver: Douglas & McIntyre, 2000), 215.

21 Robert Bringhurst, *A Story as Sharp as a Knife: The Classical Haida Myth Tellers and their World* (Vancouver: Douglas & McInytre, 1999), 68.

22 Carved from mature cedar trees, full size totem poles originally represented the story of a family or clan and were often part of the west coast potlatch ceremony. Mortuary poles, which were also removed from Haida Gwaii and displayed in museums, were carved and raised to honour a deceased elder or other highly respected member of the community.

23 Diamond Jenness, "Canadian Indian Religion," *Anthropologica*, First Series, 1 (1955): 8–14 cited in J.R. Miller, *Shingwauk's Vision: A History of Native Residential Schools* (Toronto & Buffalo: University of Toronto Press, 1996), 31.

24 Robert A. Williams, Jr., *Linking Arms Together: American Indian Treaty Visions of Law and Peace, 1600–1800* (New York: Routledge, 1999), 83.

25 Chief John Snow, *These Mountains Are Our Sacred Places: The Story of the Stoney People* (Toronto & Sarasota: Samuel Stevens, 1977), 5–6.

26 Thomas R. Berger, *Northern Frontier, Northern Homeland.* Vol. 1. Report of the Mackenzie Valley Pipeline Inquiry (Ottawa: Minister of Supply & Services, 1977), 90.

27 Brody, *The Other Side of Eden*, 215.

28 See, for example, J.M. Miller, *Shingwauk's Vision*.

29 United Church of Canada Archives, Toronto. Sutherland Papers. B.C. Conference Archives, Vancouver School of Theology. Extracts from a letter regarding the Indian Homes at Port Simpson, B. C. written by Mrs. Elizabeth Shaw to Mrs. T. G. Williams and read to the Executive of the Women's Missionary Society on 19 April 1899.

30 Brian Maracle, *Crazywater: Native Voices on Addiction and Recovery* (Toronto: Viking, 1993), cited in Miller, *Shingwauk's Vision*, 427.

31 Stan McKay, "Calling Creation into Our Family" in Diane Engelstad and John Bird, eds, *Nation to Nation: Aboriginal Sovereignty and the Future of Canada* (Concord, ON: Anansi, 1992), 30.

32 Brody, *The Other Side of Eden*, 168.

33 One of the primary concerns for the Inuit in their negotiations for Nunavut and territorial sovereignty was the preservation of their language and way of life.

34 Brody, *The Other Side of Eden*, 211–12.

35 Gisday Wa and Delgam Uukw, *The Spirit in the Land, Statements of the Gitksan and Wet'suwet'en Hereditary Chiefs in the Supreme Court of British Columbia, 1987–1990* (Gabriola, B.C.: Reflections, 1992), 97.

CHAPTER ONE: THE LAND AND THE PEOPLE

1 Peter Slingsby, *Rock Art of the Western Cape, Book One: The Seville Trail and Travelers' Rest* (Sandvlei, South Africa: The Fontmaker, 1999), 1.

2 Bartolomeu de Novaes Dias (c.1450–1500) was the Commander of the first European ship to round the southern tip of Africa. He dropped anchor in Mossel Bay at the beginning of February 1488. Dias named the Cape *Cabo de boa Esperance* because "it promised the discovery of India so-longed for and for so many years sought after." See Major R. Ravenhart, *Before Van Riebeeck: Callers at South Africa from 1488 to 1652*. Original documents translated from Dutch, Portuguese, German, French, Italian, Spanish and Danish (Cape Town: C. Struik, 1967), 2.

3 Mostert, *Frontiers*, 35.

4 By the turn of the twentieth century, the word "Kaffer" had become a pejorative term for African people used by white supremacist South Africans in the same way that "Nigger" came to be used in the United States.

5 Ravenhart, *Before Van Riebeeck*, 99.

6 Ibid., 180.

7 Donald Moodie, *The Record: Specimens of the Authentic Records of the Colony of the Cape of Good Hope Relative to the Aboriginal Tribes* (Cape Town, Cape of Good Hope: A.S. Robertson; London: J. Richardson, 1841), 4.

8 Richard Elphick and Hermann Giliomee, *The Shaping of South African Society, 1652–1840* (Middletown, CT: Wesleyan University Press, 1989), 27.

9 John Barrow, *An Account of Travels into the Interior of Southern Africa in the Years 1797 and 1798* (London, 1801; 1806), 123, quoted in ibid., 30.

10 Egbertus Bergh, *Memoirs* (Cape Town: 1802), cited in André Du Toit & Hermann Giliomee, *Afrikaner Political Thought: Analysis and Documents, Volume One, 1780–1850* (Berkeley & Los Angeles: University of California Press, 1983), 205.

11 Table Mountain, so-named because of its distinctive flat top, lies at the southern tip of Africa. Rising a sheer 1,066m from the coast, the mountain forms a dramatic backdrop to the city of Cape Town and its harbour.

12 T.R.H. Davenport, "Some Reflections on the History of Land Tenure in South Africa, seen in the Light of Attempts by the State to Impose Political and Economic Control," *Acta Juridica* (1985): 54.

13 O.F. Mentzel, *Description of the Cape of Good Hope*, Part 1, 36, cited in T.R.H. Davenport and K.S. Hunt, eds., *The Right to the Land: Documents on Southern African History* (Cape Town: David Philip, 1974), 11.

14 Olive Patricia Dickason, *Canada's First Nations: A History of Founding Nations from Earliest Times*, 3rd ed. (Don Mills, ON: Oxford University Press, 2002), 5–6.

15 Slaves in west coast societies were usually prisoners of war, but sometimes people lost status because of debt. A person could also be born into slavery, one of the few regions in North America where this happened. See ibid., 49.

16 Grace Rajnovich, *Reading Rock Art: Interpreting the Indian Rock Paintings of the Canadian Shield* (Toronto: Natural Heritage / Natural History Inc., 1994), 9.

17 Robert T. Boyd, "Demographic History, 1774–1874," in Wayne Suttles, ed., *Handbook of North American Indians*, vol. 7: *Northwest Coast* (Washington: Smithsonian Institution, 1990), 135, cited in ibid., 63.

18 Jay Miller, *Tsimshian Culture: A Light Through the Ages* (Lincoln and London: University of Nebraska Press, 1997), 12.

19 Dickason, *Canada's First Nations*, 3rd ed., 63.

20 Henry P. Biggar, ed., *The Voyages of Jacques Cartier*, with Introduction by Ramsay Cook (Toronto: University of Toronto Press, 1993), 49.

21 Robin Fisher, *Contact and Conflict: Indian-European Relations in British Columbia, 1774–1890* (Vancouver: UBC Press, 1977), 3.

22 Robert Surtees, *The Original People* (Toronto: Holt, Rinehart & Winston, 1971), ix.

23 Dickason, *Canada's First Nations* (Toronto: McClelland & Stewart, 1992), 95. (1st edition.)

24 Sir Richard Whitbourne, *A Discourse and Discovery of New-found-land, with many reasons to prove how worthy and beneficiall a Plantation may there be made, after a better manner than now is* (London: Felix Kyngston, 1620), 2–4, cited in ibid., 96.

25 Sir Richard Henry Bonnycastle, *Newfoundland in 1842: A Sequel to The Canadas in 1841*, vol. 2 (London: Henry Colburn, 1842), 252.

26 It is believed that the term "panis" was derived from "Pawnee" since members of this tribe were frequently enslaved by other North American nations. See J.R. Miller, *Skyscrapers Hide the Heavens: A History of Indian-White Relations in Canada*, rev. ed. (Toronto: University of Toronto Press, 1991), 45.

27 James C. Armstrong and Nigel A. Worden, "The Slaves, 1652–1834," in Elphick and Giliomee, eds., *The Shaping of South African Society*, 109–10.

28 Davenport and Saunders, *South Africa: A Modern History*, 5th ed., 25.

29 Eric Williams, author of *Capitalism and Slavery* (1944) and Prime Minister of Trinidad and Tobago wrote: "Slavery was not born of racism, rather racism was a consequence of slavery," cited in Robin W. Winks, ed., *Slavery: A Comparative Perspective, Readings on Slavery from Ancient Times to the Present* (New York: New York University Press, 1972).

30 Elphick and Giliomee, eds., *The Shaping of South African Society*, 541.

31 T.R.H. Davenport, *South Africa: A Modern History*, 3rd ed. (Toronto University of Toronto Press, 1987), 26–27.

32 Kerry Ward and Nigel Worden, "Commemorating, Suppressing, and Invoking Cape Slavery," in Sarah Nuttall and Carli Coetzee, eds., *Negotiating the Past: The Making of Memory in South Africa* (Cape Town: Oxford University Press, 1998), 202.

33 Robin Blackburn, *The Overthrow of Colonial Slavery, 1776–1848* (London: Verso, 1988), 78.

34 Bridglal Pachai, *Beneath the Clouds of the Promised Land: The Survival of Nova Scotia s Blacks*, vol. 2: 1880–1989 (Halifax: The Black Educators Association of Nova Scotia, 1990), 32.

35 It is not clear what proportion of the slaves emancipated under the Act were in the Cape of Good Hope. While slavery formally ended in the Cape on December 1, 1834, they were apprenticed to their owners for a further period of four years. In theory this transitional period was intended to prepare them for a useful existence as freed men, but in practice they continued to work as before. Freedom of movement and the right to demand wages did not come until 1838. See Armstrong and Worden, "The Slaves, 1652–1834," in Elphick and Giliomee, eds., *The Shaping of South African Society*, 167.

36 Cited in Dickason, *Canada's First Nations*, 1st edition, 181.

37 This correspondence is among the manuscripts of Bouquet and Haldiman Papers, No. 21. 634 at the British Museum, cited in Francis Parkman, *The Conspiracy of Pontiac and the Indian War after the Conquest of Canada*, vol. 2, 9th ed. (London: Musson Book Co. & Little, Brown & Company, 1886), 40.

38 Cited in Richard H. Bartlett, *Indian Reserves and Aboriginal Lands in Canada: A Homeland,* (Saskatoon: University of Saskatchewan Native Law Centre, 1990), 10.

39 The significance of the totemic symbols may well have reflected the clan or family affiliation, and may also have suggested the territorial or community ancestry of the signatory. However, they may have had a more personal significance and referred to the name or characteristics of the individual who adopted the symbol. See Greg Curnoe, *Deeds/Nations* (London, ON: Ontario Archaeological Society, Occasional Publications of the London Chapter, OAS, No. 4, 1996), xv.

40 Moodie, ed. *The Record*, 34. Extract of a letter from the Landdrost and Heemraden of Swellendam to Governor Plettenburg, 25 October 1774.

41 *Report of the Select Committee on Aborigines (British Settlements), Vol. 16 (London: 1836)* 2372. Evidence of Captain Andries Stockenstrom, 4 March 1836.

42 D.N. Sprague, *Canada and the Metis, 1869–1885* (Waterloo: Wilfrid Laurier University Press, 1985), 37.

43 Dickason, *Canada's First Nations*, 3rd ed. (Oxford University Press, 2002), 295.

44 Davenport, *South Africa*, 3rd ed., 145.

45 The Rehoboth Basters retained their identity through their constitutionally established

Paternal Laws, which required them to marry within their own community. Intermarriage with Germans and other communities did take place, however. See Rudolph Britz, Hartmut Land & Cornelia Limpricht, *A Concise History of the Rehoboth Basters until 1990* (Windhoek, Göttingen: Klaus Hess, 1999).

CHAPTER TWO: LAND RIGHTS AND TREATIES

1   C. Buxton, ed., *Memoirs of Sir Thomas Fowell Buxton* (London, 1848), 360, cited in Reynolds, *The Law of the Land*, 8.

2   Aborigines Protection Society, *First Annual Report* (London, 1838), 7, cited in ibid., 87.

3   In response to Mi'kmaq attacks, Governor Edward Cornwallis (1713–1776) issued a proclamation commanding settlers to "annoy, distress, take or destroy the Savages commonly called Mic-macks, wherever they are found." During this period both French and English colonial authorities paid bounties for scalps – no questions asked. See Dickason, *Canada's First Nations*, 5th ed., 136.

4   *Journal of the Legislative Assembly of Nova Scotia*, 1846, Appendix 24, 118, cited in Peter A. Cumming and Neil H. Mickenberg, eds., *Native Rights in Canada*, 2nd ed. (Toronto: The Indian-Eskimo Association of Canada in association with General Publishing Co., 1972).

5   One hundred thousand United Empire Loyalists entered the Maritimes, Quebec and Rupert's Land (the only British footholds in North America) after the American War of Independence.

6   Report by M. H. Perley, Commissioner for Indian Affairs for New Brunswick, 3 April 1848, cited in Cumming and Mickenberg, eds., *Native Rights in Canada*, 102.

7   *Journal of the Legislative Assembly of Nova Scotia*, 1845, p. 70, cited in ibid., 105.

8   In 1871, the United States ceased making treaties with the Indians and the subsequent Indian Wars are infamous, the Battle of Big Horn (1876) and the Massacre at Wounded Knee (1890) being the best known.

9   House of Commons, Dominion of Canada, Parliamentary Debates, 4th Session, 1871 at p. 341, cited in Cumming and Mickenberg, eds., *Native Rights in Canada*, 73.

10   Chris Arnett, *The Terror of the Coast: Land Alienation and Colonial War on Vancouver Island and the Gulf Islands, 1849–1863* (Vancouver: Talonbooks, 1999), 45.

11   Ibid., 45.

12   Alexander Morris, *The Treaties of Canada with the Indians of Manitoba and the North-West Territories including the Negotiations on which they were Based* (Toronto: Belfords, Clarke & Co., 1880; reprint, Saskatoon: Fifth House, 1991), 95–96.

13   T.R.L. MacInnes, "A History of Indian Administration in Canada," a paper presented at the Annual Meeting of the Canadian Political Science Association in Toronto, 24 May 1946.

14   Moodie, *The Record*, 205, cited in Mostert, *Frontiers*, 135.

15   Ibid., 62: Instructions for the Commandants of the Eastern Country, 5 December 1780.

16   *Report of the Select Committee*, 836, i, 659. Testimony of Reverend Samuel Young, a Wesleyan missionary, cited in Davenport and Hunt, *The Right to the Land*, 13.

17   Cited in Mostert, *Frontiers*, 375.

18   Republic of South Africa. State Archives, Cape Town: Kreli Treaty, 1844. G.H. 19/5.

19   William MacMillan, *Bantu, Boer and Briton*, rev. ed. (Oxford: Oxford University Press, 1963), 301.

20   Thomas Baines, *Journal of Residence in Africa, 1842–1853, Volume Two* (Cape Town: The Van Riebeeck Society, 1964), 303.

21   Aborigines' Protection Society, "The Native Policy of the Dutch Boers in the Transvaal." Memorandum to the Earl of Kimberley, Principal Secretary of State for the Colonies, 1881, 6.

22   Transvaal Archives (Pretoria), Superintendent of Native Affairs (T.A., S.N. 31, S.R. 260/95, Penzhorn to S.N. 6.2. 1895), cited in Peter Delius, *The Land Belongs to Us: The Pedi Polity, the Boers and the British in the Nineteenth-century Transvaal* (Berkeley, Los Angeles: University of California Press, 1984), 135.

23   This rule prevailed until it was challenged in court by the Reverend Tsewu in 1905. In this

celebrated case, the Transvaal Supreme Court found that the law did permit Africans to register land in their own names. For details about the Tsewu case see Donald Denoon, *A Grand Illusion: The Failure of Imperial Policy in the Transvaal Colony during the Period of Reconstruction 1900–1905* (London: Longman, 1973), 120.

24 Aborigines' Protection Society, "The Native Policy of the Dutch Boers," 4.

25 George McCall Theal, *History of South Africa from 1873 to 1884: Twelve Eventful Years.* Vol.10 (London: Allen & Unwin, 1919), 143–44.

26 The myth of the "empty land," that Bantu-speaking peoples arrived as immigrants on the lands north of the Vaal River at about the same time as the Europeans first settled in Table Bay, was finally exposed by historians in the 1970s. See Davenport, *South Africa*, 7.

27 Historian Julian Cobbing questions the entire notion of the Mfecane and argues that the motor for the disruptions (where they occurred) are to be found within white colonial society and the need for labour to ensure its continued commercial success. See Saunders and Southey, *A Dictionary of South African History*, 112.

28 Speech by Dr. Dönges at Burgersdorp on 26 July 1962 cited in Govan Mbeki, *South Africa: The Peasants' Revolt* (London: International Defence and Aid Fund for Southern Africa, 1984), 16.

29 Colonial Office. 879/14/164. Memorandum on the Zulu question. T. Shepstone, nd, 1878, cited in Delius, *The Land Belongs to Us*, 225.

30 Cited in Cumming and Mickenberg, *Native Rights in Canada*, 174.

31 Williams, *Linking Arms Together*, 5.

32 See Sarah Carter, *Lost Harvests: Prairie Indian Reserve Farmers and Government Policy* (Montreal and Kingston: McGill-Queen's University Press, 1990), 55.

33 D.J. Hall, "Serene Atmosphere: Treaty One Revisited" in Samuel W. Corrigan and Joe Sawchuck, eds., *The Recognition of Aboriginal Rights.* Case Studies 1, 1996 (Brandon, MB: Bearpaw Publishing, 1996), 20.

34 John L. Tobias, "Canada's Subjugation of the Plains Cree, 1879–1885" *Canadian Historical Review*, 64, no. 4 (December 1983): 519–48.

35 *Report of the Select Committee.* Testimony of Captain Robert Scott Aitcheson of the Cape Mounted Regiment, 31 July 1835, 2.

36 Some cautious colonists obtained and appended a certificate to the treaty document, signed by a neighbouring chief, stating that the chief they were dealing with was entitled to dispose of the land in question. See J.A.I. Agar-Hamilton, *The Native Policy of the Voortrekkers: An Essay on the History of the Interior of South Africa, 1836–1858* (Cape Town: Maskew Miller, 1928), 21.

37 Delius, *The Land Belongs to Us*, xi.

38 Cited in Davenport and Hunt, eds., *The Right to the Land*, 19.

39 Ibid., 19 & 20.

40 Agar-Hamilton, *The Native Policy of the Voortrekkers*, 21.

41 The practice of forcing Africans to go down on their hands and knees when paying taxes which began in the 1890s continued until well into the twentieth century. See David Welsh, *The Roots of Segregation: Native Policy in Natal (1894–1910)* (Cape Town: Oxford University Press, 1971), 297 and Denoon, *A Grand Illusion*, 98.

42 Cited in Bradford W. Morse, ed., *Aboriginal Peoples and the Law: Indian, Métis and Inuit Rights in Canada* (Ottawa: Carleton University Press, 1985), 331.

43 Cited by Bruce H. Wildsmith, "Pre-Confederation Treaties," in Morse, ed., *Aboriginal Peoples and the Law*, 126.

44 See Bradford W. Morse, "The Resolution of Land Claims," in Morse, ed., *Aboriginal Peoples and the Law*, 620.

45 Ibid., 623.

46 Re *Paulette et al v. The Queen* (1977), 2 R.S.C., 628, cited in Peter Cumming, "Canada's North and Native Rights," in Morse, ed., *Aboriginal Peoples and the Law*, 702.

47 Wildsmith, "Pre-Confederation Treaties," in ibid., 127.

48 Cumming and Mickenberg, *Native Rights in Canada*, 275.

CHAPTER THREE: SOVEREIGNTY AND SEGREGATION

1 H. B. Hawthorn, *A Survey of the Contemporary Indians of Canada: Economic, Political, Educational Needs and Policies* (Ottawa: Indian Affairs Branch, 1966–1967), vol. 1, 1967, 253.

2 J. Westlake, *International Law* (Cambridge: Cambridge University Press, 1904), 105–7, cited in Reynolds, *The Law and the Land*, 12.

3 Richard H. Bartlett, "Reserve Lands," in Morse, ed., *Aboriginal Peoples and the Law*, 469.

4 Dickason, *Canada's First Nations*, 1st ed., 286.

5 Cited in John Leslie and Ron Maguire, "The Historical Development of the Indian Act," 2nd ed. (Ottawa: Indian and Northern Affairs, Treaties and Historical Research Centre, 1979), 191.

6 Bartlett, "Parallels in Aboriginal Land Policy in Canada and South Africa," 34.

7 Michael C. Coleman, *Presbyterian Missionary Attitudes Towards American Indians, 1837–1893* (Jackson & London: University Press of Mississippi, 1985), 5–9.

8 Donald B. Smith, *Sacred Feathers: The Reverend Peter Jones (Kahkewaquonaby) and the Mississauga Indians* (Toronto: University of Toronto Press, 1987), 241.

9 *Select Committee Report*, 527. Testimony of Rev. John Beecham, 8 June 1836.

10 Ibid., 529. Extract of a letter addressed to the Reverend John Beecham, by the Chippeway Indian Chief Kahkeaquonaby, otherwise known as Peter Jones; dated at Credit Mission, Upper Canada, 16 February, 1836.

11 John MacLean, *Canadian Savage Folk: The Natives of Canada* (Toronto: Thomas Briggs, 1896), 547.

12 Canada. *Department of Indian Affairs Annual Report*, 1920 (Ottawa: King's Printer, 1920), 7.

13 Eleanor Brass, *I Walked in Two Worlds* (Calgary: Glenbow Museum, 1987), 71.

14 NAC. RG 10, Volume 6811, File 470-2-3, Pt. II, 7 March 1946. Letter from C. Wilmott Maddison, Vice President and Commentator of the Army, Navy and Air Force Veterans Association in Canada, Vancouver Unit Number 277 to J. Allison Glen, Minister of Indian Affairs Branch, Department of Mines and Resources.

15 Willard W. Beatty, "The Goal of Indian Assimilation," *Canadian Journal of Economics and Political Science* 12 (1946): 339.

16 Canada. Parliament. House of Commons Debates. 15 May 1951, Vol. II, 3072.

17 Canada. Parliament. House of Commons Debates, 21 June 1950, Vol. IV, 3965.

18 Canada. Parliament. House of Commons Debates, 21 June 1950, Vol. II, 3976.

19 Jean Chrétien, "Statement of the Government of Canada on Indian Policy,1969." Presented to the First Session of the Twenty-eighth Parliament, by the Honourable Jean Chrétien, Minister of Indian Affairs and Northern Development, 5.

20 Bruce Clark, *Native Liberty, Crown Sovereignty: The Existing Aboriginal Right of Self-Government in Canada* (Montreal and Kingston: McGill-Queen's University Press, 1990), 199.

21 By attaching a number of ingenious conditions to the franchise, 99 percent of voters in 1907 were white; only 6 Africans managed to avoid restrictions. See John Dugard, *Human Rights and the South African Legal Order* (Princeton, NJ: Princeton University Press, 1978), 18.

22 Ibid.,19.

23 André Odendaal, *Vukani Bantu! The Beginnings of Black Protest Politics in South Africa to 1912* (Cape Town: David Philip, 1984), 37.

24 Cited in Denoon, *A Grand Illusion*, 32.

25 Cited in John Eddy and Deryck Schreuder, eds, *The Rise of Colonial Nationalism: Australia, New Zealand, Canada and South Africa First Assert their Nationalities, 1880–1914* (Sydney: Allen & Unwin, 1988), 218.

26 Cited in Mostert, *Frontiers*, 1275.

27 Jordan K. Ngubane, *An African Explains Apartheid* (London: Pall Mall Press, 1963), 12.

28 Mzala, *Gatsha Buthelezi: Chief with a Double Agenda* (London: Zed Books, 1988), 31.

29 Cited in Davenport, *South Africa*, 134.

30 *Natal. Kaffir Commission Report*, 1853, 47, cited in H. J. Simons, *African Women: Their Legal Status in South Africa* (London: C. Hurst, 1968), 22.

31 Ibid., 21.

32 Daryl M. Balia, *Black Methodists and White Supremacy in South Africa* (Durban: Madiba Publishers for the Institute of Black Research, University of Natal, 1991), 63.

33 Blue Book on Native Affairs, Cape of Good Hope. Report of Chief Magistrate Fitz E.C. Bell, District of Kentani, 4 January 1893.

34 Monica Wilson, "The Growth of Peasant Communities," in Monica Wilson and Leonard Thompson, eds., *The Oxford History of South Africa*, volume 2, 1870–1966 (Oxford: University of Oxford Press, 1971), 65.

35 Cited in Odendaal, *Vukani Bantu!*, 140.

36 Union of South Africa. U.G. 2. 6/11: Stone to Colonial Secretary, Lord Glenelg, 29 July 1903, cited in Denoon, *A Grand Illusion*, 98.

37 Union of South Africa. *The Union Statutes, 1910–1947*. Classified and Annotated. Reprint of vol. 3 (Cape Town: Government Printer, 1950), 531.

38 Cited in John W. Cell, *The Highest Form of White Supremacy: The Origins of Segregation in South Africa and the American South* (Cambridge: Cambridge University Press, 1982), 225.

39 Colin Bundy, *The Rise and Fall of the South African Peasantry* (London: Heinemann, 1979), 239.

40 See Carter, *Lost Harvests*, 156.

41 See Bundy, *The Rise and Fall of the South African Peasantry*, 210. Also see Native Labour in South Africa. Report of a Public Meeting Convened jointly by the Aborigines Protection Society and the British and Foreign Anti-Slavery Society held at Claxton Hall, Westminster, 29 April 1903. (Reprinted by the State Library, Pretoria, 1964.)

42 Monica Wilson, " The Growth of Peasant Communities," in Wilson, *Oxford History of South Africa*, vol. 2, 55.

43 Van Onselen, *The Seed is Mine*, 6.

44 Timothy Keegan, introduction to *Natives Land Act 1913: Specific Cases of Evictions and Hardships, etc.* collected and compiled by R. W. Msimang (Cape Town: Friends of South African Library, 1996), vi.

45 Sol T. Plaatje, *Native Life in South Africa* (Harlow, England: Longman, 1987), 265.

46 Laurine Platzky and Cherryl Walker, *The Surplus People: Forced Removals in South Africa* (Johannesburg: Ravan Press for the Surplus People Project, 1985), 38.

47 Allen Cook, *Akin to Slavery: Prison Labour in South Africa* (London: International Defence and Aid Fund for Southern Africa, 1982), 2.

48 Philip Frankel, "The Politics of Passes: Control and Change in South Africa," *The Journal of Modern African Studies* 17, no. 2 (June 1979): 201.

49 G. Eloff, *Rasse en Rassevermenging* (Races and Race Mixing), cited in Leonard Thompson, *The Political Mythology of Apartheid* (New Haven, CT: Yale University Press, 1985), 41.

50 Cited in Barbara Rogers, *Divide and Rule: South Africa's Bantustans* (London: International Defence and Aid Fund for Southern Africa, 1980), 8.

51 Cited in Brian Bunting, *The Rise of the South African Reich* (London: International Defence and Aid Fund for Southern Africa, 1984), 129.

52 D. Hobart Houghton, *The Tomlinson Commission: A Summary of the Findings and Recommendations in the Tomlinson Commission Report* (Johannesburg: South African Institute of Race Relations, 1956), 3–4.

53 Ibid., 14.

54 Mbeki, *South Africa: The Peasants' Revolt*, 16.

55 *Nelson Mandela, The Struggle is my Life: His speeches and writings brought together.* (London: International Defence & Aid Fund for Southern Africa, 1978), 61–61.

56 Cited in Cosmas Desmond, *The Discarded People: An Account of African Resettlement in South Africa* (Middlesex, England: Penguin, 1971), 33.

57 Cited in Rogers, *Divide and Rule*, 17.

58 Cell, *The Highest Form of White Supremacy*, 7. See also Jim Hoagland, *South Africa: Civilizations in Conflict* (Boston: Houghton Mifflin, 1972), xxii.

59 See George M. Fredrickson, *White Supremacy: A Comparative Study in American and South African History* (New York & Oxford: Oxford University Press, 1981).

60 Jack and Ray Simons, *Class and Colour in South Africa 1850–1950* (London: International Defence and Aid Fund, 1983), 7.

61 Odendaal, *Vukani Bantu!*, 63.

62 Ibid., 6.

63 Cited in ibid., 273.

64 The Native Commissioner in Witzieshoek, Mr M. Smit, stopped pension payments to residents when he discovered that some of the money was being spent on paying a lawyer to fight the case of a suspended teacher. See RG 10, Vol. 8588, File 1/1-10-4, Pt. 1. Confidential Report of the High Commissioner for Canada, Pretoria, South Africa, 21 December 1950.

65 Cited in Anthony Sampson, *Mandela: The Authorized Autobiography* (London, England: Harper Collins, 1999), 92.

66 *Nelson Mandela: The Struggle is my Life*, 84.

67 Proclamation R400 gave the Transkei police the right to detain persons without trial and extended a number of arbitrary powers to the chiefs.

68 Rogers, *Divide and Rule*, 75.

69 Mbeki, *The Peasants' Revolt*, 137.

70 Ibid., 22.

71 The fact that the violent attacks by hostel dwellers were orchestrated by the apartheid state as part of the contest for power between Inkatha and the African National Congress was exposed in the Goldstone Commission Report (1992) and later in the hearings of the TRC. See, for example, Kadar Asmal, Louise Asmal and Ronald Saresh Roberts. *Reconciliation Through Truth: A Reckoning of Apartheid s Criminal Governance* (Cape Town: David Philip in association with Mayibuye Books, 1996), 109.

72 Extract from President Nelson Rolihlahla Mandela's address to the Constitutional Assembly after the members had voted their approval of the constitution on May 8, 1996. Cited in *The Making of the Constitution: The Story of South Africa's Constitutional Assembly, May 1994 to December 1996* (Cape Town: Published for the Constitutional Assembly by Churchill Murray Publications, March 1997), 6.

73 *Citizens Plus*, Response of the Indian Association of Alberta to the Rt. Hon. P. E. Trudeau and the Government of Canada, 1970, 19–20.

74 Peter H. Russell, *Constitutional Odyssey: Can Canadians Become a Sovereign People?* (Toronto: University of Toronto Press, 1992), 94.

75 Thomas R. Berger, *A Long and Terrible Shadow: White Values, Native Rights in the Americas 1492–1992* (Vancouver: Douglas & McIntyre; Seattle: University of Washington Press, 1991), 153.

CHAPTER FOUR: LITIGATION

1 *Calder v. Attorney General of British Columbia* (1973) S.C.R. 313 at 156 cited in Dickason, *Canada's First Nations*, 5th ed., 349.

2 The Bear Island Decision, *Ontario Reports*, second series, 49, part 7, 17 May 1985: 353–490 cited in ibid., 333.

3 Christopher McKee, *Treaty Talks in British Columbia: Negotiating a Mutually Beneficial Future* (Vancouver: UBC Press, 1996), 28. See also, Augie Fleras and Jean Leonard Elliott, *The Nations Within : Aboriginal-State Relations in Canada, the United States and New Zealand* (Toronto: Oxford University Press, 1992), 44–45.

4 *R v. Van Der Peet* (1996) 2 S.C.R. 507, para 30 cited in *Delgamuukw v. British Columbia* (1997) 3 S.C.R. 1010, File 23799.

5 Gisday Wa and Delgam Uukw, *The Spirit in the Land*, 11–12.

6 Ibid., 66.

7 The spelling of the name "Gitxsan" has replaced the former "Gitksan" and the name "Carrier" is no longer used by the Wet'suwet'en. See Don Monet and Skanu'u (Ardythe

Wilson), *Colonialism on Trial: Indigenous Land Rights and the Gitsxan and Wet'suwet'en Sovereignty Case* (Philadelphia, PA and Gabriola Island, B.C.: New Society Publishers, 1992), 15.

8 Kenny (Earl) Muldoe inherited the name of Delgam Uukw and all its duties from Albert Tait, who died before the trial began.

9 In his remarks at the opening of the case in Smithers, Wet'suwet'en Chief Gisday Wa pointed out that the Smithers courthouse itself stood on the land of the Wet'suwet'en Chief Gyolughet, in Kyas Yux, also known as Chief Woos' House. See Gisday Wa and Delgam Uukw, *The Spirit in the land*, 5.

10 Ibid., 7–9.

11 *Delgamuukw v. British Columbia* (1997) 3 S.C.R. 1010, File #23799.

12 Gisday Wa and Delgam Uukw, *The Spirit in the Land*, 92.

13 Ibid., 93.

14 Stan Persky, com., *Delgamuukw: The Supreme Court of Canada Decision on Aboriginal Title* (Vancouver: Douglas & McIntyre; Greystone Books, David Suzuki Foundation, 1998), 49.

15 Ibid., 12–13.

16 Ibid., 19.

17 Ibid., 16.

18 Ibid., 13.

19 Ministry of Forestry / Treaty Negotiations Office, Government of British Columbia. News Release, "Gitxsan Agreement is Economic Step Forward in Northwest," 1 June 2003.

20 See Surplus People Project, *Land Claims in Namaqualand* (Cape Town: Surplus People Project, 1995), 34.

21 Cape Archives. Letter Book re Namaqualand. SBK 5/1/1, 154. Letter to the Hon. Colonial Secretary, Josias Rivers, Civil Commissioner, Springfontein, 28 April 1857.

22 *Report of Surveyor General Charles Bell on the Copper Fields of Little Namaqualand, 1855*, cited in Surplus People Project, *Land Claims in Namaqualand*, 35.

23 Surveyor S. Melville's conclusions may have been influenced by a letter from the civil commissioner in Springbokfontein, J. T. Eustace who wrote to Melville in 1888. Referring to the fertility of the Orange River mouth, Eustace writes: "While in no sense advising that the Native population be forbidden use of the land they are justly entitled to, I think with increasing European and a decreasing Native population the sooner the boundaries of their larger location be defined the better." SG 1/1/1/93, 16 May 1888 1/SBK Cited in Surplus People Project, *Land Claims in Namaqualand*, 36.

24 U.G. Coloured Mission Stations, Reserves and Settlements. Inter-Departmental Inquiry, Section 1, 1945, 11.

25 South African Archives (Central Archives Depot, Pretoria) TES 2607 File No. F10/217, cited in Surplus People Project, *Land Claims in Namaqualand*, 38.

26 Peter Carstens, *In the Company of Diamonds: De Beers, Kleinzee, and the Control of a Town* (Athens, OH: Ohio University Press, 2001), 110.

27 Section 2 of the Alexander Bay Development Corporation Act 46 of 1989 established Alexkor as a corporate body and provided for the transfer to it of all assets, liabilities, rights and obligations of the state in the State Alluvial Diggings which the Minister (of Economic Affairs) with the concurrence of the Minister of Finance may determine. See Land Claims Court, Case Number LCC 151/98. Summary of the Plaintiffs Submission, 57.

28 The sixth plaintiff is listed as "The Adult Members of the Richtersveld Community." It was agreed between the parties that the persons on the list are inhabitants of the Richtersveld Reserve. The list was up-dated to reflect the changes which occurred in the community since its original submission due to deaths, people moving in or out, or children growing up and becoming adult members of the community. See ibid., 3.

29 The state-run mine Alexkor is supposed to pay 30 percent of its profits into the Alexkor Development Trust. But, according to the mine, it makes no profit and the fund is therefore dormant. See Paul Weinberg, *Once We Were Hunters: A Journey with Africa s Indigenous People* (Amsterdam: Mets and Schilt; Cape Town: David Philip, 2000), 68.

30 Ibid., 68–69.

31 During 1998–2000, Ms. Berzborn did extensive research (including anthropological fieldwork) on the social and economic structures and land use patterns prevalent in the Richtersveld. To facilitate her task, she learnt Nama and Afrikaans. She then lived with a family and moved about with them. See Land Claims Court. Case Number: LCC 151/98. Judgement of Gildenhuys, AJ, 22 March 2001, 9.

32 Land Claims Court. Summary of Plaintiffs Submissions, Case LCC 151/98, 73.

33 Ibid., 25.

34 Ibid., 77.

35 The plaintiffs claimed ownership of the subject land by virtue of the fact that the Common Law of the Cape colony when the Richtersveld was annexed in 1847 was Roman Dutch Law. Under Roman Dutch Law, the ownership of *terra nullius* can be acquired by *occupatio*. The land claimed by the Richtersveld community was *terra nullius* in the sense that nobody owned it, and thus they acquired ownership of the land by right of occupation. See Land Claims Court. LCC 151/98, 32.

36 *Calder v. Attorney-General of British Columbia* (1-DLR (3d) 145 (SCC)98-199 and *Guerin v. The Queen* (1984) 13 DLR 321 (SCC) 336 cited in ibid., 38.

37 Land Claims Court. LCC 151/98, 32.

38 *R v. Adams [1996] 3 S.C.R.* cited in ibid., 47.

39 Land Claims Court. LCC 151/98, 30.

40 In his ruling, Lord Sumner stated that the plaintiffs in this case were " incapable of arguing, and perhaps unconscious of possessing, any case at all… Some of the tribes are so low in the scale of social organization that their usages and conceptions of rights and duties are not to be reconciled with the institutions and laws of civilized society. Such a gulf cannot be bridged." See *In re Southern Rhodesia* (1919) AC 211 (PC) cited in ibid., 39.

41 *Alexkor Ltd v. Richtersveld Community and Others*, Constitutional Court – CCT 19/03.

42 Rory Carrole, "South Africa: Tribe Wins Rights to Diamond-Rich Land," *The Guardian*, London, 15 October 2003.

43 Patrick Macklem, "First Nations Self-Government and the Borders of the Canadian Legal Imagination," *McGill Law Journal* 36 (1991): 382.

44 Brent Olthuis, "Defrosting Delgamuukw (or How to Reject a Frozen Rights Interpretation of Aboriginal Title in Canada)," *National Journal of Constitutional Law/ Revue Nationale de Droit Constitutionnel* 12 (2000–2001): 422–23.

45 David W. Elliot, "Delgamuukw: Back to Court?" *Manitoba Law Journal* 26, no. 1 (2000): 131–32.

46 Gurston Dacks, "British Columbia after the *Delgamuukw* Decision: Land Claims and other Processes," *Canadian Public Policy - Analyse de Politique* 28, no. 2 (2002): 246.

CHAPTER FIVE: NEGOTIATING RESTITUTION

1 *Surplus People Project Annual Report, 2000* (Athlone, Cape Town: Surplus People Project, 2001), 1.

2 Andries du Toit, " The End of Restitution: Getting Real about Land Claims." Paper prepared for the Land and Agrarian Reform Conference, Pretoria, 26–28 July 1999.

3 *Transvaal Agricultural Union v. Minister of Land Affairs and the Commission on Restitution of Land Rights (1996)* Constitutional Court - CCT 21/96.

4 Arthur Ndlovu, "Land Claim a Resounding Success." Press Release issued by the Department of Housing and Land Administration, Mpumalanga Province, 3 February 2001.

5 Chris McGreal, "White Farmers denounce ANC land grab : South Africa is accused of following Zimbabwe's example after a farm is returned to its original owners." *The Guardian*, 17 March 2001.

6 Danielle Owen, "South Africa's Gender-unfriendly land reform programme," *Woza Forum On-line*, 23 March 2001.

7 Catherine Cross and Michelle Friedman, "Women and tenure: marginality and the left-hand power" in Shamim Meer, ed., *Women, Land and Authority: Perspectives from South Africa* (Claremont, South Africa: David Philip, 1997), 17.

8   Mariette Louw, "Farmers 'must ask less for land,'" *Beeld*, 14 April 2003.
9   The Black Sash was an organization of white women that conducted silent protests against the unjust laws of apartheid and assisted black South Africans in a variety of ways.
10 African National Congress. Statement to the Truth and Reconciliation Commission, August 1996.
11 Transvaal Rural Action Committee, 1985, 21, cited in Elaine Unterhalter, *Forced Removal: The Division, Segregation and Control of South Africa* (London: International Defence and Aid Fund, 1987), 118.
12 Marlene Winberg and Paul Weinberg. *Back to the Land* (Johannesburg: The Porcupine Press, 1996), 45.
13 Unterhalter, *Forced Removals*, 118.
14 Winberg and Weinberg, *Back to the Land*, 42.
15 Ibid., 44.
16 Interview with Z. Hadebe by Cherryl Walker cited in Cherryl Walker, "The Cremin Land Claim: From Resistance to Reconstruction." Paper presented at the conference "Ten Years of Democracy in Southern Africa" held at Queen's University, Kingston, Ontario on 3 May 2004, 19.
17 Rodney Davenport: personal communication, April 2000.
18 Surplus People Project, *Land Claims in Namaqualand*, 106.
19 Winberg and Weinberg, *Back to the Land*, 12–14.
20 Ibid., 74.
21 Ibid., 78.
22 Donovan Kotze, "Organic Gold," *Mail & Guardian*, Johannesburg, 27 May 2004.
23 Thembela Kepe, "Land Restitution and Biodiversity Conservation in South Africa: An Analysis of Challenges and the Case of Mkambati, Eastern Cape Province," Paper presented at the conference "Ten Years of Democracy in Southern Africa," held at Queen's University, Kingston, Ontario, 3 May 2004.
24 Lubicon Lake Cree Nation, Band Prepared History, 1989, 11, cited in Rosemary Brown, "The Exploration of the Oil and Gas Frontier: Its Impact on Lubicon Cree Lake Women," in Christine Miller and Patricia Chuchryk, eds., *Women of the First Nations: Power, Wisdom and Strength*, (Winnipeg: University of Manitoba Press, 1996), 153.
25 John Goddard, *Last Stand of the Lubicon Cree* (Vancouver & Toronto: Douglas & McIntyre, 1991), 210.
26 Ibid., 210.
27 Ibid., 210.
28 Ibid., 213.
29 Paul Bucci, "Minister Backs Lubicon," *Edmonton Sun*, 3 February 1993.
30 Amnesty International, Canada, "Time is Wasting : Respect for the Land Rights of the Lubicon Cree Long Overdue." (London, United Kingdom: International Secretariat, AI Index: AMR 20/001/2003, April 2003), 9.
31 United Nations: Commission on Human Rights. Indigenous Issues. "Human Rights and Indigenous Issues: Report of the Special Rapporteur on the Situation of human rights and fundamental freedoms of Indigenous People, Rodolpho Stavenhagen." Addendum: Mission to Canada. E/CN.4/2005/88/Add.3, 2 December 2004.

CHAPTER SIX: SELF-GOVERNMENT

1   John Ibbitson, "First Native Bank a Canadian First," *The Gazette*, Montreal, 10 December 1996.
2   William I.C. Wuttunee, *Ruffled Feathers: Indians in Canadian Society* (Calgary: Bell Books, 1971), 111.
3   J. Rick Ponting and Roger Gibbins, "Thorns in the Bed of Roses: A Socio-Political View of the Problems of Indian Government" in Leroy Little Bear, Menno Boldt and J. Anthony Long eds., *Pathways to Self-Determination : Canadian Indians and the Canadian State* (Toronto: University of Toronto Press, 1984), 125–34.

4   See for example *Native Women's Association of Canada Newsletter*, January 1992, 7.

5   Frank Cassidy, ed. *Aboriginal Self-Determination* (Halifax: Institute of Research on Public Policy, 1991), cited in Stephen Brooks, *Public Policy in Canada: An Introduction*, 3rd ed., (Toronto: Oxford University Press, 1998), 213.

6   See, for example, Brooks, *Public Policy in Canada*, 204. See also John Stackhouse, "Canada's Apartheid," a 14-part series of articles published in the *Globe and Mail*, November 3 to December 15, 2001.

7   Douglas Sanders, "An Uncertain Path: The Aboriginal Constitutional Conferences," in Joseph M. Weiler & Robin M. Elliot, eds. *Litigating the Values of a Nation: The Canadian Charter of Rights and Freedoms* (Toronto: 1986), 22–23, cited in Alan C. Cairns, *Disruptions: Constitutional Struggles, from the Charter to Meech Lake* (Toronto: McClelland & Stewart, 1991), 210.

8   Canada. Indian Self-Government in Canada, *Minutes and Proceedings of the Special Committee on Indian Self-Government*, no. 40, 12 and 20 October 1983.

9   Miller, *Skyscrapers Hide the Heavens*, 246.

10 Cited in John P. Taylor and Gary Paget, " Federal/Provincial Responsibility and the Sechelt (Draft)." Paper prepared for the National Conference on Federal and Provincial Governments and Aboriginal Peoples held at Carleton University, Ottawa, October 1988.

11 David Crombie, " Policy Statement on Indian Self-Government in Canada: Minister of Indian Affairs and Northern Development." (Ottawa: Department of Indian Affairs and Northern Development, 1986).

12 Taylor and Paget, "Federal/Provincial Responsibility and the Sechelt," 1988.

13 Print-making, while it capitalized on traditional skills, was only developed after European contact and paper became available.

14 Inuit Tapirisat of Canada, *The Inuit of Canada*, 5.

15 There were also over-lapping claims from other non-Inuit groups, such as the Chipenyan nation, which had to be considered.

16 Nungaq, "Kicking the Tires of History," 32.

17 Nunavut. *Nunavut Implementation Commission: A Comprehensive Report from the Nunavut Implementation Commission to the Department of Indian Affairs and Northern Development, Government of the Northwest Territories and Nunavut Tunngavik Incorporated concerning the establishment of the Nunavut government*, 1995, 2.

18 Nunavut. *Annual Report of the Nunavut Tunngavik Incorporated*, 1993.

19 *Nunavut Implementation Commission: A Comprehensive Report*, 1995, 6.

20 Ibid., 67.

21 Rosalie Kingwill, "Land Issues Scoping Study: Communal Land Tenure Areas." Paper prepared for the Department for International Development (RFID) Southern Africa, November 2003.

22 M. Mamdani, *Citizen and Subject: Contemporary Africa and the Legacy of Late Colonialism* (Princeton, NJ: Princeton University Press, 1996), 23, cited in Lungisile Ntsebeza, "Traditional Authorities, Local Government, and Land Rights," Paper presented at the Land and Agrarian Reform Conference held in Pretoria, 26–28 July 1999, 3.

23 Ibid., 4.

24 Ibid.,14.

25 Sipho Sibanda, "Proposals for the Management of Land Rights in Rural South Africa." Paper presented at the Land and Agrarian Reform Conference held in Pretoria, 26–28 July 1999, 1.

26 Drew Forrest, "Uproar over Land Bill," *Mail & Guardian*, Johannesburg, 23 November 2001.

27 Thoko Didiza, Speech on Communal Land Rights Bill, 12 February 2004.

CHAPTER SEVEN: RESTORING DIGNITY

1   Mathatha Tsedu, untitled article prepared for a seminar attended by academics, journalists, artists and writers on the social engagement of African intellectuals, held on the island of Gorée off the coast of Senegal, 20 December 1998.

2   Assembly of First Nations. Speech by Chief Matthew Coon Come in Fort McMurray, 26
    October 2000, 2.
3   United Nations. Commission on Human Rights. "Human Rights and Indigenous Issues:
    Report of the Special Rapporteur on the Situation of Human Rights and Fundamental
    Freedoms of Indigenous People, Rodolfo Stavenhagen." Addendum: Mission to Canada,
    E/CN.4/2005/88/Add.3, 2 December 2005.
4   From 1980–1985 the infant mortality rate among First Nations was 19.6 per 1,000 births.
    During the same period, the rate for non-natives was 7.9 per 1,000 births. See Geoffrey
    York, *The Dispossessed: Life and Death in Native Canada* (London: Vintage, 1990), 75.
5   John R. Williams, "Ethics and Human Rights in South African Medicine," *Canadian
    Medical Association Journal* 162, no. 8 (18 April 2000): 1169.
6   Cited in Canada. *Royal Commission on Aboriginal Peoples*, vol. 3 (Ottawa: Minister of
    Supply and Services Canada, 1996), 17.
7   Will Horter, "UN Report confirms Exploitation of First Nations," *Peace, Earth and Justice
    News*, Victoria, B.C., 13 April 2005.
8   See Geoffrey York, *The Dispossessed: Life and Death in Native Canada* (London: Vintage,
    1990), 76.
9   George Erasmus, "Twenty Years of Disappointed Hopes," in Boyce Richardson, ed.,
    Drumbeat: Anger and Renewal in Indian Country (Toronto: Summerhill Press, The
    Assembly of First Nations, 1989), 1–2.
10 "Harry Oppenheimer Obituary," *The Economist*, 26 August 2000, 76.
11 John Pilger, article in *Mail and Guardian*, Johannesburg, 21 April 1998.
12 South African Institute of Race Relations, *Survey of Race Relations in South Africa*,
    Johannesburg, 1983, cited in Roger Omond, *The Apartheid Handbook: A Guide to South
    Africa's Everyday Racial Policies* (Harmondsworth, England: Penguin, 1986), 80.
13 South Africa. House of Assembly Debates, 21 February 1985, col. 218 cited in ibid., 81.
14 Laurel Baldwin-Ragaven, Jeanelle de Gruchy and Leslie London, *An Ambulance of the
    Wrong Colour: Health Professionals, Human Rights and Ethics in South Africa* (Cape Town:
    University of Cape Town Press, 1999), 3.
15 Robert Carty, "Whose Hand on the Tap?" CBC Radio, February 2003.
16 Nicol Degli Innocenti, "South Africa proceeds with Launch of Free Aids Drugs," *Financial
    Times*, 20 November 2003.
17 Anna Strebel. "Women and Aids: Women are more Vulnerable," *Sash* 36, no. 3 (January
    1994): 38.
18 The construction of the hostels, and the regulations governing such accommodation, were
    provided for under the Natives (Urban Areas) Act 21 of 1923. In the 1960s, 166 dormitories
    (hostels) were built every year, housing 2,652 African men per hostel. In 1965–66, a total
    of 61,620 persons (listed by tribal affiliation) were accommodated in single-sex hostels
    for migrant workers in urban locations across the country. See Republic of South Africa.
    Bantu Resettlement Board Annual Report, 1964–65, 76.
19 Neville Alexander, who spent ten years as a prisoner on Robben Island (1964–1974),
    confirmed the importance of imagination in coping with space constraints: "One creates
    imaginary boundaries around oneself. Body language is an important part of the strategies
    used. Just turning one's shoulders slightly establishes private conversation space." See
    Mamphele Ramphele, *A Bed Called Home: Life in the Migrant Labour Hostels of Cape Town*
    (Cape Town: David Philip, 1993), 23.
20 Ibid., 134.
21 Ibid.,116.
22 Peter Carstens, *The Queen's People: A Study of Hegemony, Coercion, and Accommodation
    among the Okanagan of Canada* (Toronto: University of Toronto Press, 1991), 287–88.
23 Maria Campbell, *Half-Breed* (Halifax, NS: Goodread Biographies, 1973), 159.
24 Peter Carstens, "An Essay on Suicide and Disease in Canadian Indian Reserves: Bringing
    Durkheim Back in," *The Canadian Journal of Native Studies* 20, no. 2 (2000): 327.
25 S. Steele, *The Content of our Character: A New Vision of Race in America* (New York: St.
    Martin's Press, 1990), cited in Ramphele, *A Bed Called Home*, 117.

26 Maura Andrews, Charlie Shackleton and Andrew Ainslie, "Land Use and Rural Livelihoods: Have They Been Enhanced through Land Reform?" Policy Brief: Debating Land Reform and Rural Development, Programme for Land and Agrarian Studies, School of Government, University of the Western Cape, No. 5, August 2003.

27 David Mayson, "Joint Ventures," *Policy Brief: Debating Land Reform and Rural Development*, Programme for Land and Agrarian Studies (PLAAS), School of Government, University of the Western Cape, No. 8, February 2004.

28 United Nations. Human Rights Commission. "Human Rights and Indigenous Issues," 7.

29 Alan C. Cairns, *Citizens Plus: Aboriginal Peoples and the Canadian State* (Vancouver: UBC Press, 2000), 45.

30 George Soros, Chairman's Statement, "Building Open Societies." *Soros Foundations Report, 1995*, 16.

CHAPTER EIGHT: RECONCILIATION

1 RCAP. *People to People, Nation to Nation: Highlights from the Report of the Royal Commission on Aboriginal Peoples* (Ottawa: Minister of Supply and Services, 1996), 1.

2 Examples of previous inquiries are: the Royal Commission on the Settlement of Indian Reserves in the Province of British Columbia (1916); Royal Commission on the Condition of Half-Breeds in Alberta (1934); Mackenzie Valley Pipeline Inquiry (1974–1977); and the Special Parliamentary Committee on Indian Self-government (1983).

3 Determined to protect their ancestral land from being taken over for the extension of a golf course by the municipality of Oka, the Mohawk of Kanesetake confronted first the Quebec police and then the Canadian Armed Forces. When the neighbouring reserve of Kahnawake built barricades across the Mercier Bridge (obstructing commuter traffic to and from Montreal) in solidarity with the people of Kanesetake, news coverage showed angry "white" Canadians stoning the cars of Mohawk residents (many of them elderly and ill) leaving the reserve under police escort. See Dickason, *Canada's First Nations*, 3rd ed., 329.

4 Royal Commission on Aboriginal Peoples. *People to People, Nation to Nation: Highlights from the Royal Commission on Aboriginal Affairs* (Ottawa: Minister of Supply & Services, 1997), 126.

5 RG 33, File 3038-2, RCAP Public Hearings, Winnipeg, Manitoba, 22 April 1992 (Ottawa: Libraxus Inc. CD-ROM, 1997).

6 RG 33, File 3014-2, RCAP Hearings, Kingsclear, N.B., 19 May 1992 (Ottawa: Libraxus Inc. CD-ROM, 1997).

7 RCAP. *People to People*, 147.

8 RG 33, File 3090-2, RCAP Hearings, Sudbury, Ontario, 31 May 1993 (Ottawa: Libraxus Inc. CD-ROM, 1997).

9 RG 33, File 3031-2, RCAP Hearings, Teslin, Yukon, 26 May 1992 (Ottawa: Libraxus Inc. CD-ROM, 1997).

10 United Nations. Commission on Human Rights. "Human Rights and Indigenous Issues," 6.

11 RCAP. *People to People*, 116.

12 Roland Chrisjohn and Sherri L.Young with Michael Maraun, *The Circle Game: Shadows and Substance in the Indian Residential School Experience in Canada* (Penticton, B.C.: Theytus Books, 1997), 110.

13 For detailed descriptions of the situation in South Africa on the eve of the 1994 elections see, for example, George Bizos, *No One to Blame? In Pursuit of Justice in South Africa* (Cape Town: David Philip Publishers & Bellville: Mayibuye Books, University of the Western Cape, 1998), 231. Also, Allister Sparks, *Tomorrow is Another Country: The Inside Story of South Africa s Negotiated Revolution* (Sandton: Struik Book Distributors, 1994), 187.

14 Research Institute on Christianity in South Africa, Faith Communities and Apartheid. A Report prepared for the Truth and Reconciliation Commission, cited in James

Cochrane, John de Gruchy and Stephen Martin, eds., *Facing the Truth: South African Faith Communities and the Truth and Reconciliation Commission* (Cape Town: David Philip; Athens, OH: Ohio University Press, 1999), 67.

15 Antjie Krog, *Country of my Skull* (Johannesburg: Random House, 1998), Publisher s Note, vii.

16 Elizabeth Kiss, "National Reconciliation: Is Truth Enough?" *The Economist*, August/ September 2000, 72.

17 Among these were the sisters of Ashley Kriel when his killer, the notorious police torturer Jeffrey Benzien was granted amnesty for his death. See Orr, *From Biko to Basson* (Saxonwold, South Africa: Contra, 2000), 123.

18 Ibid.,123.

19 Alex Boraine, Janet Levy and Ronel Scheffer, eds., *Dealing with the Past: Truth and Reconciliation in South Africa*, 2nd ed. (Cape Town: Institute for Democracy in South Africa, 1997), xii.

20 *Transforming Society through Reconciliation: Myth or Reality?* Proceedings of a public discussion on the Truth and Reconciliation Commission held at the University of Cape Town, 12 March 1998, 12–13.

21 Antjie Krog, *Country of my Skull*, 278–79.

22 *Transforming Society through Reconciliation*, public discussion, 14–15.

23 Editorial, *The Argus*, Cape Town, 12 August 1999.

24 Emsie Ferreira, "Government Spits in Face of Apartheid Victims," *Mail and Guardian*, Johannesburg, 28 April 2000.

25 Alex Boraine et al., *Dealing with the Past*, 122–23.

26 Breytenbach, Appendix 1 in ibid., 161.

27 F. W de Klerk, *The Last Trek – A New Beginning: The Autobiography* (New York: St. Martin's Press, 1999), 382.

28 Ibid., 381.

29 Verne Harris, " 'They Should Have Destroyed More': The Destruction of Public Records by the South African State in the Final Years of Apartheid, 1990–1994." Paper presented to the Conference "TRC: Commissioning the Past," held at the University of the Witwatersrand, Johannesburg, 11–14 June 1999, 14.

30 South Africa. *Truth and Reconciliation Commission Report*, vol. 5, 345 cited in ibid., 14.

31 Boraine et al., *Dealing with the Past*, 29.

32 Ibid., 23–24.

33 DIAND. Statement by Bob Watts, Assistant Deputy Minister, Lands and Trusts Services, Department of Indian and Northern Affairs Canada, to the United Nations Working Group on Indigenous Populations, 16th session, Geneva, 28 July 1998.

34 Laura Landen, "Legacy of Racism," *The Ottawa Citizen*, 9 September 2000, B3.

35 Ibid.

36 Cited in Boyce Richardson, *People of Terra Nullius: Betrayal and Rebirth in Aboriginal Canada* (Vancouver: Douglas & McIntyre, 1993), 102.

37 Don Posterski, "A Conversation with Elijah Harper," *Envision* (World Vision Canada) (Spring 2000): 10–11.

38 Paul Tennant, "Aboriginal Rights and the Penner Report on Indian Self-Government," in Menno Boldt and Anthony J. Long, eds. *The Quest for Justice: Aboriginal Peoples and Aboriginal Rights* (Toronto: University of Toronto Press, 1985), 327–28.

39 Boraine et al., *Dealing with the Past*, 67–68.

40 Ibid., 128.

41 Aboriginal Rights Coalition. Brief to the United Nations Committee on Human Rights by the Aboriginal Rights Coalition, 26 March 1999.

42 Boraine et al., *Dealing with the Past*, 9.

43 Mosala, "The Meaning of Reconciliation: Black Perspective," *Journal of Theology for Southern Africa* 59 (June 1987): 19–25, cited in Cochrane *et al.*, *Facing the Truth*, 103.

44 RG 33, File 3017-2. RCAP Hearings, Charlottetown, 5 May 1992. Testimony of John Joe Sark, Mi kmaq Grand Council (Ottawa: Libraxus Inc., CD-ROM, 1997).

CONCLUSION

1 Quoted in Winberg and Weinberg, *Back to the Land*, Back Cover.
2 Land Charter: Final List of Demands Adopted at the Community Land Conference (Unedited). A document compiled from demands that were agreed to by 135 communities at the Community Land Conference on 12 February 1994 in the Bloemfontein City Hall, South Africa.
3 Nelson Mandela, "We are Committed to Building a Single Nation in our Country." Speech at rally in Durban, 25 February 1990 in Greg McCartan, *Nelson Mandela: Speeches 1990* (New York: Pathfinder Press, 1990), 34.
4 John Battersby, "Mandela, back in the Maelstrom," *The Christian Science Monitor*, 28 March 2002.
5 Cited in Adrian Hadland and Jovial Rantao, *The Life and Times of Thabo Mbeki* (Rivonia, South Africa: Zebra Press, 1999), 153–58.
6 In 1995 an Afrikaans-speaking performer wrote a one-woman show in which Krotoä is referred to as *onse ma* (our mother). See Carli Coetzee, "Krotoä Remembered: a Mother of Unity, a Mother of Sorrow," in Nuttall and Coetzee, eds., *Negotiating the Past*, 112–19.
7 Feature article, "Museum Offers Chilling Trip into Belly of Apartheid," *Business Day*, Johannesburg, 6 December 2001.
8 Cairns, *Citizens Plus*, 86.
9 RCAP. *People to People*, 126.
10 Ovide Mercredi was speaking at an Indigenous Peoples' Conference "Strengthening the Spirit: Beyond 500 Years" held in Ottawa in November 1991.

APPENDIX: AUSTRALIA AND NEW ZEALAND

1 Reynolds, *The Law of the Land*, 8.
2 Clive Turnbull, *Black War: The Extermination of the Tasmanian Aborigines* (Melbourne and London: F.W. Cheshire, 1948), 8.
3 *Mabo and Others v. Queensland (No. 2) (1992)* 175 C.L.R. 1FC 92/014.
4 Jacqui Katona, "Hylus Marcus Memorial Lecture," delivered in Melbourne, Australia, 1999, 9. *Author's note: Katona, a Mirrar woman born in New South Wales, worked on Australia's Royal Commission into Aboriginal Deaths in Custody and as a "stolen generation" researcher before taking on the work of communicating the Mirrar story to the international community.*
5 The Human Rights and Equal Opportunities Commission of Inquiry report, "Bringing them Home: Report of a National Inquiry into the Separation of Aboriginal and Torres Strait Islander Children from Their Families" was published in 2000.
6 Senator John Herron, Australia's Aboriginal Affairs minister, raised a public outcry by questioning the accuracy of the term "stolen generations" (and thus the legitimacy of the project) in his report to a Senate Committee. See Tony Wright and Kerry Taylor. "Fury over 'stolen' denial" *The Age*, Melbourne, Australia, 3 April 2000, 14.
7 Michael Gordon, "Another blow to process of healing," *The Age*, Melbourne, Australia, 3 April 2000, 9.
8 Apart from incidents involving shooting, kidnapping and thefts, Cook acted at most times with restraint and common sense during his three visits to New Zealand (which he apparently failed to do in Hawaii where he met his death in 1779). See Michael King, *One Thousand Years of Maori History: Nga iwi o te motu* (Aukland: Reed Books, 1997), 25.
9 As Michael King explains it, paradoxically there were no Maori in New Zealand before there were Europeans. New Zealand Polynesians did not begin to use this name for themselves until 1840. "Maori" means "normal" or "usual;" as in "tangata Maori," an ordinary man. There was no need to distinguish such ordinary people from others until the land was shared by others. See ibid., 10.
10 Cited in R. J. Walker, "The Treaty of Waitangi as the Focus of Māori Protest," in Kawhuru, ed., *Waitangi*, 266.

11 Ibid., 269.
12 Ibid., 272.
13 Allan Ward, *A Show of Justice: Racial 'Amalgamation' in Nineteenth Century New Zealand* (Canberra: Australian National University Press, 1974), 308–9.
14 Ibid., 310.
15 Ibid., 312–14.

Bibliography

ARCHIVAL SOURCES

Canada

National Archives of Canada, Ottawa

Records of the Department of Indian Affairs and Northern Development
RG 10, Volume 6823, File 495-5-1, Pt. 1.
RG 10, Volume 7982, File 1/19-2-1, Pts. 1 & 2.
RG 10, Volume 7984, File 1/19-2-10, vol. 1.
RG 10, Volume 8588, File 1/1-10-3, vols. 1-3.
RG 10, Volume 8588, File 1/1-10-4, Pt. 1.
RG 10, Volume 6811, File 470-2-3, Pt. 2.

Royal Commission on Aboriginal Peoples. Hearings (Transcripts)
RG 33, Series 157. File 3014-2
RG 33, Series 157. File 3015-2
RG 33, Series 157. File 3017-2
RG 33, Series 157. File 3031-2
RG 33, Series 157. File 3038-2
RG 33, Series 157. File 3090-2

United Church of Canada Archives, Vancouver
B.C. Conference Archives, Vancouver. Sutherland Papers.

Republic of South Africa

Cape Archives, Cape Town
British and Cape of Good Hope Parliamentary Papers. Blue Book on Native
    Affairs, Cape of Good Hope, 1893.
    ———. Letterbook re Namaqualand. SBK 5/1/1. 1855–1857.
Cape of Good Hope. Glen Grey Commission. Fifth Session of Parliament, CPP.
    1/1/83, 1883
Cape of Good Hope. House of Assembly and Report of Select Committees. Third
    Session of Parliament, Vol. 1, 1806.
Cape of Good Hope. Minutes of Evidence of Select Committee on Namaqualand
    Mission Lands and Reserves, 1 June 1896.
Colonial Office. Aborigines' Protection Society, "The Native Policy of the Dutch
    Boers in the Transvaal," Memorandum to the Earl of Kimberley, Principal
    Secretary of State for the Colonies, 1881.
National Archives of South Africa, Pretoria
BTS Foreign Affairs, File 1/28/3.30. July 1960. Papers of Dirkse van Schalkwyk.

ALPHABETICAL LIST

Aboriginal Rights Coalition. *Brief to the United Nations Committee on Human Rights*. Ottawa, 26 March 1999.

Adams, Howard. *Prison of Grass: Canada from the Native Point of View*. Toronto: General Publishing, 1975.

Angus, Murray. *"...And the last shall be first": Native Policy in an Era of Cutbacks*. Ottawa: The Aboriginal Rights Coalition (Project North), 1990.

The Argus, Cape Town. Editorial. 12 August 1999.

Arnett, Chris. *The Terror of the Coast: Land Alienation and Colonial War on Vancouver Island and the Gulf Islands, 1849–1863*. Vancouver: Talonbooks, 1999.

Asmal, Kadar, Louise Asmal and Ronald Saresh Roberts. *Reconciliation Through Truth: A Reckoning of Apartheid's Criminal Governance*. Cape Town: David Philip in association with Mayibuye Books, 1996.

Balia, Daryl M. *Black Methodists and White Supremacy in South Africa*. Durban: Madiba Publishers for the Institute of Black Research, University of Natal, 1991.

Baldwin-Ragaven, Laurel, Jeannelle de Gruchy, and Leslie London. *An Ambulance of the Wrong Colour: Health Professionals, Human Rights and Ethics in South Africa*. Cape Town: University of Cape Town Press, 1999.

Bannister, S. *Humane Policy; Or Justice to the Aborigines of New Settlements Essential to a due expenditure of British money, and to the best interests of the settlers with suggestions how to civilize the Natives by an improved administration of existing means by S. Bannister, Late Attorney-Governor in New South Wales*. London: 1830; Reprint, 1968.

Barrell, Howard. Article in *The Mail and Guardian*, Johannesburg, 31 January 2000.

Barron, Laurie. "The Indian Pass System in the Canadian West, 1882–1988." *Prairie Forum* 13 (1) Spring 1988: 25–42.

Bartlett, Richard H. *Indian Reserves and Aboriginal Lands in Canada: A Homeland*. Saskatoon: University of Saskatchewan Native Law Centre, 1990.

————. "Parallels in Aboriginal Land Policy in Canada and South Africa." *Canadian Native Law Review* 4, 1988: 1–35.

Battersby, John. "Mandela, Back in the Maelstrom." *The Christian Science Monitor* 28 March 2002.

Beatty, Willard W. "The Goal of Indian Assimilation." *Canadian Journal of Economics and Political Science* 12, 1946: 396–404.

Beinart, William, and Colin Bundy. *Hidden Struggles in Rural South Africa*. London: James Currey, 1987.

Beinart, William, Peter Delius, and Stanley Trapido, eds. *Putting the Plough to the Ground: Accumulation and Dispossession in Rural South Africa, 1850–1930*. Johannesburg: Ravan Press, 1986.

Benson, Mary, ed. *The Sun Will Rise: Statements from the Dock by Southern African Political Prisoners*. Revised ed. London: International Defence and Aid Fund for Southern Africa, 1981.

Berger, Thomas R. *A Long and Terrible Shadow: White Values, Native Rights in the Americas 1492–1992*. Vancouver: Douglas & McIntyre; Seattle: University of Washington Press, 1991.

————. "Native Rights and Self Determination." *The Canadian Journal of Native Studies* III (2) 1983: 363–375.

————. *Northern Frontier, Northern Homeland*. Vols. 1 & 2. Report of the Mackenzie Valley Pipeline Inquiry. Ottawa: Minister of Supply & Services, 1977.

Bethune, Brian. "Mystery of the First North Americans." *Maclean's* 19 March 2001: 2–29.

Bliss, Michael. *Canadian History in Documents, 1763–1966* Toronto: The Ryerson Press, 1966.

Bizos, George. *No One to Blame? Pursuit of Justice in South Africa*. Cape Town: David Philip; Bellville: Mayibuye Books, University of the Western Cape, 1998.

Blackburn, Robin. *The Overthrow of Slavery, 1776–1848*. London: Verso, 1988.

Boldt, Menno and J. Anthony Long with Leroy Little Bear, eds. *The Quest for Justice: Aboriginal Peoples and Aboriginal Rights*. Toronto: University of Toronto Press, 1985.

Bonnycastle, Sir Richard Henry. *Newfoundland in 1842: A Sequel to the Canadas in 1841*. Volume II. London: Henry Colburn, 1842.

Boraine, Alex, Janet Levy and Ronel Scheffer, eds. *Dealing with the Past: Truth and Reconciliation in South Africa*. Johannesburg: IDASA, 1997.

Bourgeault, Ron. "Canada Indians: The South Africa Connection." *Canadian Dimension* 21 (8) 1988: 6–10.

Brass, Eleanor. *I Walked in Two Worlds*. Calgary: Glenbow Museum, 1987.

Bringhurst, Robert. *A Story as Sharp as a Knife: The Classical Haida Myth Tellers and their World*. Vancouver: Douglas & McIntyre, 1999.

Brittain, Victoria. "Truth and Reconciliation in South Africa." *Le Monde diplomatique*, December 1998.

Britz, Rudolph, Hartmut Land and Cornelia Limpricht. *A Concise History of the Rehoboth Basters until 1990*. Verlag, Windhoek, Namibia: Klaus Hess, 1999.

Brody, Hugh. *Maps and Dreams: Indians and the British Columbia Frontier*. Vancouver: Douglas & McIntyre, 1981.

————. *The Other Side of Eden: Hunters, Farmers and the Shaping of the World*. Vancouver: Douglas & McIntyre, 2000.

Brooks, Stephen. *Public Policy in Canada: An Introduction*, 3rd ed. Toronto: Oxford University Press, 1998.

Business Day, Johannesburg. Feature article, "Museum offers Chilling Trip into Belly of Apartheid," 6 December 2001.

Bundy, Colin. *The Rise and Fall of the South African Peasantry*. London: Heinemann, 1979.

Bunting, Brian. *The Rise of the South African Reich*. London: International Defence and Aid Fund for Southern Africa, 1986.

Butler, Jeffrey, Robert I. Rotberg, and John Adams. *The Black Homelands of South Africa: The Political and Economic Development of Bophuthatswana and KwaZulu*. Berkeley: University of California Press, 1977.

Buyers, Robin, and Ann Pohl. "Report from the Coalition for a Public Inquiry into the Death of Dudley George." Submitted to the United Nations Committee on Human Rights, New York, March 1999.

Cairns, Alan C. *Citizens Plus: Aboriginal Peoples and the Canadian State*. Vancouver: UBC Press, 2000.

Canada. Department of Indian Affairs Annual Report, 1920.

————. Department of Indian and Northern Affairs (IANA) Report, "Aboriginal Agenda: Renewing the Partnership," 1997.

Canada. House of Commons Debates, 21 June 1950, Vol. 4, 3965.

———. House of Commons Debates, 15 May 1951, Vol. 2, 3072.

———. The Indian Act: A Simplified Version. Indian and Northern Affairs Canada, Saskatchewan Region, December 1982.

———. Royal Commission on Aboriginal Peoples. *People to People, Nation to Nation: Highlights from the Royal Commission on Aboriginal Affairs*. Ottawa: Minister of Supply & Services, 1997.

———. Royal Commission on Aboriginal Peoples Report. Vols. 1–5. Ottawa: Minister of Supply & Services, 1997.

Canadian Medical Association. *Bridging the Gap: Promoting Health and Healing for Aboriginal Peoples of Canada*. Ottawa: Canadian Medical Association, 1994.

Cardinal, Harold. *The Unjust Society: The Tragedy of Canada's Indians*. Edmonton: Hurtig, 1969; Reprint, 1999.

Carter, Gwendolen M., Thomas Karis, and Newell M. Schultz. *South Africa's Transkei: The Politics of Domestic Colonialism*. London: Heinemann, 1967.

Campbell, Maria. *Half-Breed*. Toronto: McClelland & Stewart, 1973; Reprint, Halifax, NS: Goodread Biographies, 1983.

Carter, Sarah. *Aboriginal People and Colonizers of Western Canada to 1900*. Toronto: University of Toronto Press, 1999.

———. *Lost Harvests: Prairie Indian Reserve Farmers and Government Policy*. Montreal and Kingston: McGill-Queen's University Press, 1990.

Carstens, Peter. *In the Company of Diamonds: De Beers, Kleinzee, and the Control of a Town*. Athens: Ohio University Press, 2001.

———. "An Essay on Suicide and Disease in Canadian Indian Reserves: Bringing Durkheim Back in." *Canadian Journal of Native Studies* 20 (2) 2000, 309–345.

———. *The Queen's People: A Study of Hegemony, Coercion, and Accommodation among the Okanagan of Canada*. Toronto: University of Toronto Press, 1991.

Cassidy, Frank, ed. *Aboriginal Self-Determination: Proceedings of a Conference held September 30 to October 3, 1990*. Lantzville, B.C. & Halifax, N.S.: Oolichan Books and the Institute for Research on Public Policy, 1991.

Cell, John W. *The Highest Form of White Supremacy: The Origins of Segregation in South Africa and the American South*. Cambridge: Cambridge University Press, 1982.

Chrétien, Jean. "Statement of the Government of Canada on Indian Policy, 1969." Presented to the First Session of the Twenty-eighth Parliament by the Minister of Indian Affairs and Northern Development.

———. "The Unfinished Tapestry – Indian Policy in Canada." A speech by the Minister of Indian Affairs and Northern Development given at Queen's University, 17 March 1971.

Chrisjohn, Roland, and Sherri L. Young with Michael Maraun. *The Circle Game: Shadows and Substance in the Indian Residential School Experience in Canada*. Penticton, BC: Theytus Books, 1997.

Citizens Plus. A Presentation by the Indian Chiefs of Alberta to Right Honourable P.E. Trudeau, Prime Minister and the Government of Canada, June 1970.

Clark, Bruce. *Native Liberty, Crown Sovereignty: The Existing Aboriginal Right of Self-Government in Canada*. Montreal and Kingston: McGill-Queen's University Press, 1990.

Cochrane, James, John de Gruchy, and Stephen Martin, eds. *Facing the Truth: South African Faith Communities and the Truth and Reconciliation*

Commission. Cape Town: David Philip & Athens, OH: Ohio University Press, 1999.

Coleman, Michael C. *Presbyterian Missionary Attitudes Towards American Indians, 1837–1893*. Jackson & London: University Press of Mississippi, 1985.

Coney, Sandra. *Standing in the Sunshine: A History of New Zealand Women Since They Won the Vote*. Auckland, New Zealand: Penguin, 1993.

Cook, Allen. *Akin to Slavery: Prison Labour in South Africa*. Fact Paper on Southern Africa No. 11. London: International Defence and Aid Fund for Southern Africa, 1982.

Coon Come, Matthew. Speech given to the Canadian Bar Association, Toronto, 1 October 2001. Ottawa: Assembly of First Nations, National Indian Brotherhood, 2001.

———. Speech at Fort McMurray, 26 October 2000. Ottawa. Assembly of First Nations, October 2000.

Corringan, Samuel W., and Joe Sawchuck, eds. *The Recognition of Aboriginal Rights*. Case Study 1, 1996. Brandon, Manitoba: Bearpaw Publishing, 1996.

Crombie, David. "Policy Statement on Indian Self-Government in Canada: Minister of Indian Affairs and Northern Development." Ottawa: Department of Indian Affairs and Northern Development, 1986.

Cumming, Peter A., and Neil H. Mickenberg, eds. *Native Rights in Canada*. 2nd ed. Toronto: The Indian-Eskimo Association of Canada in association with General Publishing, 1972.

Davenport, T.R.H. "Some Reflections on the History of Land Tenure in South Africa, seen in the Light of Attempts by the State to Impose Political and Economic Control." *Acta Juridica* (1985).

———. *South Africa: A Modern History*. 3rd ed. Toronto: University of Toronto Press, 1985.

Davenport, T.R.H. and K.S. Hunt, eds. *The Right to the Land: Documents on Southern African History*. Cape Town: David Philip, 1974.

Davenport, Rodney, and Christopher Saunders. *South Africa: A Modern History*. 5th ed. London: Macmillan Press, 2000.

de Klerk, F.W. *The Last Trek – A New Beginning: The Autobiography*. New York: St. Martin's Press, 1999.

de Toit, Andries. "The End of Restitution: Getting Real about Land Claims." Paper prepared for the Land and Agrarian Reform Conference, Pretoria, 26–28 July, 1999.

Delius, Peter. *The Land Belongs to us: The Pedi Polity, the Boers and the British in the Nineteenth Century Transvaal*. Berkeley, Los Angeles: University of California Press, 1983.

Denoon, Donald. *A Grand Illusion: The Failure of Imperial Policy in the Transvaal Colony during the Period of Reconstruction 1900–1905*. London: Longman, 1973.

Desmond, Cosmas. *The Discarded People: An Account of African Resettlement in South Africa*. Middlesex, England: Penguin Books, 1971.

Dickason, Olive Patricia. *Canada's First Nations: A History of Founding Peoples from Earliest Times*. Toronto: McClelland & Stewart, 1992; Reprint, Toronto: Oxford University Press, 2002.

Du Toit, André, and Hermann Giliomee, eds. *Afrikaner Political Thought: Analysis and Documents, Volume One, 1780–1850*. Berkeley & Los Angeles: University of California Press, 1983.

Dubow, S. *Racial Segregation and the Origins of Apartheid in South Africa, 1919–1936*. Basingstoke, England: Macmillan in association with St. Anthony's College, Oxford, 1989.

Dueck, Lorna. "Sorry Isn't Good Enough." *The Globe and Mail*, Toronto, 31 October 2000, A 21.

Dugard, John. *Human Rights and the South African Legal Order* Princeton, NJ: Princeton University Press, 1978.

Duly, L.C. *British Land Policy in the Cape, 1795–1844*. Cape Town: 1968.

Dyck, Noel. *Indigenous Peoples and the Nation-State: 'Fourth World' Politics in Canada, Australia and Norway*. Social and Economic Papers Number 14. St. John's: Institute of Social and Economic Research, Memorial University of Newfoundland, 1985.

Eddy, John, and Deryck Schreuder, eds. *The Rise of Colonial Nationalism: Australia, New Zealand, Canada and South Africa First Assert Their Nationalities, 1880–1914*. Sydney: Allen & Unwin, 1988.

Elphick, Richard, and Hermann Giliomee, eds. *The Shaping of South African Society, 1652–1840*. Middletown, Connecticut: Wesleyan University Press, 1989.

Engelstad, Diane, and John Bird, eds. *Nation to Nation: Aboriginal Sovereignty and the Future of Canada*. Concord, ON: Anansi Press, 1992.

Ferreira, Emsie. "Government Spits in Face of Apartheid Victims." *Mail and Guardian*, Johannesburg, 28 April 2000.

Fisher, Robin. *Contact and Conflict: Indian-European Relations in British Columbia, 1774–1890*. Vancouver: University of British Columbia Press, 1977.

———. "The Impact of European Settlement on the Indigenous Peoples of Australia, New Zealand, and British Columbia: Some Comparative Dimensions." *Canadian Ethnic Studies* XII (1) 1980: 1–14.

Fleras, Augie, and Jean Leonard Elliott. *The 'Nations Within': Aboriginal-State Relations in Canada, the United States and New Zealand*. Toronto: Oxford University Press, 1992.

Forrest, Drew, "Uproar over land bill," *Mail & Guardian*, Johannesburg, 23 November 2001.

Frankel, Philip. "The Politics of Passes: Control and Change in South Africa." *Journal of Modern African Studies* 17 (2) June 1979: 199–218.

Frederikse, Julie. *The Unbreakable Thread: Non-Racialism in South Africa*. Johannesburg: Ravan Press, 1992.

Fredrickson, George M. *White Supremacy: A Comparative Study in American and South African History*. New York: Oxford University Press, 1981.

Frideres, James. "Native Rights and the 21st Century: The Making of Red Power." *Canadian Ethnic Studies* XXII (3) 1990: 1–7.

Fumoleau, René, OMI. *As Long as This Land Shall Last: A History of Treaty Eight and Treaty Eleven, 1870–1939*. Toronto: McClelland & Stewart, 1973.

Gay, G. Fay, and Alison Brookman. *Race Relations in Australia – The Aborigines*. Sydney, Australia: McGraw-Hill Book Company, 1975.

Gerhart, Gail M. *Black Power in South Africa: The Evolution of an Ideology*. Berkeley: University of Los Angeles Press, 1978.

Getty, Ian A.L., and Antoine S. Lussier, eds. *As Long as the Sun Shines and the Water Flows*. Vancouver: University of British Columbia Press, 1983.

Gisday Wa, and Delgam Uukw. *The Spirit in the Land: Statements of the Gitxsan and Wet'suwet'en Hereditary Chiefs in the Supreme Court of Canada of British*

Columbia, 1987–1990. Gabriola, BC: Reflections, 1992.

Glavin, Terry. *A Death Feast in Dimlahamid*. Vancouver: New Star Books, 1990.

Goddard, John, *Last Stand of the Lubicon Cree*. Vancouver & Toronto: Douglas & McIntyre, 1991.

Godwin, Peter. "Bushmen: Last Stand for Southern Africa's First People." *National Geographic*, February 2001.

Gordon, Michael. "Another Blow to Process of Healing." *The Age*, Melbourne, 3 April 2000, 9

Great Britain. Report of the Select Committee on Aborigines (British Settlements). London, 1836.

Hadland, Adrian, and Jovial Rantao. *The Life and Times of Thabo Mbeki*. Rivonia, South Africa: Zebra Press, 1999.

Hargreaves, Samantha, and Shamim Meer, "Out of the Margins and in to the Centre: Gender and Institutional Change." Unpublished paper prepared for a National Gender Strategy Workshop, 2000.

Harris, Verne. "'They Should Have Destroyed More': The Destruction of Public Records by the South African State in the Final Years of Apartheid, 1990–1994." Unpublished essay, July 2001.

Hawthorn, Harry B. *A Survey of the Contemporary Indians of Canada: Economic, Political, Educational Needs and Policies*, Vols. I and II. Ottawa: Indian Affairs, 1966 and 1968.

Houghton, D. Hobart. *The Tomlinson Commission: A Summary of the Findings and Recommendations in the Tomlinson Commission Report*. Johannesburg: South African Institute of Race Relations, 1956.

Indian Association of Alberta. *Citizens Plus*. Response of the Indian Association of Alberta to the Rt. Hon. P.E. Trudeau and the Government of Canada, 1970.

Inuit Tapirisat of Canada. *The Inuit of Canada*. Ottawa: Inuit Tapirisat of Canada, 1995.

Jamieson, Kathleen. *Indian Women and the Law in Canada: Citizens Minus*. Ottawa: Ministry of Supply & Services for the Advisory Council on the Status of Women and Indian Rights for Women, 1978.

Johnstone, Frederick. *Class, Race and Gold: A Study of Class Relations and Racial Discrimination in South Africa*. London: Routledge & Kegan Paul, 1976.

Katona, Jacqui. "Hylus Marcus Memorial Lecture." Melbourne, Australia, 1999.

Kawhuru, I.H., ed. *Waitangi: M ori and P keh Perspectives of the Treaty of Waitangi*. Auckland, New Zealand: Oxford University Press, 1989.

Kingston-Ontario Whig Standard. Editorial, 24 July 1964.

Kiss, Elizabeth, "National Reconciliation: Is Truth Enough?" *The Economist*, August 26/September 1, 2000, 73.

Krog, Antjie. *Country of my Skull*. Johannesburg: Random House, 1998.

Lahiff, Edward, "Land Reform in South Africa: Is it Meeting the Challenge?" Policy Brief Number 1. PLAAS (Programme for Land and Agrarian Studies), School of Government, University of the Western Cape, Bellville, South Africa. September 2001.

Land and Rural Digest 18 (May/June 2001).

Landen, Laura. "Legacy of Racism." *The Ottawa Citizen*, 9 September 2000, B3.

Laurence, Patrick. *The Transkei: South Africa's Politics of Partition*. Johannesburg: Ravan Press, 1976.

Law Commission of Canada. "Restoring Dignity: Responding to Child Abuse in

Canadian Institutions." Executive Summary. Ottawa: Minister of Public Works and Government Services, March 2000.

Leslie, John, and Ron Maguire. "The Historical Development of the Indian Act." 2nd ed. Treaties and Historical Research Centre, Indian and Northern Affairs, 1979.

Lipschultz, Mark R., and R. Kent Rasmussen. *Dictionary of African Biography*. 2nd ed. Berkeley: University of California Press, 1989.

Little Bear, Leroy, Menno Boldt, and J. Anthony Long, eds. *Pathways to Self-Determination: Canadian Indians and the Canadian State*. Toronto: University of Toronto Press, 1984.

Luthuli, Albert. *Let My People Go: An Autobiography*. Johannesburg & London: Collins, 1967.

Mabandla, Bridgette. "Sucking the Poison of Apartheid Science." *Sunday Independent*, Johannesburg, 21 July 1998.

MacLean, John. *Canadian Savage Folk: The Natives of Canada*. Toronto: Thomas Briggs, 1896.

Macmillan, William. *Bantu, Boer and Briton: The Making of the South African Native Problem*. Oxford: Clarendon Press, 1963.

Makin, Kirk, and Robert Matas, "Reserve Land Worth Half the Market Value: Court," *The Globe and Mail*, Toronto, 10 November 2000, A3.

Marks, Shula. "The Myth of the Empty Land." *History Today* 30 (January 1980): 7–12.

Mbeki, Govan. *South Africa: The Peasants' Revolt*. London: International Defence and Aid Fund for Southern Africa, 1984.

McGreal, Chris, "White Farmers Denouce ANC 'Land Grab:' South Africa is accused of following Zimbabwe's example after a farm is returned to its original owners." *The Guardian*, London, 17 March 2001.

McInnis, Edgar. *Canada: A Political and Social History*. Toronto: Clarke, Irwin and Company, 1947; Reprint, 1959.

McCartan, Greg, ed. *Nelson Mandela: Speeches 1990*. New York: Pathfinders, 1990.

McKee, Christopher, *Treaty Talks in British Columbia: Negotiating a Mutually Beneficial Future*. Vancouver: UBC Press, 1996.

McLeod, Clay. "The Oral History of Canada's Northern People, Anglo-Canadian Evidence Law and Canadian Fiduciary Duty to the First Nations: Breaking Down the Barriers of the Past." *Alberta Law Review* 20 (4) 1992: 1276–1290.

Meer, Shamim, ed. Women, Land and Authority: Perspectives from South Africa. Claremont, South Africa: David Philip, 1997.

Mercredi, Ovide, and Mary Ellen Turpel. *In the Rapids: Navigating the Future of First Nations*. Toronto: Viking/Penguin, 1993.

Miller, Christine, and Patricia Chuchryk, eds. *Women of the First Nations: Power, Wisdom and Strength*. Winnipeg: University of Manitoba Press, 1996.

Miller, J.R. *Shingwauk's Vision: A History of Native Residential Schools*. Toronto: University of Toronto Press, 1996.

———. *Skyscrapers Hide the Heavens: A History of Indian-White Relations in Canada*. Toronto: University of Toronto Press, 1989.

———. ed. *Sweet Promises: A Reader on Indian-White Relations in Canada*. Toronto: University of Toronto Press, 1991.

Minkley, Gary, Ciraj Rassool, and Leslie Witz. "Thresholds, Gateways and Spectacles: Journey Through South Africa's Hidden Pasts and Histories in the

Last Decade of the Twentieth Century." Paper presented at the Conference "The Future of the Past: The Production of History in a Changing South Africa" held at the University of the Western Cape, Bellville, South Africa, 10–12 July 1996.

Mofina, Rick, "Nault Ready to Table long-awaited bill on native claims." *The Ottawa Citizen*, 13 May 2002.

Monet, Don, and Skanu'u (Ardythe Wilson). *Colonialism on Trial: Indigenous Lan Rights and the Gitsxan and Wet'suwet'en Sovereignty Case*. Philadelphia and Gabriola Island, B.C.: New Society Publishers, 1992.

Moodie, Donald, ed. *The Record: or a Series of Official Papers Relative to the Condition and Treatment of the Native Tribes of South Africa*. London: J. Richardson; Cape Town, Cape of Good Hope: A.S. Robertson, 1838, 1841.

Morris, Alexander. *The Treaties of Canada with the Indians of Manitoba and the Northwest Territories including the Negotiations on which they were based*. Toronto: Belfords, Clarke & Co. 1880; Reprinted, Saskatoon: Fifth House, 1991.

Morse, Bradford W., ed. *Aboriginal Peoples and the Law: Indian, Métis and Inuit Rights in Canada*. Ottawa: Carleton University Press, 1985.

Mostert, Noël. *Frontiers: The Epic of South Africa's Creation and the Tragedy of the Xhosa People*. London: Pimlico, 1992.

Msimang, R.W., comp. *Natives Land Act 1013: Specific Cases of Evictions and Hardships, etc.* with introduction by Timothy Keegan. Cape Town: Friends of South African Library, reprinted in 1996.

Mzala. *Gatsha Buthelezi: Chief with a Double Agenda*. London: Zed Books, 1988.

Naidoo, Jay. *Tracking Down Historical Myths*. Johannesburg: A.D. Donker, 1989.

Native Women's Association of Canada Newsletter, January 1992, 7.

Ndlovu, Arthur, "Land Claim a Resounding Success." Press release by the Department of Housing and Land Administration, Mpumalanga Province, 3 February 2001.

Nelson Mandela: The Struggle is My Life: His Speeches and writings brought together with historical documents and accounts of Mandela in prison by fellow-prisoners. London: International Defence and Aid Fund for Southern Africa, 1986.

Ngubane, Jordan K. *An African Explains Apartheid*. London: Pall Mall Press, 1963.

Ntsebeza, Lungisile. "Traditional Authorities, Local Government, and Land Rights." Paper presented at the Land and Agrarian Reform Conference, Pretoria, 26–28, 1999.

Nunavut. Annual Report of the Nunavut Tungngavik Incorporated, 1993.

Nunavut Implementation Commission. A Comprehensive Report from the Nunavut Implementation Commission to the Department of Indian Affairs and Northern Development, Government of the Northwest Territories and Nunavut Tunngavik Incorporated concerning the establishment of the Nunavut government, 1995.

Nunavut News, Iqaliut, Nunavut, 4 January 2002.

Nungaq, Zebedee. "Kicking the Tires of History." *Nunavut*, Special Edition, 85 (1999): 20–21.

Nunsiaq News. Iqaliut, Nunavut, January , 2002.

Nuttall, Sarah, and Carli Coetzee, eds. *Negotiating the Past: The Making of Memory in South Africa*. Cape Town: Oxford University Press, 1998.

Odendaal, André. *Vukani Bantu!: The Beginnings of Black Protest Politics in South Africa to 1912*. Cape Town & Johannesburg: David Philip, 1984.

Olivier, Paul. "TRC to Probe San 'Executions' SADF under Spotlight." *Cape Argus*, Cape Town, 13 September, 1997.

Omond, Roger. *The Apartheid Handbook: A Guide to South Africa's Everyday Racial Policies*. Harmondsworth, UK: Penguin, 1986.

Oppenheimer, Harry. Obituary. *The Economist*. August 26/September 1, 2000, 76.

Orr, Wendy. *From Biko to Basson*. Saxonwold, South Africa: Contra, 2000.

Ossenberg, Richard J., ed. *Canadian Society: Pluralism, Change, and Conflict*. Scarborough, ON: Prentice-Hall, 1971.

Owen, Daniel, "South Africa's Gender-unfriendly land reform programme." Woza Forum On-line, 23 March 2001.

Pachai, Bridglal. *Beneath the Clouds of the Promised Land: The Survival of Nova Scotia's Blacks*. Vol. 2: 1880–1989. Halifax: The Black Educators Association of Nova Scotia, 1990.

Parkman, Francis. *The Conspiracy of Pontiac and the Indian War after the Conquest of Canada*, vol. 2, 9th ed. London, Toronto & Boston: Musson Book Company & Little, Brown & Company, 1886.

Pelot, Bernard J. "The Buckskin Curtain: Canada's Indians from Government Wards ... to Feudal Lords?" A discussion paper on the Aboriginal Rights in the Constitution, February 1985.

Persky, Stan, Commentary. *Delgamuukw: The Supreme Court of Canada Decision on Aboriginal Title*. Vancouver: Douglas & McIntyre Greystone Books for David Susuki Foundation, 1998.

Pilger, John. Article in *The Mail and Guardian*, Johannesburg, 21 April 1998.

Plaatje, Sol T. *Mhudi: An Epic of South African Native Life a Hundred Years Ago*. Lovedale Press, 1930. Reprint, Jeppestown, South Africa: A.D. Donker, 1989.

———. *Native Life in South Africa*. London: P.S. King and Co., 1917; Reprinted London: Longman, 1987.

Platzky, Laurine, and Cherryl Walker. *The Surplus People: Forced Removals in South Africa*. Johannesburg: Ravan Press for Surplus People Project, 1985.

Ponting, Rick. "The Sociological Impact of Aboriginal Self-Government on Aboriginal Communities." Paper presented to a joint session of the Canadian Sociology and Anthropology Association and the Canadian Political Science Association, Annual Meetings of the Learned Societies, l'Université de Montréal, Montreal, Quebec, 31 May 1985.

Posterski, Greg. "A Conversation with Elijah Harper." Envision (World Vision Canada) Spring 2000, 10–11.

Pritzker, Barry M. *A Native American Encyclopedia: History, Culture and Peoples*. Oxford: Oxford University Press, 2000.

Purich, Donald. *Our Land: Native Rights in Canada*. Toronto: James Lorimer, 1986.

Rajinovich, Grace. *Reading Rock Art: Interpreting the Indian Rock Paintings of the Canadian Shield*. Toronto: Natural Heritage; Natural History Inc., 1994.

Ramphele, Mamphele. *A Bed Called Home: Life in the Migrant Labour Hostels of Cape Town*. Cape Town: David Philip, 1993.

Raven-Hart, Major R. *Before Van Riebeeck: Callers at South Africa from 1488 to 1652. Original documents translated from the Dutch, Portuguese, German, French, Italian, Spanish and Danish*. Cape Town: C. Struik, 1967.

Republic of South Africa. Bantu Resettlement Board Annual Report, 1964–65.

———. Commission on Restitution to Land Rights, Annual Report, 1999–2000.

———. Constitution of South Africa, 1996.

———. Constitutional Assembly. *The Making of a Constitution: The Story of South Africa's Constitutional Assembly, May 1994 to December 1996.* Cape Town: Published for the Constitutional Assembly by Churchill Murray Publications, 1997.

———. House of Assembly Debates, 12 February 1973.

———. House of Assembly Debates, 2 March 1984.

———. Land Claims Commission. Land Claims Court, Case Number LCC 151/98.

———. Republic of South Africa. Statutes – Constitutional Law.

———. Republic of South Africa, Constitution Act, No. 32 of 1961.

———. Republic of South Africa, Constitution Act, No. 110, 1983.

———. Truth and Reconciliation Commission of South Africa Report. 5 Volumes. Cape Town, 1998.

Reynolds, Henry. *The Law of the Land.* 2nd ed. Ringwood, Victoria, Australia: Penguin, 1992.

Richardson, Boyce, ed. *Drumbeat: Anger and Renewal in Indian Country.* Toronto: Summerhill Press, Assembly of First Nations, 1989.

———. *People of Terra Nullius: Betrayal and Rebirth in Aboriginal Canada.* Vancouver: Douglas & McIntyre, 1993.

Rogers, Barbara. *Divide and Rule: South Africa's Bantustans.* London: International Defence and Aid Fund for Southern Africa, 1980.

Rose, Brian, and Raymond Turner, eds. *Documents in South African Education.* Johannesburg: A.D. Donker, 1975.

Russell, Peter H. *Constitutional Odyssey: Can Canadians be a Sovereign People?* Toronto: University of Toronto Press, 1992.

Sampson, Anthony. *Mandela: The Authorized Biography.* London: Harper Collins, 1999.

Saunders, Christopher, and Nicholas Southey. *A Dictionary of South African History.* Cape Town: David Philip, 1998.

Sibanda, Sipho. "Proposals for the Management of Land Rights in Rural South Africa." Paper presented to the Land and Agrarian Reform Conference, Pretoria, 26–28 July 1999.

Simons, H.J. *African Women: Their Legal Status in South Africa.* London: C. Hurst and Co., 1968.

Simons, Jack, and Ray. *Class and Colour in South Africa 1850–1950.* London: International Defence and Aid Fund for Southern Africa, 1983.

Sinclair, Donna. "Reliving the Nightmare." *United Church Observer* 64 (2) September 2000, 24–25.

Slingsby, Peter. *Rock Art of the Western Cape. Book One: The Sevilla Trail and Travelers' Rest.* Sandvlei, South Africa: The Fontmaker, 1999.

Smith, Bernard. *The Spectre of Treganni.* 1980 Boyer Lectures. Sydney: The Australian Broadcasting Commission, 1980.

Smith, Donald B. *Sacred Feathers: The Reverend Peter Jones (Kahkewaquonaby) and the Mississauga Indians.* Toronto: University of Toronto Press, 1987.

Smith, Henk. Affidavit in Application for the Right to Appeal Directly to the Constitutional Court of South Africa in the case of *Richtersveld v. Alexkor Corporation and the Government of South Africa.* August 2001.

Snow, Chief John. *These Mountains Are Our Sacred Places: The Story of the Stoney People.* Toronto & Sarasota: Samuel Stevens, 1977.

Soros, George. Chairman's Statement. *Building Open Societies. Soros Foundation Report, 1995.* New York: Open Society Institute, 1996.

South Africa. See under Republic of South Africa and Union of South Africa.

Sparks, Allister. *The Mind of South Africa.* New York: Ballantine Books, 1990.

———. *Tomorrow is Another Country: The Inside Story of South Africa's Negotiated Revolution.* Sandton: Struik Book Distributors, 1994.

Sprague, D.N. *Canada and the Métis, 1869–1885.* Waterloo, Ontario: Wilfrid Laurier University Press, 1985.

Stackhouse, John, "Canada's Apartheid," 14-part series published in the Globe and Mail, November 3 to December 15, 2001.

Steckley, John. *Beyond Their Years: Five Native Women's Stories.* Toronto: Canadian Scholars' Press Inc., 1999.

Sterritt, Neil J. "Aboriginal Rights Recognition in Public Policy: A Canadian Perspective." Paper presented to the Aboriginal and Torres Strait Islander Commission National Policy Conference held in Canberra, Australia, 8 March 2002.

Strebel, Anna. "Women and Aids: Women are more Vulnerable." *Sash* 36 (3) January 1994, 38.

Strehlow, T.G.H. *Assimilation Problems: The Aboriginal Viewpoint.* Adelaide, Australia: Aborigines Advancement League Inc. of South Australia, 1964.

Stultz, Newell M. *Transkei's Half Loaf: Race Separatism in South Africa.* New Haven & London: Yale University Press, 1979.

Surplus People Project. *Land Claims in Namaqualand.* Cape Town: Surplus People Project, 1995.

Surtees, R.J. "Development of an Indian Reserve Policy in Canada." *Ontario History* 61 (2) June 1969.

Taylor, John L. "Canadian Indian Policy During the Inter-War Years, 1918–1939." Ottawa: Department of Indian and Northern Affairs, Treaties and Historical Research Branch, 1984.

Taylor, John P., and Gary Paget. "Federal/Provincial Responsibility and Sechelt." Draft paper prepared for National Conference on Federal and Provincial Government and Aboriginal Peoples at Carleton University, Ottawa, October 1988.

Theal, George McCall. *History of South Africa from 1873 to 1884: Twelve Eventful Years.* Volume 10. London: George Allen & Unwin, 1919.

Tobias, John L. "Canada's Subjugation of the Plain's Cree, 1879–1885." *Canadian Historical Review* 64 (4) December 1983: 519–548.

Townsend, J. *Autobiography of the Reverend J. Townsend and Reminiscences of his missionary labours in Australia.* 2nd ed. London: W. Reed, United Methodist Free Churches' Book Room, 1869.

"Transforming Society through Reconciliation: Myth or Reality?" Proceedings of a public discussion on the Truth and Reconciliation Commission held in Cape Town, 12 March 1998.

Trapido, Stanley. "South Africa in a Comparative Study of Industrialization." *Journal of Development Studies* 7 (1971): 309–320.

Tsedu, Mathatha, Untitled article prepared for a seminar attended by academics, jurnalists, artists and writers on the social engagement of African intellectuals, held at Gorée off the coast of Senegal, 20 December 1998.

Turnbull, Clive. *Black War: The Extermination of the Tasmanian Aborigines.* Melbourne & London: F.W. Cheshire, 1948.

Union of South Africa. Coloured Mission Stations, Reserves and Settlements. Inter-Departmental Committee of Inquiry, 1945–1947.

———. The Union Statues, 1910–1947, Volume 3. Classified and Annotated. Cape Town: Government Printer, 1950.

United Church of Canada. *Justice and Reconciliation: The Legacy of Indian Residential Schools and the Journey Towards Reconciliation.* Etobicoke, Ontario: United Church of Canada, 2001.

Unterhalter, Elaine. Forced Removal: The Division, Segregation and Control of South Africa. London: International Defence and Aid Fund for Southern Africa, 1987.

Van Onselen, Charles. *The Seed is Mine: The Life of Kas Maine, a South African Sharecropper, 1894–1985.* New York: Hill and Wang, 1996

Vickery, Kenneth P. "'Herrenvolk' Democracy and Egalitarianism in South Africa and the U.S. South." *Comparative Studies in Society and History* 16 (1974): 309–328.

Victims or Victors? The Story of the Victorian Aborigines Advancement League. South Yarra, Victoria: Hyland House, 1985.

The Voyages of Jacques Cartier, with Introduction by Ramsay Cook. Toronto: University of Toronto Press, 1993.

Walker, Cherryl, "Relocating Restitution," *Transformation: Critical Perspectives on Southern Africa.* Durban: University of Durban. 4 (2000): 1–16.

Ward, Allan. *A Show of Justice: Racial 'Amalgamation' in Nineteenth Century New Zealand.* Canberra: Australian University Press, 1974.

Watts, Robert. Statement by Bob Watts, Assistant Deputy Minister, Lands and Trusts Services, Department of Indian Affairs and Northern Development, to the United Nations Working Group on Indigenous Populations, Sixteenth Session, Geneva, 28 July 1988.

Weinberg, Paul. *Once We Were Hunters: A Journey with Africa's Indigenous People.* Amsterdam: Mets and Schilt; Cape Town: David Philip, 2000.

Williams, John R. "Ethics and Human Rights in South African Medicine." *Canadian Medical Association Journal* 162 (8) 18 April 2000.

Williams, Robert A., Jr. *Linking Arms Together: American Indian Treaty Visions of Law amd Peace, 1600–1800.* New York & London: Routledge, 1999.

Wilson, Monica, and Leonard Thompson, eds. *The Oxford History of South Africa.* Vols. I & II. New York & Oxford: Oxford University Press, 1971.

Winberg, Marlene, and Paul Weinberg. *Back to the Land.* Johannesburg: The Porcupine Press, 1996.

Winks, Robin W., ed. *Slavery: A Comparative Perspective, Readings on Slavery from Ancient Times to the Present.* New York: New York University Press, 1972.

Wolpe, Harold. "Capitalism and Cheap Labour-power in South Africa: From Segregation to Apartheid." *Economy and Society* 1 (4) 1972: 425–456.

Wright, Ronald. *Stolen Continents: The "New World" Through Indian Eyes.* Toronto: Penguin, 1993.

Wright, Tony, and Kerry Taylor. "Fury over 'stolen' denial." *The Age,* Melbourne, 3 April 2000, 14.

Wuttunee, William I.C. *Ruffled Feathers: Indians in Canadian Society.* Calgary: Bell Books, 1971.

York, Geoffrey. *The Dispossessed: Life and Death in Native Canada.* London: Vintage U.K., 1990.

Index

AFRICA: MISSING VOICES SERIES

Donald I. Ray & Peter Shinnie, general editors.

ISSN 1703-1826

University of Calgary Press has a long history of publishing academic works on Africa. *Africa: Missing Voices* illuminates issues and topics concerning Africa that have been ignored or are missing from current global debates. This series will fill a gap in African scholarship by addressing concerns that have been long overlooked in political, social, and historical discussions about this continent.

Grassroots Governance?: Chiefs in Africa and the Afro-Caribbean. Edited by D.I. Ray and P.S. Reddy. Copublished with the International Association of Schools and Institutes of Administration (IASIA), No. 1.

The African Diaspora in Canada: Negotiating Identity and Belonging. Edited by Wisdom Tettey and Korbla Puplampu, No. 2.

A Common Hunger: Land Rights in Canada and South Africa by Joan G. Fairweather, No. 3.

www.ingramcontent.com/pod-product-compliance
Lightning Source LLC
Chambersburg PA
CBHW050633280326
41932CB00015B/2626